Hard-to-Teach
BIOLOGY
CONCEPTS

A Framework to Deepen Student Understanding

Hard-to-Teach BIOLOGY CONCEPTS

A Framework to Deepen Student Understanding

By Susan Koba with Anne Tweed

NSTA press
National Science Teachers Association
Arlington, Virginia

National Science Teachers Association

Claire Reinburg, Director
Jennifer Horak, Managing Editor
Judy Cusick, Senior Editor
Andrew Cocke, Associate Editor

ART AND DESIGN
Will Thomas Jr., Director, cover and interior design
Tim French, Senior Graphic Designer, interior design

PRINTING AND PRODUCTION
Catherine Lorrain, Director
Jack Parker, Electronic Prepress Technician

SCILINKS
Tyson Brown, Director
Virginie L. Chokouanga, Customer Service and Database Coordinator

NATIONAL SCIENCE TEACHERS ASSOCIATION
Francis Q. Eberle, PhD, Executive Director
David Beacom, Publisher

LIBRARY OF CONGRESS CATALOGING-IN-PUBLICATION DATA
Koba, Susan.
  Hard-to-teach biology concepts : a framework to deepen student understanding / by Susan Koba, with Anne Tweed.
     p. cm.
  Includes bibliographical references and index.
  ISBN 978-1-933531-41-0
  1. Biology--Study and teaching (Secondary) I. Tweed, Anne. II. Title.
  QH315.K58 2009
  570.71'2--dc22
                        2009007877

NSTA is committed to publishing material that promotes the best in inquiry-based science education. However, conditions of actual use may vary, and the safety procedures and practices described in this book are intended to serve only as a guide. Additional precautionary measures may be required. NSTA and the authors do not warrant or represent that the procedures and practices in this book meet any safety code or standard of federal, state, or local regulations. NSTA and the authors disclaim any liability for personal injury or damage to property arising out of or relating to the use of this book, including any of the recommendations, instructions, or materials contained therein.

PERMISSIONS
You may photocopy, print, or email up to five copies of an NSTA book chapter for personal use only; this does not include display or promotional use. Elementary, middle, and high school teachers *only* may reproduce a single NSTA book chapter for classroom or noncommercial, professional-development use only. For permission to photocopy or use material electronically from this NSTA Press book, please contact the Copyright Clearance Center (CCC) (*www.copyright.com*; 978-750-8400). Please access *www.nsta.org/ permissions* for further information about NSTA's rights and permissions policies.

Featuring sciLINKS®— Up-to-the minute online content, classroom ideas, and other materials. For more information go to www.scilinks.org/faq/moreinformation.asp.

Contents

About the Authors ix

Introduction xi
- Science Education Reform and Conceptual Understanding xiii
- Hard-to-Teach Biology Concepts—*Why* Are They Hard? xiv
- Why Aren't Students Learning? xv
- Organization of the Book xv

Part I: The Toolbox: A Framework and Strategies 1

Chapter 1. The Instructional Planning Framework: Addressing Conceptual Change 3
- Why Are There Hard-to-Teach Biology Concepts? 4
- Introducing the Instructional Planning Framework 5
- The Research Behind the Framework 7
- Endnotes 12

Chapter 2. Instructional Approaches to Promote Student Understanding 15
- Overview 16
- Instructional Strategy Sequencing Tool 16
- Metacognitive Approach Tools 17
- Standards-Based Approach Tools 19
- Sense Making: Linguistic and Nonlinguistic Representational Tools 23
- A Note on Technology 27
- Some Thoughts on Assessment 27
- Instructional Tools 2.1–2.14 29
- Recommended Resources 87
- Endnotes 89

Part II: Toolbox Implementation: The Framework and Strategies in Practice 91

Chapter 3. Reproduction: Meiosis and Variation 93
- Why This Topic? 94
- Overview 94
- Case Study: Setting the Stage 95
- Instructional Planning Framework: *Predictive Phase* 96
  - What Is the Conceptual Target? 96
  - What Is a Logical Learning Sequence? 102
  - What Criteria Should We Use to Determine Understanding? 105
- Instructional Planning Framework: *Responsive Phase* 108
- Tables 3.1–3.2 110
- Recommended Resources 115
- Endnotes 116

Contents

Chapter 4. Flow of Energy and Matter: Photosynthesis 119
- Why This Topic? 120
- Overview..121
- Instructional Planning Framework: *Predictive Phase*..122
- Instructional Planning Framework: *Responsive Phase* 125
  - Identifying Preconceptions...125
  - Learning About Research-Identified Misconceptions 125
  - Identifying Our Students' Preconceptions..127
  - Description of Assessment for Preconceptions..129
- Eliciting and Confronting Preconceptions..130
- Completing the *Responsive Phase*: Sense Making and Demonstrating Understanding......132
- Tables 4.1–4.3..133
- Recommended Resources 141
- Endnotes 141

Chapter 5. Evolution: Natural Selection 143
- Why This Topic? 144
- Overview..144
- Instructional Planning Framework: *Predictive Phase*..146
- Instructional Planning Framework: *Responsive Phase* 148
  - Identifying Preconceptions...148
  - Eliciting and Confronting Preconceptions and Sense Making 151
- Tables 5.1–5.3..159
- Recommended Resources 166
- Endnote...167

Chapter 6. Molecular Genetics: Proteins and Genes..169
- Why This Topic? 170
- Overview..170
- Instructional Planning Framework: *Predictive Phase*..171
- Instructional Planning Framework: *Responsive Phase* 173
  - Identifying, Eliciting, and Confronting Preconceptions 173
  - Sense Making: Strategies to Address Preconceptions 175
  - Demonstrating Understanding..176
  - Sense Making and Demonstrating Understanding for the Learning Targets 178
- Table 6.1 183
- Recommended Resources 188
- Endnotes 189

Contents

Chapter 7. Interdependence: Environmental Systems and Human Impact 191
- Why This Topic? 192
- Overview 193
- Instructional Planning Framework: *Predictive Phase* 193
  - What Are the Conceptual Targets? What Are the Essential Understandings? 194
  - What Is a Logical Learning Sequence? 199
  - What Criteria Should We Use to Determine Understanding? 200
- Instructional Planning Framework: *Responsive Phase* 201
  - Identifying Preconceptions 202
  - Eliciting and Confronting Preconceptions, Sense Making, and Demonstrating Understanding 206
- Closing 215
- Tables 7.1–7.3 217
- Recommended Resources 226
- Endnotes 228

References 229

Appendix A1: Teacher Work Template (Blank) 244

Appendix A2: Steps of the Planning Process 246

Appendix B1: Concept Map for Flow of Matter and Energy: "Flow of Matter in Ecosystems" 248

Appendix B2: Concept Map for Evolution of Life: "Natural Selection" 249

Appendix B3: Concept Map for Cells: "Cell Functions" 250

Index 251

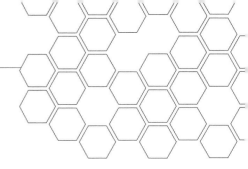

About the Authors

Susan Koba, a science education consultant, works primarily with the National Science Teachers Association (NSTA) on its professional development website, The NSTA Learning Center. She recently retired after 30 years in the Omaha Public Schools (OPS), having taught on the middle and high school levels for 20 years and then having served as a curriculum specialist and district mentor. Koba ended her service to OPS as project director and professional development coordinator for the OPS Urban Systemic Program, serving 60 schools.

Koba has been named Alice Buffett Outstanding Teacher, Outstanding Biology Teacher for Nebraska, Tandy Technology Scholar, and Access Excellence Fellow. She is also a recipient of a Christa McAuliffe Fellowship and of a Presidential Award for Excellence in Mathematics and Science Teaching. She received her BS in biology from Doane College, MA in biology from the University of Nebraska-Omaha, and PhD in science education from the University of Nebraska-Lincoln.

Koba has published and presented on many topics, including school and teacher change, equity in science, inquiry, and action research. She has developed curriculum at the local, state, and national levels and served as curriculum specialist for a U.S. Department of Education Technology Innovation Challenge Grant. A past director of coordination and supervision on the NSTA Board and a past president of her state NSTA chapter, she currently serves NSTA on the Nominations Committee. Other past NSTA work includes serving as the conference chairperson for the 2006 Area Conference in Omaha and on the Budget and Finance Committee. She also serves on the National Science Education Leadership Association (NSELA) Board of Directors as the Region E Director.

Anne Tweed, a principal consultant with Mid-continent Research for Education and Learning (McREL) in Aurora, Colorado, also serves as the associate director of the North Central Comprehensive Center in St. Paul, Minnesota. Her work at McREL supports professional development in the areas of formative assessment, high-quality instructional practices, teaching reading in content areas, effective science instruction, analyzing instructional materials, and audits of science curricula and programs.

Tweed is a past president of the National Science Teachers Association (NSTA) (2004–2005). A veteran high school science educator and department coordinator, she spent the majority of her 30-year teaching career with the Cherry Creek School District in Colorado. She earned a BA in biology from Colorado College, an MS in botany from the University of Minnesota, and a teaching certificate from the University of Colorado.

Tweed has held several leadership positions with NSTA and with the Colorado Association of Science Teachers and the Colorado Alliance for Science. She also was on the review committee for the National Science Education Standards and was a contributor to the Colorado Model Content Standards for Science. In addition, she served on the program-planning team that revised the 2009 NAEP Framework for Science. She has received the Distinguished High School Science Teaching Award from NSTA and the Outstanding Biology Teacher Award for Colorado and is a state Presidential Award for Excellence in Mathematics and Science Teaching honoree.

* * * * * * *

Contributors

Kelly Gatewood, PhD, assistant professor of graduate studies, Peru State College, Peru, Nebraska.

Frank Tworek, PhD, science teacher, King Science and Technology Magnet Center, Omaha, Nebraska.

Susan Van Gundy, director of education and strategic partnerships at the National Science Digital Library, Boulder, Colorado, and principal and founder of Eduvate Consulting, Golden, Colorado.

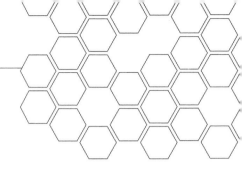

Introduction

"Biology has become the most active, the most relevant, and the most personal science, one characterized by extraordinary rigor and predictive power."
—John A. Moore, 1993

"A pessimist sees the difficulty in every opportunity; an optimist sees the opportunity in every difficulty."
—Winston Churchill (1874–1965)

Biology is a science in which the curriculum continuously changes. New knowledge and emerging content have an enormous impact on our lives. With each new discovery, biologists develop new questions, which lead to more new knowledge. As biology teachers, we constantly learn new content and develop not only our own understanding of biological concepts but also ways to best teach that content to our students.

This book does not contain a recipe to follow as you plan and deliver lessons. Nor is it a set of predesigned lessons for use in biology classrooms. Instead, it features both an instructional framework you can use as you plan—our Instructional Planning Framework (for a visual representation of the framework, see Figure 1.1, p. 6)—and sets of strategies and resources you can select from to help your students learn. We believe that the framework can be used by both new and veteran teachers alike to develop students' conceptual understanding of five hard-to-teach biology topics: reproduction, photosynthesis, natural selection, molecular genetics, and interdependence of living things. We do not expect you to completely change what you do already. By using the examples provided in the content chapters (Chapters 3–7) as a guide and tackling one piece at a time, you can make adjustments to your planning and teaching that, we believe, will result in improved conceptual understanding for your students.

We begin by looking at what is known biologically. From there we must determine what and how we should teach to develop our students' biological literacy (essential biology concepts) and appreciation of the living world. Obviously we all want students to understand ideas such as genetic engineering, stem cell research, and evolutionary biology. But before students can learn about genetic engineering, they have to understand how DNA (deoxyribonucleic acid) and RNA (ribonucleic acid) work and how they provide the genetic information in all living things. To understand stem cells, students have to understand the process of cell division and differentiation. Making sure that students understand the fundamentals of biology is not a simple process and therein lays the dilemma we all face.

Introduction

Learning biology is clearly a struggle for many of our students, as evidenced by biology achievement scores across the country. In other words, if you have trouble teaching your students the basic principles of biology, you're not alone! What might be the reasons for these difficulties? With the advent of state standards and high-stakes assessments, biology teachers are finding it difficult to teach in ways that worked for them in the past. A common complaint of both students and teachers is that there is so much content to cover that there is not enough time to do the experiments and inquiry activities that engage students with the ideas. Biology teachers know that laboratory experiences help students learn complex concepts (Singer, Hilton, and Schweinbruger 2007), yet we get caught up in the attempt to cover so many topics and lists of vocabulary that, on average, students are only provided one laboratory experience each week. In the classroom, we often focus on the names and labels for living organisms or steps in processes, and our students get lost in details without learning the important, essential biological principles.

With this book, the authors seek to help all biology teachers to teach the five hard-to-teach biology concepts listed on the previous page. Although this book is not about providing teachers with scripted lessons, it does include much that we have learned from our own experiences and from recent research findings. Science research that focuses on how students learn recommends certain strategies that teachers can use to help develop and implement effective instructional methods. In this book, we do not tackle all the issues in high school biology. Rather we focus on selected research that informs our Instructional Planning Framework.

We realize that teachers' implementation of selected instructional strategies impacts the effectiveness of a strategy in the classroom. Even with research-based strategies and tools, we need to figure out ways to use them in the best way possible. For example, we know that classroom discourse (discussion) helps students think about their ideas and supports sense making. But if we just ask students to discuss a question or problem without setting a time limit, establishing the groups they will work with, and determining how they will report-out to the class, then classroom discourse won't help students make sense of the hard-to-teach biology concepts.

We love teaching biology, and we want to provide opportunities for you to meet the challenges posed when teaching hard-to-teach biology concepts. We were prompted to write this book because guidance for teachers is located in so many different places; our hope was to put all of the findings together into a model that made sense to us and would support your work. This book presents a framework for planning, shares appropriate approaches to develop student understanding, and provides opportunities to reflect on and apply those approaches to specific, hard-to-teach concepts and topics. It is more about helping you learn how to improve your practice than it is about providing sample lessons that recommend a "best" way to provide instruction. Clearly, you must decide what works best for you.

NATIONAL SCIENCE TEACHERS ASSOCIATION

Science Education Reform and Conceptual Understanding

At that same time that our students struggle to master biology concepts, many states require students to pass high-stakes tests in order to graduate. Science reform efforts stress science understanding by all citizens; unfortunately, little impact is made on persistent achievement gaps (Chubb and Loveless 2002). However, the current cycle of science education reform that resulted in the Benchmarks for Science Literacy (AAAS 1993) and the National Science Education Standards (NRC 1996) expects, among other things, (1) meaningful science learning for all students at all grade levels, (2) that students are able to discriminate among science ideas, and (3) that they are able to build connections among ideas, moving past recall and into more sophisticated understandings of science. To meet the standards, it is critical that all of us work to implement strategies shown as effective to build these types of student understandings.

We know that serious change takes time, often seven to ten years to move from establishing goals to changing teacher practice and curriculum materials that meet the needs of our students (Bybee 1997). One major obstacle to change is the lack of support for teachers to fully understand ways to teach hard-to-teach concepts (Flick 1997). School structures in the United States do not adequately provide professional support for us to engage in new learning to improve our teaching. We are rarely provided the time to work individually or collaboratively to inquire into our own teaching and our students' learning (Fisher, Wandersee, and Moody 2000). So what makes current reform efforts any different from those in the past? Perhaps the standards, political influences, and the growing body of research provide an answer.

Hope for change begins with the standards because we now at least have common targets for both teaching and learning. We know the content learning goals for our students and the teaching and assessment goals we should meet. We also know the programmatic and systemic educational support expected to implement the content and teaching standards. But achieving these goals requires support even beyond our school systems.

The next ray of hope is that the political focus on science education has grown dramatically over the past few years, as evidenced by the 2007 report by the National Academy of Sciences (NAS), *Rising Above the Gathering Storm: Energizing and Employing America for a Brighter Economic Future* (NAS 2007). The federal government's growing focus on the needs in mathematics and science has resulted in increased funding for science education efforts in support of science, technology, engineering and mathematics (STEM) education.

What should directly impact us, as educators, is a growing body of research on teaching and learning in general (Bransford, Brown, and Cocking 1999) and science teaching and learning in particular (NRC 2005). Also, we now have access to a considerable body of research on the understandings and skills required for meaningful learning in biology (Fisher, Wandersee, and Moody 2000; Hershey 2004), inquiry (Anderson 2007), and the nature of science (Lederman 2007). Finally, there is an increasing understanding of conceptual change (Driver 1983; Hewson 1992; Lemke 1990; Mortimer 1995; Scott, Asoko, and Driver 1992, Strike and Posner 1992), as well as research on common misconceptions and strategies to address them (Committee on Undergraduate Science Education 1997; Driver et. al. 1994, Mortimer and Scott 2003; NAS 1997; Tanner and Allen 2005).

But hope, by itself, is not a method. Because biology is the most common entry course for science in secondary schools, it is essential that changes in science teaching and learning begin with us, the biology teachers. It is the goal of this book to support your walk down the path to more effective teaching and learning in biology.

Hard-to-Teach Biology Concepts—*Why* Are They Hard?

Traditionally students struggle to learn some of the basic ideas taught in high school biology classes. To understand why, we must analyze not only the content itself but also the classroom conditions and learning environment. One concern cited by biology teachers is the "overstuffed" biology curriculum. Because of the sheer amount of information that is taught related to each topic, even good students find it difficult to retain what they learn (NRC 2001b). Because of an emphasis on a fact-based biology curriculum, instruction often relies on direct instruction to cover all of the material. As a result, students have limited experiences with the ideas and rarely retain what they learned past the quiz or unit test.

Certain biology topics are hard for students to learn because students aren't given the time they need to think and process learning. We must give students multiple opportunities to engage with ideas. Research suggests that students need at least four to six experiences in different contexts with a concept before they can integrate the concept and make sense of what they are learning (Marzano, Pickering, and Pollock 2001).

Another reason that there are hard to teach (and learn) topics relates to the prior knowledge of our students. High school students are far from being blank slates; they come to us with their own ideas and explanations about biology principles. After all, everyone knows something about biology and our students have had a variety of experiences both as they have grown up outside school and in previous science classrooms. Student preconceptions can be incomplete and students often hold onto them tenaciously. One classic research study was captured in the video *A Private Universe: Minds of Our Own* (Harvard-Smithsonian Center for Astrophysics 1995). In one segment, researchers asked Harvard graduates where the mass of a log came from. The response was water and nutrients from the soil. Students and even college graduates hadn't learned the fundamental concept that photosynthesis requires carbon dioxide from the air to manufacture carbohydrates, which are the basis for the vast majority of a tree's mass.

This example relates to two additional reasons why some biology topics are hard to teach. One, many biology lessons are highly conceptual and students can't visualize what is taking place on a microscopic level. And two, some biology teachers are not aware of strategies that engage students with a scientific way of knowing (Banilower et al. 2008; Lederman 2007). Such strategies include asking questions, inferring from data, challenging each other's ideas, communicating inquiry results, and synthesizing student explanations with scientific explanations.

When we consider these various impeding factors, it is no wonder that students struggle in our biology classes.

Why Aren't Students Learning?

Science research helps us answer the question about why students aren't learning.

- Students may not learn because of their learning environments. The meta-analyses of the research in *How People Learn: Brain, Mind, Experience, and School* (Bransford, Brown, and Cocking 1999) and *How Students Learn: Science in the Classroom* (NRC 2005) report that the instructional environment must be learner-, not teacher-, centered. Students come to school with conceptions of biological phenomena from their everyday experiences and teachers need to take into account such preconceptions. Furthermore, what we teach is often too hard for students because they lack the necessary backgrounds on which the hard-to-teach topics are based.

- Several studies have shown that high school students perceive science knowledge as either right or wrong (NRC 2005). Unfortunately, biology concepts are rarely this clear-cut and the body of knowledge in biology is ever changing. Biological systems are dynamic, and long-term observations are often needed to understand and make sense of the evidence. The norm in many classrooms, however, is to come up with a correct answer, which is not reasonable or possible in biology classrooms, where we look at probabilities, changes over time, and trends. Quantitative and qualitative data can be ambiguous. This can be very uncomfortable for students who ask us, Why don't you just tell me the answer? While biologists, like other scientists, give priority to evidence to justify explanations, students think that we should have THE answer to biology questions and problems. Students may believe that biology is really a collection of facts because we often use direct instruction to cover the biology facts and vocabulary that may be addressed in state assessments.

- Students learn best when they are able to work collaboratively with other students. With only one investigation per week in the average biology classroom, students may not receive sufficient opportunities to engage in interactive work.

Organization of the Book

Hard-to-Teach Biology Concepts: A Framework to Deepen Student Understanding is designed to support biology teachers as they plan and implement lessons that will intellectually engage students with the biology concepts that most students find challenging. To develop successful learners, teachers must identify prior student conceptions and research-identified misconceptions related to the concept being taught and then select instructional approaches to dispel those misconceptions and promote students' conceptual understanding.

The book is made up of two parts: Part I, The Toolbox: A Framework and Strategies (Chapters 1 and 2), and Part II, Toolbox Implementation: The Framework and Strategies in Practice (Chapters 3–7).* In Part I, we share a research-based framework to address conceptual change—the Instructional Planning Framework—as well as specific instructional approaches shown to dispel preconceptions. Chapter 1 outlines the Instructional Planning Framework and gives an overview of (1) the identification of conceptual targets and preconceptions, (2) the importance of confronting preconceptions, (3) sense-making strategies to address preconceptions, and (4) best ways in which students can demonstrate understanding. Chapter 2 discusses specific instructional approaches that teachers might use to dispel preconceptions: metacognitive approaches, standards-based approaches, and specific strategies for sense making. Though the framework can be followed in a linear manner, it is not really intended as a stepwise process. Instead, it is important for you to reflect on the framework presented in Chapter 1, adapting it for your use and selecting strategies from Chapter 2 most appropriate for your own classroom.

Part II is organized to model use of this framework through its application in the analysis of five hard-to-teach topics. The topics were carefully chosen to reflect the grade-level-appropriate content common to both the National Science Education Standards (NSES) and the Benchmarks for Science Literacy (NRC 1996; AAAS 1993). Each topic, in its own chapter, is used to model a specific aspect of the framework. Each chapter also provides opportunities for personal reflection. Recommended resources, including technology applications and websites, will be found at the end of each chapter in Part II.

Chapter 3 focuses on meiosis and variation, specifically looking at the first aspect of the framework: conceptual targets, the learning sequence, and criteria for understanding. Chapter 4 looks carefully at ways to identify and confront preconceptions, using the hard-to-teach concepts associated with photosynthesis. Chapter 5 focuses on evolution (specifically, natural selection), and looks carefully at specific sense-making approaches to address research-identified misconceptions. Chapter 6 addresses molecular genetics (specifically, the relationship of genes and proteins) and considers both sense-making strategies and ways to demonstrate understanding. Finally, in Chapter 7, the topic of interdependence of organisms is modeled with a review of the entire framework. The appendixes enhance our understanding of the framework and its application.

---

* The Instructional Tools in Chapter 2 and all tables in Chapters 3–7 are located at the end of each chapter.

PART I
The Toolbox:
A Framework and Strategies

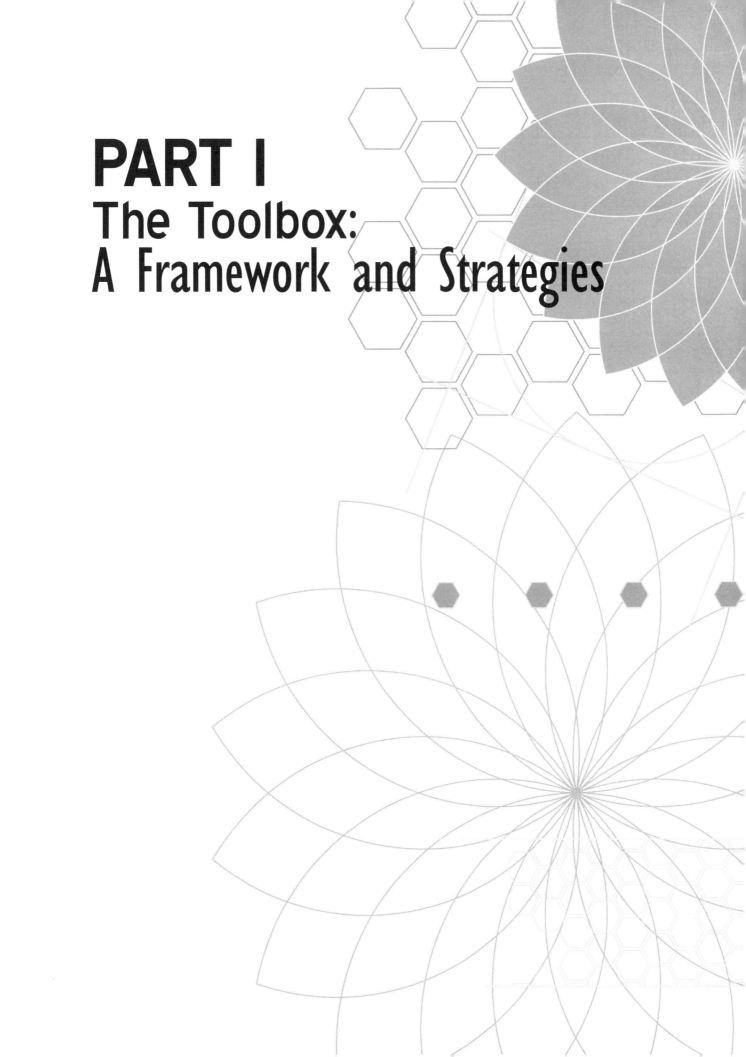

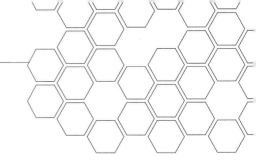

Instructional Planning Framework

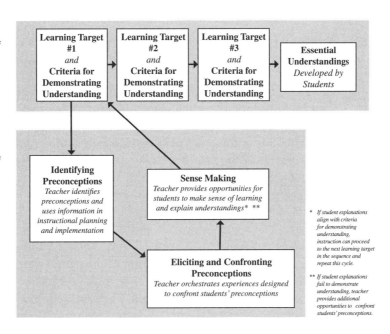

Predictive Phase
The teacher determines the lesson's essential understandings, the sequence of learning targets that lead toward those understandings, and the criteria by which understanding is determined.

Learning Target #1 *and* **Criteria for Demonstrating Understanding**

Learning Target #2 *and* **Criteria for Demonstrating Understanding**

Learning Target #3 *and* **Criteria for Demonstrating Understanding**

Essential Understandings *Developed by Students*

Responsive Phase
Building on the foundation of the predictive phase, the teacher plans for and implements instruction during the responsive phase, one learning target at a time.

Identifying Preconceptions *Teacher identifies preconceptions and uses information in instructional planning and implementation*

Sense Making *Teacher provides opportunities for students to make sense of learning and explain understandings* ***

Eliciting and Confronting Preconceptions *Teacher orchestrates experiences designed to confront students' preconceptions*

* *If student explanations align with criteria for demonstrating understanding, instruction can proceed to the next learning target in the sequence and repeat this cycle.*

** *If student explanations fail to demonstrate understanding, teacher provides additional opportunities to confront students' preconceptions.*

Chapter 1

The Instructional Planning Framework: Addressing Conceptual Change

"Students come to the classroom with preconceptions about how the world works. If their initial understanding is not engaged, they may fail to grasp the new concepts and information that are taught, or they may learn them for purposes of a test but revert to their preconceptions outside the classroom."
—*Donovan, Bransford, and Pellegrino 1999, p. 10*

High school biology teachers know that certain biology concepts are particularly difficult for their students. Yet these same students depend on their teachers to teach and assess them so that they can progress in their biology learning. Teachers also know that the reality of the world in which we live is that societal, economic, and technological changes shape the skills and understanding required in the future (Bransford, Brown, and Cocking 1999; Bureau of Labor Statistics 2000). With the No Child Left Behind legislation requirements and expectations, teachers are focused on standards and on identifying what students should know and be able to do in core subjects such as science (NRC 1996; AAAS 1993). Such reforms have called on teachers to place more emphasis on learning important concepts than on rote learning. This change is particularly significant in biology because of the difficulty that students often have with biology concepts. The Instructional Planning Framework (Figure 1.1, p. 6) on which this book is based incorporates research findings and implications for biology teachers in regard to the five hard-to-teach biology concepts we have selected: reproduction, photosynthesis, evolution, molecular genetics, and interdependence of living things.

Why Are There Hard-to-Teach Biology Concepts?

As we discussed in the introduction, learning biology is hard for many students. Students often say that learning biology is like learning a foreign language—that mastering the vocabulary alone is a struggle. Some say that they just don't understand science and they were never any good at it anyway. What are teachers to do about unfamiliar terminology and students who believe they are not capable of learning biology? How might they address their students' needs as well as their own? Research-based strategies such as those described in this book offer answers to these important questions.

According to *Teaching with the Brain in Mind* (Jensen 1998, p. 39), "Since what is challenging for one student may not be challenging for another ... [teachers must provide] more variety in the strategies used to engage learners better." As you think about the differences among your students, we're sure that it is obvious that all students do not face the same challenges. What makes certain biology concepts more challenging for some students other than their beliefs that they are just too hard? In some instances, it is the content itself that cannot be studied directly. Students may not have the ability to study the scientific phenomena through direct observations, so they say that the ideas are just too conceptual and that they can't visualize what is happening. Often the biological system being studied is very complex and cannot be understood easily without understanding the pieces and parts of the system and how they interact.

To further complicate matters, biological concepts require understanding chemistry ideas. As a result, students' preconceptions include incomplete foundational knowledge that causes them to struggle to understand complex biological concepts. Our approach here is not only to engage students intellectually with the ideas in ways that get them to think about their thinking but also to provide strategies that will increase student motivation to learn and bring about conceptual change.

Introducing the Instructional Planning Framework

We draw from the research base that supports a conceptual change framework. According to this research, change in students' preconceptions can occur if teachers use a conceptual change process that addresses the following conditions:

- Students must be aware of their personal conceptual understandings.
- Students must become dissatisfied with their existing views through the introduction of new evidence.
- New conceptions (scientific viewpoints) must appear somewhat plausible.
- New conceptions must be more attractive in order to replace previous conceptions. (Strike and Posner 1985)

Students develop their own ideas about and explanations for many of our hard-to-teach biology concepts. Their learning is an additive process and the experiences that teachers provide must be incorporated into their existing conceptions. Their preconceptions may even contain faulty reasoning that they developed during previous classes or from their own observations. Ultimately, students must reconstruct their ideas and revise their mental models and conceptual frameworks. Revealing student thinking and adding to their ideas is an essential part of our instructional framework.[1]

In this chapter, we elaborate on the steps of our research-based Instructional Planning Framework. Figure 1.1 provides a diagrammatic representation of the framework. Based on the framework and the research cited throughout the book, biology teachers can select strategies to support development of student conceptual understanding. Chapter 2 provides Instructional Tools (pp. 29–87) that support specific instructional approaches that have been shown to address preconceptions.

Figure 1.1

Instructional Planning Framework

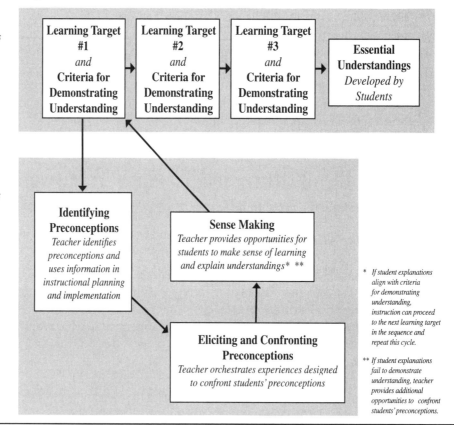

Predictive Phase

The teacher determines the lesson's essential understandings, the sequence of learning targets that lead toward those understandings, and the criteria by which understanding is determined.

Responsive Phase

Building on the foundation of the predictive phase, the teacher plans for and implements instruction during the responsive phase, one learning target at a time.

In this chapter, we outline the Instructional Planning Framework and provide an overview of its five components.

1. *Identify the conceptual target, learning sequence, and criteria to demonstrate understanding*
The framework acts as a logic model diagram. Refer to the four white boxes at the top of Figure 1.1. We refer to these aspects as the *predictive phase* of the framework. During this phase, we first clarify the conceptual target—that is, the essential understandings we want students to develop, as well as the knowledge and skills to be taught and learned in order to develop these understandings. We are then able to identify the steps in the learning sequence (the learning targets) needed to build student understanding. Finally, it is critical to provide the criteria for demonstrating conceptual understanding by students so that they can know what successful performance looks like. To measure progress to the desired outcome, we create checkpoints for the students and provide feedback so that they know how to improve.

Now, refer back to Figure 1.1 and consider the *responsive phase*. While the *predictive phase* is research-based, the *responsive phase* implements a research-based plan and *responds* to our students' ideas. We explore this phase in the steps #3–#5, below.

2. *Identify preconceptions*

We recognize that, in the ideal, teachers should elicit their students' preconceptions and use these preconceptions to plan instruction. However, we also understand the importance of long-term planning. This step is designed to help you study the research base as well as identify your students' initial ideas so that you can outline instruction focused on the conceptual target. Operationally, the first part of the *responsive phase* is to identify preconceptions, including common, research-identified misconceptions and the preconceptions of your own students. This is essential as a foundation for planning instruction as we move forward with the framework steps.

3. *Elicit and confront preconceptions*

We begin instruction by eliciting our students' preconceptions and discussing those preconceptions with our students. Although this step may require you to make some modifications along the way to your initial plan, it should serve you reasonably well because now your plan uses both research-identified misconceptions and preconceptions[1] as well as those of your students. Once you know what conceptual understandings your students already have related to the concepts, you can use the tools in Chapter 2 to select strategies that address the conceptual change process.

4. *Use sense-making strategies to address preconceptions*

This step in the process is at the core of the framework. Teachers need to provide opportunities for students to make sense of the ideas they learn because it is unlikely that students will draw the appropriate conclusions on their own. Teachers must select strategies that engage students through questioning, discussions, and other methods so that students can make connections between their ideas and what they are meant to learn. Later, you will ask students to think about their initial ideas, relate them to their current learning, and then determine how their thinking has changed.

5. *Connect learning to the criteria for developing understanding*

To complete the framework, student learning must match the criteria for developing student conceptual understanding. If it does not, you will need to revisit the final steps in the *responsive phase* and select additional tools to help students understand the concepts.

The Research Behind the Framework

Broad research supports the *predictive* and *responsive phases* of the Instructional Planning Framework. The Instructional Tools and strategies in Chapter 2 build on this research and provide effective methods to support student learning. We don't make recommendations for specific strategies. Instead, we model the use of the tools in the content chapters (Chapters 3–7), providing suggestions and inviting you to make your own selections based on the part of the framework addressed.

At this point, we ask you to consider both cognitive and metacognitive processes (learning and thinking about your thinking) as we explore each part of the planning sequence. Cognitively, teachers need to determine their own conceptual understandings about how students learn biology concepts in order to think about how to teach students to make sense of their learning. We also use a self-reflection process in each of the content chapters to address the metacognitive aspect of the book. We ask you to start this process by being very clear about why you are teaching what you are teaching. In essence, we hope that using the self-reflection process helps you become more metacognitive. How have you taught in the past? How can you engage in a critical-thinking process as you also learn about the research findings that support the framework?

The Predictive Phase

Let's look again at the *predictive phase* of the framework (Figure 1.1). Recall that this phase includes three important themes: the importance of (1) identifying essential learning(s) or learning goals in a topic; (2) focusing in depth on the progression of the related learning targets; and (3) determining criteria for demonstrating understanding for each of the learning goals (Bransford, Brown, and Cocking 1999; Heritage 2008; Masilla and Gardner 2008; Michaels, Shouse, and Schweingruber 2007; Vitale and Romance 2006).

Each of the content chapters (Chapters 3–7) highlights a different component of the Instructional Planning Framework. Chapter 3, for example, models the steps to take to learn about the *predictive phase*. Providing students with clear learning goals is at the heart of this part of the framework. It is a critical first step for teachers and students and, as an instructional approach, can lead to increased student achievement (Marzano, Pickering, and Pollock 2001). Many biology textbooks are beginning to identify big ideas and key concepts to help teachers with this process of identifying essential learning. Our goal is for you to think about what is really important for students to understand conceptually. Throughout the book, we refer to conceptual learning as *essential understanding*. Before students can grasp the essential understandings, we need to unpack the big ideas into a sequence of learning targets. The steps in the process to identify essential understandings and the criteria for student success are featured in Chapter 3 and reinforced in subsequent chapters.

Why is identifying essential understandings and criteria for student success the important first step in our framework? The answer is that if teachers are not clear about the concepts and subconcepts that lead to adult literacy in biology, then students will be unsure about what they are supposed to learn and will cling to facts and vocabulary without developing the fundamental understanding of the concepts. According to Margaret Heritage's (2008) work on learning progressions, teachers need to identify subgoals and sequence them to help students progress to the ultimate learning goals. Unfortunately, most state science standards do not provide clear progressions to understanding (Heritage 2008). Sometimes standards don't even make it clear what students should learn. Learning progressions provide our students with a pathway to the ultimate learning goals or big ideas we want them to learn.

We want to be very clear about the distinction between learning *progressions* (learning trajectories across grade bands or progressions within a course or grade level) and what we are calling learning *sequences* (shorter-term goals within standards). Students need these short-term goals so that the gaps between their current preconceptions and the desired learning goals are not too great. To engage them in learning, teachers must make sure that the gaps are neither so big that students give up nor so small that students quickly "get it" and are bored. But learning, presented in a sequence that helps students link their thinking to scientific ideas, should be the teacher's expected outcome. Identifying the short-term goals should also be accompanied by determining the criteria for conceptual understanding, so that students know the evidence of learning they need to show to move forward to the next short-term goal. Clear procedures for identifying the big ideas and learning target short-term goals are described in Chapters 3–7.

We need to think about the logic model for teacher planning that clearly identifies the learning targets, establishes a learning sequence, and plans for assessments (both formative and summative) that provide evidence of student learning. These steps are part of the *predictive phase,* when teachers do their unit planning. Once the pathway is clear, the teacher uses the rest of the framework to create instruction that identifies and addresses student preconceptions.

The Responsive Phase

The conceptual targets, learning sequence, and criteria for determining understanding are now all in place as a result of completing the *prescriptive phase* of the framework. Next we must flesh out a plan for instruction that aligns with the conceptual target. "By taking the time to study a topic before planning a unit, teachers build a deeper understanding of the content, connections, and effective ways to help students achieve understanding of the most important concepts and procedures in that topic" (Keeley and Rose 2006, p. 5). Teachers need to know and understand the content themselves so that they are certain that they know what students should learn.

During the *predictive phase*, you began to clarify the content. But you also need to know *when* and *how* to best teach those concepts to your students. So we now look at effective instructional strategies in the *responsive phase*. The Instructional Strategy Sequencing Tool (Table 2.1, p. 29) is the core tool we developed to assist you as you learn about and reflect on the selection and sequencing of strategies. The tool, further explained in Chapter 2, is based on our research review and organized by the phases of the Instructional Planning Framework.

We know that teachers are experts and students are novices in terms of understanding biology concepts. Based on our extensive teaching and learning experiences, we can anticipate many of the conceptual barriers our students face. We can also put our own understanding together in ways that our students cannot because they don't see the patterns and features that we do (Bransford, Brown, and Cocking 1999). But we are responsible for helping our students to develop these understandings. The keys to their successful learning are for us to plan experiences that let students grapple with important science concepts and for us to ensure that they make sense of the concepts (Weiss et al. 2003).[2]

In the *responsive phase* we first identify student preconceptions (i.e., what are the students' ideas about the biology concepts?). Getting students to make their thinking visible is a critical next step. The research into how people in general learn—and in particular how students learn—recommends that teachers determine prior knowledge so they know where to begin instruction (Bransford, Brown, and Cocking 1999; Donovan, Bransford, and Pellegrino 1999). A teacher doesn't really know what his or her students are thinking unless that teacher uses strategies to find out. The teacher can reflect on the strategies he or she currently uses that support a learner-centered classroom. In terms of the Instructional Planning Framework, the teacher now finds out about possible student preconceptions, determines student prior knowledge, and plans and delivers instruction that engages students intellectually with the content in ways that both confront their existing ideas and help them make sense of their learning.

Once we identify the nature of any differences between students' thinking and the science viewpoint, it becomes easier to plan activities (using the Instructional Tools on pp. 33–87) (Driver et al. 1994). Identifying the gap in student conceptual understanding helps determine the specific instructional strategies we can use to scaffold our students' learning. But not all students are in exactly the same place with their understanding. Ways to support these differences and focus on student sense making and metacognition are modeled in Chapters 3–7.

Teachers need to determine how best to use formative assessment strategies based on student feedback. "Probes" are among the many strategies described in Chapter 2 that serve as formative assessments of students' ideas. They, like other strategies, are useful at the beginning of a unit (to determine students' current conceptual understandings), in the middle of a unit (to determine where learning is clear and where students may be stuck or still clinging to misconceptions), and at the end of a unit (to determine if students are ready for a summative assessment). This type of assessment can be used diagnostically because it provides information to the teacher about student thinking related to a concept in science. "Probes are concerned less with the correct answer or quality of the student response and focus more on what students are thinking about a concept or phenomenon and where their ideas may have originated" (Keeley and Eberle 2008, p. 207). Many of the Instructional Tools can be used formatively or to promote conceptual understanding.

It goes without saying that understanding is more than just knowing facts. Confronting student's preconceptions is very different from direct instruction, which calls on teachers to tell students the scientific viewpoints and expect that they will gain comprehension through this direct presentation of information. Instead, we know that students need to engage with the content so that they can integrate conceptual learning into their brains in ways that result in durable understanding. One set of strategies featured in the Instructional Tools derives from the science standards and includes inquiry as well as the history and nature of science. Through scientific inquiry, students make observations and gather evidence that can change their ideas, deepen their understanding of important scientific principles, and develop important abilities such as reasoning, careful observing, and logical analysis (Minstrell 1989). Inquiry-based learning engages students in the lesson and arouses their interest, promotes teamwork, makes sense out of what is otherwise mystifying, and prepares students to successfully defend findings before an audience of their peers (Layman, Ochoa, and Heikkinen 1996). Inquiry-based learning is featured in each of the content chapters. Students connect their thinking to the inquiry investigations (through hands-on investigations and/or virtual simulations) and create mental models that lead to understanding. Students who use inquiry-based materials understand science concepts more deeply and thoroughly than students who learn through more traditional methods (Thier 2002).

The biggest challenge for science teachers is to build student knowledge and understanding so that students learn the accepted scientific explanations that relate to the hard-to-teach biology concepts. However, students build new understanding based on what they already know and believe, which may be inconsistent with the scientific viewpoint. Students see their preconceptions as reasonable and appropriate, and they may apply them inappropriately to learning situations (Driver et al. 1994).

The research into conceptual change, described earlier in this chapter, reminds us that to change students' ideas that are inconsistent with the scientific ideas we must present new conceptions that appear plausible to our students. This change rarely occurs unless students have a chance to engage in inquiries. The new observations and new evidence must get them to think about their thinking in ways that result in the new explanation becoming the more logical or attractive explanation (Strike and Posner 1985). If teachers do not explicitly address student's everyday conceptions in meaningful ways and ultimately replace their previous conceptions with scientifically more accurate viewpoints, then students will continue to struggle with the conceptual understanding of our hard-to-teach biology concepts (NRC 2005).

The *responsive phase* is all about developing student understanding, and so it is during this phase that the teacher must get the students actively engaged in learning. The work of the teacher is partially to plan for the learning, but within the classroom, the teacher's major responsibility is to facilitate the work of the students. After all, teachers can't learn biology for them. But they can provide a variety of learning experiences that generate discussions among students. Using the research on how students learn science and the findings from a wide variety of instructional strategies, the *responsive phase* of the Instructional Planning Framework can help all students learn essential biology concepts.

The framework itself is an iterative process and many of the steps can either lead you to the next step or return you to a previous step. Whether you move on or revisit previous steps depends on the depth of your students' understandings. We cannot prescribe these steps for you. We instead encourage you to use the framework and tools to determine next steps in the learning for *your* students because the context in which you teach is unlikely to be the same as that of other biology teachers.

Chapters 3–7 each focus on a different piece of the framework. The final chapter puts it all together and provides a review of all of the elements in the framework. The chapter content topics are not sequenced in an order that you would typically teach them in your class. Rather we match the content topic with the part of the framework that it best models so that you gain a clearer understanding of the process. For example, one topic was rife with research-based misconceptions (Chapter 4, "Flow of Energy and Matter: Photosynthesis") and another (Chapter 6: "Molecular Genetics: Proteins and Genes") was ideal to demonstrate the use of computer simulations in sense making and constructing mental models.

We realize that there are other hard-to-teach biology concepts that we could have included in this book, but we picked some of our favorites for which there was a clear research base about students' ideas. In fact, we hope that you will become sufficiently adept at the process that you will be able to apply it to other units that you teach. The framework is designed to help us, as teachers, but the greatest expected outcome is improved student achievement and understanding of five complicated biology concepts.

Endnotes

1. As revealed in a study of the research, various terms are used for the explanations that students create for themselves as they make sense of scientific phenomena. All of the terms relate to the understanding students have when they arrive in our classrooms. The most prevalent terms are the following:

Preconceptions. This term refers to student ideas that were formed through life experiences and earlier learning.

Alternative conceptions. This term refers to the variety of ideas that students have that differ from scientific explanations.

Naive conceptions. These are usually incompletely formulated or simplistic representations of student conceptual understanding.

Misconceptions. This term refers to students' wrong explanations and errors in thinking. (Naive conceptions, preconceptions, and alternative conceptions may also include wrong explanations, but students view those terms less negatively than they do *misconceptions*.)

For our purposes, we use the term *preconceptions* to refer to the thinking that we hope to get students to reveal as we implement the Instructional Planning Framework. We use the term *misconceptions* specifically when referring to misconceptions that have been identified by the considerable research into students' ideas at different grade levels.

2. Another key to successful learning is that students feel safe to share ideas and express themselves. For example, students need to be able to practice sharing the results of investigations, their individual or team visual representations, or the results of consensus discussions. So that they can do these things without fear of rebuke, teachers must teach the strategies, model them, practice them, and reinforce them so that safe dialogue occurs within the class. For that risk-free environment, we should also include processing time for student sense making.

Getting students to be metacognitive must be taught and practiced. How to develop student metacognitive strategies is discussed in Chapter 2; we include strategies such as providing time for journaling (thinking creatively), conducting self-assessments (thinking critically), and goal setting based on what students don't understand (self-regulated thinking) (Marzano 1997). These metacognitive strategies are a key piece of the *responsive phase* because they guide students forward from what they understand for sure, to what they think they understand, to what they know is still confusing, and finally to knowing what they need to do next to develop conceptual understanding.

Instructional Planning Framework

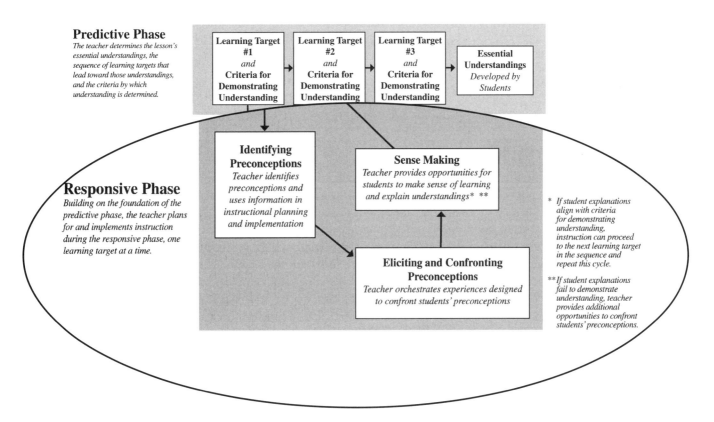

Predictive Phase
The teacher determines the lesson's essential understandings, the sequence of learning targets that lead toward those understandings, and the criteria by which understanding is determined.

Learning Target #1 *and* **Criteria for Demonstrating Understanding**	Learning Target #2 *and* **Criteria for Demonstrating Understanding**	Learning Target #3 *and* **Criteria for Demonstrating Understanding**	**Essential Understandings** *Developed by Students*

Identifying Preconceptions
Teacher identifies preconceptions and uses information in instructional planning and implementation

Sense Making
Teacher provides opportunities for students to make sense of learning and explain understandings * ***

Responsive Phase
Building on the foundation of the predictive phase, the teacher plans for and implements instruction during the responsive phase, one learning target at a time.

Eliciting and Confronting Preconceptions
Teacher orchestrates experiences designed to confront students' preconceptions

* *If student explanations align with criteria for demonstrating understanding, instruction can proceed to the next learning target in the sequence and repeat this cycle.*

** *If student explanations fail to demonstrate understanding, teacher provides additional opportunities to confront students' preconceptions.*

Chapter 2

Instructional Approaches to Promote Student Understanding

15

"Science teachers have always used multiple strategies, so we need not make a decision about the one best strategy for teaching science. There isn't one; there are many strategies that can be applied to achieve different outcomes. Science teachers should try to sequence them in coherent and focused ways. This is how inquiry can contribute to the prepared mind."

—*Bybee 2006, p. 456*

Overview

As teachers, we all know various strategies. As we also know, the strategies themselves are not the solution to learning for our students. What we must do is select strategies that best fit our instructional goals and sequence them to support students' conceptual understandings.

In this chapter, we build on the Instructional Planning Framework explained in Chapter 1 and provide Instructional Tools and strategies to put the framework into practice. This chapter is grounded in research about constructivist practices in general and science teaching and learning in particular.[1] The *predictive phase* of the Instructional Planning Framework will not be covered here but is explained in Chapter 3. We focus here on the *responsive phase* of the framework because it is during initial planning for and implementation of instruction that research-based strategies come into play. At this point, your review of this chapter is important so that you understand the Instructional Tools, strategies, and resources, as well as why we have developed them. However, your actual implementation of the Instructional Tools will not occur until you see their applications in Part II of this book. **(Note: All the Instructional Tools—2.1–2.14—are grouped at the end of this chapter, beginning on page 29. They are followed by Recommended Resources and Endnotes.)**

Instructional Strategy Sequencing Tool

The Instructional Strategy Sequencing Tool (Instructional Tool 2.1, p. 29) is the core tool developed to assist you as you select and sequence strategies. This tool is based on the research and organized by the phases of the Instructional Planning Framework. The first row of Instructional Tool 2.1 is composed of four framework phases—identifying preconceptions, eliciting and confronting preconceptions, sense making, and demonstrating understanding—all of which are grounded in a conceptual change model (Posner et al. 1982). The phases use the thinking and some of the language of "dimensions of learning" (Marzano 1992) and "meaningful learning" (Fisher, Wandersee, and Moody 2000) and are found in the second row of Instructional Tool 2.1 (as column heads, presented vertically).[2] Specific approaches and strategies are listed according to one of three approaches—metacognitive (Instructional Tools 2.2–2.4), standards based (Instructional Tools 2.5–2.7), and sense making (Instructional Tools 2.9–2.14)—and then by categories within each approach.

In Instructional Tool 2.1, strategies identified by a checkmark have the potential, if effectively implemented, to promote student understanding. You can use this tool to identify appropriate strategies from each phase of the framework as you sequence instruction. These strategies are further explained in the individual Instructional Tools. We encourage you to select more than one or two strategies because students benefit from multiple strategies. In addition, the results from any formative assessments you use may require that you provide additional learning experiences for students.

Once you have selected possible strategies, the remaining Instructional Tools (2.2–2.14, on pp. 31–87) provide detail about strategies, the research that supports their use, implementation ideas, resources that provide information and examples, and technology applications.

In Part II, Chapters 3–7, where the five hard-to-teach biology concepts are explored, various sense-making approaches give you multiple entry points into the content. In addition, we recommend that teachers use one standards-based approach and one metacognitive approach for the five concepts in order to develop students' understandings of these approaches and to strengthen students' content understanding. The process for selecting strategies will be modeled in Part II. Now we look more closely at each of the three approaches and describe the tools we have developed for each.

Metacognitive Approach Tools

Achievement increases if teachers provide students with clear cognitive goals, support students in the sharing and development of their ideas, value the ideas they share, and use their multiple ideas to help them reflect on and move toward the goals of the class (Hipkins et al. 2002). Metacognition requires that students have knowledge about, awareness of, and control over their learning (Baird and White 1996). Furthermore, conceptual change requires that teachers elicit various student explanations for the teacher and the student to consider. Students need to reflect on and discuss their understandings, compare and contrast explanations, consider arguments to support or contradict explanations, and choose possible explanations based on the evidence they have gathered (Hewson 1996; Hipkins et al. 2002).

Some concepts seem too abstract for students to understand. Teachers can avoid these more abstract concepts until their students have developed appropriate thinking skills, or they can teach those skills (Scott, Asoko, and Driver 2007). We recommend explicitly teaching metacognitive skills. In fact, teaching metacognitive strategies is second only to classroom management in influencing student learning (Wang, Haertel, and Walberg

1993/94). Direct instruction on metacognitive skills does not seem to enhance conceptual learning, but coupling this instruction with content learning is effective. The classrooms that are most successful at metacognitive thinking are those in which teachers purposefully target both cognitive and metacognitive learning goals, formatively track students' progress, and help students reach both kinds of goals (Hipkins et al. 2002). We suggest that you target both cognitive and metacognitive goals in each lesson you teach.

How do we teach metacognition? Thinking is invisible, but there are ways that teachers can make it visible to their students, helping them to become more metacognitive and to see high school as more about exploring ideas than memorizing content. Ritchart and Perkins (2008) developed thinking routines that help in this effort. Each routine targets a type of thinking and should be used in conjunction with specific content. Some of these strategies are included in Instructional Tools 2.2, 2.3, and 2.4. Though these strategies are not guaranteed to develop metacognitive capacity, they are general areas of expertise that teachers can develop in their students. We use Marzano's (1992) habits of mind to categorize these areas in the metacognitive strategy tools (Instructional Tools 2.2–2.4) and we share strategies that support skill development in them.

Critical Thinking and Learning

"Critical thinking and learning include being accurate and seeking accuracy, being clear and seeking clarity, being open-minded, restraining impulsivity, taking a position when the situation warrants it, and being sensitive to others' feelings and level of knowledge"(Marzano 1992, pp. 133–134). Instructional Tool 2.2 on page 33 explores various strategies that promote critical thinking and learning.

Creative Thinking and Learning

"Creative thinking and learning include engaging intensely in tasks even when answers or solutions are not immediately apparent, pushing the limits of your knowledge and abilities, generating, trusting, and maintaining your own standards of evaluation, and generating new ways of viewing a situation outside the boundaries of standard conventions" (Marzano 1992, p. 134). Instructional Tool 2.3 on page 36 explores various strategies to promote creative thinking and learning.

Self-Regulated Thinking and Learning

Self-regulated thinking includes "being aware of your own thinking, planning, being aware of necessary resources, being sensitive to feedback, and evaluating the effectiveness of your actions" (Marzano 1992, p. 133). Instructional Tool 2.4 on page 38 lists various strategies to promote self-regulated thinking.

Standards-Based Approach Tools

The National Science Education Standards (NSES) (NRC 1996), which are grounded in exemplary practice and research, provide focus as science teachers contribute to the goal of a scientifically literate society. It is only natural that teachers use the NSES as one of the major approaches to teach the hard-to-teach topics in Chapters 3–7. We address the standards related to those topics in each of those chapters. We also encourage you to infuse other NSES content standards into your curriculum—especially inquiry, the history of science (HOS), and the nature of science (NOS). The standards-based approaches (Instructional Tools 2.5–2.7) are designed to help you determine which approaches are best for each topic in Part II.

Inquiry Tools

As the NSES state, "Science as inquiry is basic to science education and a controlling principle in the ultimate organization and selection of student activities" (NRC 1996, p. 105). Inquiry is much more than traditional instruction on process skills. Rather, the standards expect students to be able to use scientific inquiry and to think and act in ways associated with inquiry, using "the cognitive and manipulative skills associated with formulation of scientific explanations" (NRC 1996, p. 173). Indeed, limiting experiences to recipe-type investigations restricts students' understandings of the nature of science. Students frequently misinterpret such investigations and often do not develop even the desired basic understandings of those investigations (Hipkins et al. 2002).

By high school, students should understand that concepts are what drive inquiry and that the purpose of inquiry is to test their ideas. Successful inquiry in high school requires that students reflect on the concepts that guide inquiry (NRC 1996). Students are not exposed to inquiry just to experience it. Instead, inquiry is a process that results in conceptual understanding; it is therefore central among our standards-based approaches.

Inquiry means different things to different people, and there is extensive discussion about the merits of guided inquiry and open inquiry. We focus our Instructional Tools on the five "essential features" of inquiry outlined in *Inquiry and the National Science Education Standards* (NRC 2000, p. 29). This framework (Figure 2.1, p. 20) shows a continuum of variations that give students and teachers varying amounts of control over the inquiry process.

We believe that effective use of the framework shown in Figure 2.1 is critical to promoting inquiry. By "effective use" we mean the following:

1. It is important that teachers develop their students' understanding of and abilities in each of the five features. This process may require varying degrees of support, but ultimately teachers want their students to be able to manage their own inquiry.

Figure 2.1

Essential Features of Classroom Inquiry and Their Variations

Essential Feature	Variations			
1. Learner engages in scientifically oriented questions	Learner poses a question	Learner selects among questions, poses new questions	Learner sharpens or clarifies question provided by the teacher, materials, or other sources	Learner engages in question provided by teacher, materials, or other sources
2. Learner gives priority to **evidence** in responding to questions	Learner determines what constitutes evidence and collects it	Learner directed to collect certain data	Learner given data and asked to analyze	Learner given data and told how to analyze
3. Learner formulates **explanations** from evidence	Learner formulates explanation after summarizing evidence	Learner guided in process of formulating explanations from evidence	Learner given possible ways to use evidence to formulate explanation	Learner provided with evidence
4. Learner connects explanations to scientific knowledge	Learner independently examines other resources and forms the links to explanations	Learner directed toward areas and sources of scientific knowledge	Learner given possible connections	
5. Learner communicates and justifies explanations	Learner forms reasonable and logical argument to communicate explanations	Learner coached in development of communication	Learner provided broad guidelines to use to sharpen communication	Learner given steps and procedures for communication
More————————————Amount of Learner Self-Direction————————————Less				
Less————————————Amount of Direction From Teacher or Manual————————————More				

Source: National Research Council (NRC). 2000. *Inquiry and the National Science Education Standards.* Washington, DC: National Academy Press, p. 29.

2. Each of the variations is useful in instruction, and teachers must carefully select inquiry approaches based on the content the students are learning and on the differences among students in their classrooms.

3. Guided inquiry is the most teacher-centered form of inquiry; it allows students to develop knowledge related to a specific domain because it is goal-oriented. It is effective with diverse students, improves higher-order thinking and problem-

solving skills, and enhances conceptual understanding (Moreno and Tharp 2006). Open-ended inquiries, on the other hand, are more student-centered and directly reflect the work of scientists. They can extend learning to gifted students (among others), especially if supported by mentors from the scientific community (Hipkins et al. 2002). Since it would be counterproductive to pit direct instruction against open inquiry, we should consider instructional sequences that use a variety of strategies and allow for an inquiry approach that contributes to a "prepared mind" (Bybee 2006).

The Instructional Tool for Inquiry (Tool 2.5, p. 43) should help you select and use strategies that develop the best possible instructional sequence. Notice that this tool is organized around each of the five essential features of inquiry and provides research and classroom implications.

History and Nature of Science Tools

The NSES expect that students should understand science as a human endeavor, the nature of scientific knowledge (NOS), and the historical perspectives of science (HOS) (NRC 1996). What do we mean by the history and nature of science? And are the two related?

History of Science (HOS)

By teaching aspects of the HOS, teachers help students to learn science concepts and to see the NOS as a process. Integration of the HOS and NOS with content learning is recommended (McKinney and Michalovic 2004; Rudge and Howe 2004). Here, however, for purposes of clarity, we will discuss them separately. Instructional Tool 2.6 on page 49 outlines several strategies and resources.

The following steps are useful to consider, regardless of the strategy you select:

1. As always, identify and prioritize your lesson objectives.
2. Select a historic episode—for example, an important scientific discovery, scientific debate, serendipitous event, or how theories have changed with new evidence—that aligns with your objectives and the misconceptions that you know are typically held by students.
3. Learn about the episode and identify resources.
4. Develop and implement a related scenario that is adequate to address the objectives but not so extensive as to overwhelm your students.
5. Prepare questions that will help scaffold student learning (Rudge and Howe 2004).

Nature of Science

"A comprehensive science curriculum should include the study of both science knowledge and the nature of science (not just one of the two) as a requirement for science literacy" (Vitale and Romance 2006, p. 339). But what exactly do we mean when we use the term *the nature of science*? Different experts provide slightly different lists of the various aspects of the nature of science, but they consistently include the following aspects (Bryson 2003; Chiappetta and Koballa 2004; Colburn 2004; Lederman and Lederman 2004; McComas 2004):

1. There is no single, step-by-step method by which all science is done. Sadly, science educators often teach a single scientific method.

2. The scientific enterprise searches for and relies on empirical evidence, and all scientific knowledge, at least in part, is based on observations of the natural world. Most students do not recognize the link between theory and gathering evidence, though researchers believe this link should be a key NOS outcome (Hipkins et al. 2002).

3. There is a difference between observation and inference. "Observations are descriptive statements about natural phenomena that are 'directly' accessible to the senses (or extensions of the senses) and about which several observers can reach consensus with relative ease (e.g., descriptions of the morphology of the remnants of a once living organism). Inferences, on the other hand, go beyond the senses. For example, one may develop explanations about the observed morphology in terms of its possible contributions to function. At a higher level, a scientist can infer models or mechanisms that explain observations of complex phenomena (e.g., models of weather, evolution)" (Lederman 2007, p. 833).

4. There is a difference between scientific laws and theories. Laws are statements about relationships among natural phenomena while theories are inferred from observable phenomena. All must be checked against what happens in the natural world. One never becomes the other, though it is often taught in that way.

5. Creativity and imagination are important parts of science. But students often think that scientists are entirely objective and that science is a set of facts and conclusions rather than a dynamic body of knowledge.

6. There is subjectivity in science since humans carry on the enterprise. None of us is entirely objective. Discovery is personal and subjective, but rigor is maintained through peer review and presentation of ideas and conclusions to the larger scientific community.

7. There are historical, social, and cultural influences on science that include philosophy, religion, politics, social structures, and more. Consider the many controversial issues we face today, such as cloning and stem cell research.

8. Scientific knowledge is tentative and subject to change but it is also durable. Change occurs when new evidence is made available, so new claims are made. Science cannot absolutely prove something but does provide the best possible explanation based on current evidence.

9. Science does not presume to answer all questions. Sometimes, especially in regard to morality, ethics, and faith, we must turn to other sources for the answers we seek.

We believe that these aspects of the NOS and the HOS should be embedded in the teaching of content. This means helping our students to think scientifically and, like scientists, to pose questions using evidence in support of claims and to communicate and discuss their results. Students do not understand the NOS by doing science activities alone. Instead, selected aspects must be planned for and integrated into our lessons (Lederman and Lederman 2004). Instructional Tool 2.7 (p. 51) summarizes some strategies that can help us to just that.

A teacher's illustration and promotion of the NOS must be explicit. Many traditional science experiences inadvertently establish misconceptions about NOS. Some of the more common ways that teachers accidentally promote these misconceptions include the language that they use when teaching content, the use of cookbook labs common to textbooks, the use of texts that report the end products (facts) of science without relating how that knowledge was developed, and the use of assessment strategies that stress vocabulary and knowledge end products but not the NOS (Clough and Olson 2004). Concerted efforts to counter the impact of these influences require that teachers do not approach the NOS as an add-on strategy. Instead, it must be an overarching strategy used in a complementary way with other strategies, so that the NOS is a *process* that students learn and apply during their science learning.

Sense Making: Linguistic and Nonlinguistic Representational Tools

It is not always easy to know what your students are thinking. Their knowledge tends to be implicit, so they themselves are not entirely aware of their thinking or of assumptions they make. On top of that, they are not often encouraged to voice these thoughts, so that even when their knowledge is explicit, they learn to keep it to themselves. Finally, traditional classrooms limit opportunities for students to express themselves in nonverbal ways (Fisher, Wandersee, and Moody 2000). Yet explicit communication is essential to sense making for student learning. It is also essential for teachers so that they can recognize what their students understand and do not understand.

Strategies that support sense making are important throughout the responsive phase, but particularly when teachers confront and address preconceptions. (See the Sense-Making Strategy Instructional Tools, 2.8–2.14) There are both linguistic and nonlinguistic strategies for sense making. We categorize them using Marzano's (1992) organization: speaking (linguistic), writing (linguistic), and symbolizing (nonlinguistic). All three are not only important for learning; they are also aligned with ways in which scientists work.

Linguistic Representations

Instructional Tool 2.8 on page 55, in addition to examining speaking (including listening) and writing as ways to linguistically represent knowledge, looks at "reading to learn" and "speaking to learn." Reading, writing, speaking, and listening are essential to the stages of inquiry outlined in the NSES and can be used during engagement and exploration, designing and conducting investigations, analyzing and interpreting data, and presenting findings and understandings (Century et al. 2002). There are extensive resources available on discourse, reading, and writing to learn. In Instructional Tool 2.8 we focus our attention on those strategies that support the concurrent development of literacy and science literacy and that are foundational to meaning making through inquiry. There is more extensive research that supports the use of some of these strategies at the K–8 level, and, although that is not the grade band targeted in this book, we included those strategies that showed potential for high school teaching and learning in our Instructional Tools.

Nonlinguistic Representations

In the previous section, we discussed the use of language in learning (linguistic representation). Knowledge, as educators know, is also stored in an imagery form (nonlinguistic). The more learners use both systems of representation (linguistic and nonlinguistic), the better they think about and recall knowledge. Teachers, however, tend to use linguistic representation most often. Students typically are left on their own to develop and use nonlinguistic representations, even though the impact of nonlinguistic representations on achievement is significant (Marzano, Pickering, and Pollack 2001).

Two basic points should be made about the use of nonlinguistic representations. First, research shows that the following activities help to develop nonlinguistic representations and enhance understanding for our students:

- Creating graphic representations
- Making physical models
- Generating mental pictures
- Drawing pictures and pictographs
- Engaging in kinesthetic activity

Second, nonlinguistic representations should elaborate on students' knowledge. Teachers should ask students to explain and justify their elaborations (Marzano, Pickering, and Pollock 2001).

How can you, as a teacher, determine which strategies help to promote nonlinguistic representations? Instructional Tools 2.9–14 will help you select appropriate strategies. Here we discuss four major groupings: models; maps and graphic organizers; drawing; and kinesthetic activities.

Models (Mental, Physical, Verbal, Visual, and Dynamic)

Recall Marzano's (1992) generalization that we want our students to build nonlinguistic representations in their minds. Such "mental models" represent ideas, objects, events, processes, and systems. To help build and communicate mental models, people use expressed models that are simplified from those held in their brains (Hipkins et al. 2002). Types of expressed models are mental; physical; verbal (metaphors and analogies); visual (graphs, pictures, and diagrams); and dynamic (simulations, computer simulations, virtual manipulatives, and animations). Physical models lend themselves to building images of knowledge in students' minds (Marzano, Pickering, and Pollock 2001). Metaphors and analogies help students see how dissimilar things are similar, which is important for building mental models. Visual and dynamic models provide further representations that help students learn. See Instructional Tool 2.9, page 66, for extensive information on models.

Maps and Graphic Organizers

We recognize both the value of laboratories and other hands-on exercises and the fact that they are often underused in classrooms. But we also recognize that these experiences, alone, do not translate directly into conceptual understanding. "Doing a science activity is largely meaningless unless time is also spent making sense of the activity. This is where mapping strategies have the most to offer" (Fisher, Wandersee, and Moody 2000, p. 94).

Indeed, maps and graphic organizers are among the most commonly used strategies to help students to construct nonlinguistic representations. They combine linguistic and nonlinguistic modes since they call for words and phrases as well as symbols. They help students retrieve what they already know, activating their prior knowledge, when used as advanced organizers (Marzano, Pickering, and Pollock 2001). Furthermore, these visual thinking tools are used for storing ideas already developed and for construction of content knowledge.

Several types of visual tools promote the translation of experiential learning into semantic knowledge. We use Hyerle's (2000) classifications to discuss three types of visual tools: brainstorming webs, task-specific organizers, and thinking-process maps.

Brainstorming webs are open systems that help us think "outside the box." People often think of brainstorming as something that occurs only at the beginning of a process, but brainstorming webs can be revised as thinking changes (Hyerle 2000). They are usually unstructured diagrams that start with a central idea and support free association to create a graphic that reflects relations with other ideas (Young n.d.). Several types of brainstorming webs are outlined in Instructional Tool 2.10 on page 72.

Task-specific organizers are highly structured tools that help students see the big picture about the content that teachers want them to learn. They help organize the mind and promote "thinking *inside* the box" (Hyerle 2000). They are applied in formal, rule-based ways and used for defined tasks or in a specific knowledge area. Emphasis is on organization as specified by the teacher rather the learner's creative organization (Young n.d.). The structured nature of these tools supports development of important habits of mind, including persistence, self-control, accuracy, and precision of language and thinking. The organizers are concrete models that scaffold the work for students who might otherwise give up. They help students stay inside the box of learning that is the teacher's target. They also provide written evidence of students' ideas that students can reflect on and then, perhaps, go on to modify their thinking. Once students become familiar with these structured organizers, they are more able to create their own organizers and control their own thinking (Hyerle 2000). Several types of task-specific organizers—for general use and for use specifically in to science classrooms—are outlined in Instructional Tool 2.11 on page 75.

Thinking-process maps include concept maps and systems diagrams. In some ways they grow out of and synthesize brainstorming webs and graphic organizers, and they support thinking *about* the box. They help students do the following: define specific thinking processes as recurring patterns that can be transferred across disciplines, guide the building of simple and complex mental models, focus on evaluating their own and their peers' mental models, and reflect on their own meaning making (Hyerle 2000). Several types of thinking-process maps are reviewed in Instructional Tool 2.12 on page 79.

Drawing

Student drawings can be used to determine students' levels of conceptual understanding, observational skills, and abilities to reason, as well as their beliefs. Teachers can use drawing as a learning experience or an assessment (McNair and Stein 2001). See Instructional Tool 2.13 on page 83 for drawing activities.

Kinesthetic Activities

Kinesthetic activities are those that involve movement. The cerebellum of the brain processes both movement and learning. There is a constant interplay between movement and learning, and this relationship continues throughout our lives. Indeed, more than 80 studies "suggest strong links between the cerebellum and memory, spatial perception, language, attention, emotion, nonverbal cues, and even decision making" (Jensen 1998, p. 84). The association of movement with specific knowledge produces a mental image of that knowledge in the learner's mind (Marzano, Pickering, and Pollock 2001). Teachers need to purposefully integrate movement into their everyday instruction. Instructional Tool 2.14 on page 86 outlines two major groups of strategies that help to promote such integration: (1) hands-on experiments, activities, and manipulatives and (2) physical movement and gestures.

A Note on Technology

Rather than include a separate set of tools for applying technology to science teaching and learning, we embedded possible applications and resources in the Instructional Tools where inclusion was appropriate. We tried, in each case, to give examples of technology applications of the strategy that can be applied by teachers who have access to the appropriate technology. However, each of the strategies can be used independently of the technology application.

We encourage you to consider using technology to support inquiry-based instruction. Songer (2007, p. 283) suggests that the tools essential to inquiry that make the best use of technology are the following:

1. Modeling, simulations, and visualization tools are effective when "learners think critically about scientific ideas and/or compare to real life conditions."
2. Online critique and resources for discussion are helpful when "learners critically evaluate and communicate scientific ideas."
3. Online scaffolding tools are supportive when "learners formulate knowledge such as scientific explanations from evidence."
4. The use of calculators and/or computer based tools to collect and analyze data is appropriate when learners are called on to "gather, analyze, and interpret data."

Some Thoughts on Assessment

For this book, we could have developed additional tools for summative, formative, and peer assessment. However, the assessment focus for this book is to check for understanding. Many of the strategies found in our Instructional Tools serve as assessments for learning, that is, the findings from the assessments can be used by teachers to inform their teaching. Coffey (2006) lists the following five features of what she calls supportive assessment, each of which aligns with our Instructional Planning Framework, as we demonstrate below.

1. Involves students
2. Is organized around meaningful criteria
3. Is embedded in everyday activities
4. Provides immediate and relevant feedback to students and teachers
5. Focuses on progress and improvement

Student involvement (#1) is central in our framework, and metacognition, including peer assessment and self-assessment, is a critical part of student involvement. The *predictive phase* in the framework identifies essential understandings, which are the criteria (#2) for determining understanding *and* the learning sequence targets designed to move from goals to understanding. Perhaps most important, the strategies in each of the Instructional Tools can serve not only as teaching strategies, but as formative assessments as well. The strategies are embedded in everyday activities (#3) and provide immediate feedback to the teacher and students (#4). (Of course, feedback only helps teachers and their students if they actually *use* it.)

Finally, the iterative *responsive phase* in the framework is designed specifically to focus on progress and improvement (#5). Though we do not specifically talk about feedback to students (except in science notebooks) and grading, our intent is for each student to reach the targeted understandings. The understandings, not just grades, are the goal of our model.

Many exceptional assessment resources are available to you. Some are specific to science assessment and some are more general in nature. We recommend some of our favorite resources specific to science in Build Your Library (p. 88).

***

To summarize, during the *predictive phase* teachers clarify the learning goals, learning sequence, and criteria for demonstrating understanding. Then, in the *responsive phase*, strategies are selected for use. It is important to select multiple strategies not only for use during initial (planned) instruction, but also for possible follow-up teaching experiences, as determined by formative assessments. This supports the iterative nature of the *responsive phase*.

The upcoming chapters in the book will model aspects of the Instructional Planning Framework (Chapter 3 focuses on the *predictive phase*, and Chapters 4–7 immerse the reader in the *responsive phase*. Chapter 7 summarizes the thinking outlined in the book by modeling once more the entire Instructional Planning Framework).

Instructional Tool 2.1

Instructional Strategy Sequencing Tool

Framework Phases		Identifying Preconceptions	Eliciting and Confronting Preconceptions		Sense Making				Demonstrating Understanding	
		Bringing (by the teacher) students' preconceptions to the surface and determining prior knowledge	Eliciting preconceptions explicitly	Confronting preconceptions	Perceiving, interpreting, and organizing information	Connecting information	Retrieving, extending, and applying information	Using knowledge in relevant ways	Formative assessment	Peer and self-assessment
Approaches	Strategies									
Metacognitive										
Critical thinking	Truth Routines				√	√	√		√	√
	Fairness Routines				√	√	√		√	√
	Graphic Organizers		√		√	√			√	√
	Socratic Dialogue		√		√	√			√	
Creative thinking	Brainstorming Webs	√	√		√	√			√	
	Creativity Routines		√	√	√	√	√	√	√	√
	Self-Evaluation		√						√	√
	Socratic Dialogue		√		√	√			√	
Self-regulated thinking	Identify What You Know and What You Don't Know	√	√	√	√				√	√
	Talk About Thinking		√	√	√	√			√	√
	Thinking Journals		√		√	√			√	√
	Plan and Self-Regulate		√		√					√
	Debrief the Thinking Process				√	√	√		√	√
	Self-Evaluation		√						√	√

Instructional Tool 2.1 (continued)

Framework Phases		Identifying Preconceptions	Eliciting and Confronting Preconceptions		Sense Making				Demonstrating Understanding	
		Bringing (by the teacher) students' preconceptions to the surface and determining prior knowledge	Eliciting preconceptions explicitly	Confronting preconceptions	Perceiving, interpreting, and organizing information	Connecting information	Retrieving, extending, and applying information	Using knowledge in relevant ways	Formative assessment	Peer and self-assessment
Approaches	**Strategies**									
Standards-Based										
Inquiry	Engage in Scientifically Oriented Questions		√	√						
	Give Priority to Evidence in Responding to Questions			√	√	√				
	Formulate Explanations from Evidence				√	√	√		√	√
	Connect Explanations to Scientific Knowledge				√	√	√		√	√
	Communicate and Justify Explanations					√	√	√	√	√
History of Science	Demonstration Experiments	√		√	√	√			√	√
	Reading and Narratives			√	√	√			√	√
Nature of Science	Formal Introduction of NOS					√	√	√		
	Careful Attention to Language			√						
	Questions and Discussion	√		√	√	√			√	√
	Focusing Labs on NOS			√	√	√	√	√		√

Instructional Tool 2.1 (continued)

Framework Phases		Identifying Preconceptions	Eliciting and Confronting Preconceptions		Sense Making				Demonstrating Understanding	
		Bringing (by the teacher) students' preconceptions to the surface and determining prior knowledge	Eliciting preconceptions explicitly	Confronting preconceptions	Perceiving, interpreting, and organizing information	Connecting information	Retrieving, extending, and applying information	Using knowledge in relevant ways	Formative assessment	Peer and self-assessment
Approaches	Strategies									
Sense Making: Linguistic Representations										
Writing to Learn	Learning Logs	√	√		√	√	√		√	√
	Science Notebooks		√	√	√	√	√		√	√
	Scientific Explanations		√	√	√	√	√		√	√
	Science Writing Heuristic		√	√	√	√	√		√	√
Reading to Learn	Vocabulary Development Strategies		√		√	√			√	
	Informational Text Strategies	√	√	√	√	√	√		√	
	Reflection Strategies		√	√	√	√	√		√	√
	Thinking-Process Maps	√	√	√	√	√	√		√	√
Speaking to Learn	Large- and Small-Group Discourse (including questioning)	√	√	√	√	√	√	√	√	√
	Student Questioning		√	√					√	√
	Socratic Dialogue		√		√	√			√	

Instructional Tool 2.1 (continued)

Framework Phases		Identifying Preconceptions	Eliciting and Confronting Preconceptions		Sense Making				Demonstrating Understanding	
		Bringing (by the teacher) students' preconceptions to the surface and determining prior knowledge	Eliciting preconceptions explicitly	Confronting preconceptions	Perceiving, interpreting, and organizing information	Connecting information	Retrieving, extending, and applying information	Using knowledge in relevant ways	Formative assessment	Peer and self-assessment
Approaches	Strategies									
Sense Making: Nonlinguistic Representations										
Models	Mental Models				√	√	√			
	Physical Models			√	√	√	√		√	√
	Verbal Models: Analogies				√	√	√		√	√
	Verbal Models: Metaphors				√	√	√		√	√
	Visual Models		√	√	√	√	√		√	√
	Dynamic Models			√	√	√	√		√	√
Visual Tools	Brainstorming Webs	√	√		√	√			√	
	Task-Specific Organizers				√	√	√		√	√
	Thinking Process Maps	√	√	√	√	√	√		√	√
Drawing Out Thinking	Drawings and Annotated Drawings	√	√	√	√	√			√	√
	Concept Cartoons		√	√					√	
Kinesthetic Activities	Hands-on Experiments, Activities, and Manipulatives			√						
	Physical Movements/ Gestures		√	√	√	√			√	

Instructional Tool 2.2

Strategies That Support Critical Thinking and Learning (Metacognitive Approaches)

Sense Making: Visible Thinking: Truth Routines	Visible Thinking is a method that deepens students' subject matter understandings, increases interactions with peers, and cultivates dispositions toward thinking (Ritchart and Perkins 2008). In particular, mini-strategies called "truth routines" (see the Visible Thinking website, *www.pz.harvard.edu/vt*) are designed to help students identify truth claims and explore strategies to uncover the truth, think more deeply about the truth of something, clarify claims and sources, explore truth claims from various perspectives, and determine the various factors relevant to a question of truth and see beyond an either–or approach to truth. These routines promote critical thinking because they address seeking accuracy and clarity, being open-minded, and restraining impulsivity.
The Research	• The Visible Thinking website (*www.pz.harvard.edu/vt*) is based on years of research about thinking and learning, as well as research and development in classrooms. In all cases the research found that skills and abilities are not enough but thinking and attitudes toward thinking and learning (dispositions) are clearly important. All strategies shared on the site were developed in classrooms and revised multiple times to ensure applicability in the classroom. • These strategies allow students with disabilities and general education students to show what they know, provide gifted and talented students a way to explore ideas at a deeper level, and give teachers a window into their students' thinking, allowing them to provide targeted and differentiated instruction (Ritchart and Perkins n.d.). • Visible Thinking changes the nature of classroom discussions, making them more open, student-directed, and inclusive (Ritchart and Perkins n.d.).
Classroom Implications	• Some of these strategies work very well during inquiry when students are expected to formulate explanations from evidence and to connect their explanations to scientific knowledge. • They also work well when exploring controversial issues related to science. • The various strategies can be used with individuals or small groups as well as during whole-class discussion. • The Visible Thinking website itself is rich with descriptions of various truth routines and examples of those routines in action. We suggest you visit the site and explore it yourself.
Application Example	One strategy at the website is Claim/Support/Question. It requires students to clarify claims of truth by making a claim, identifying support for their claim, and further questioning their own claims. You can use this strategy during initial explorations of specific content. Provide students with hands-on experiences (e.g., various stations that explore osmosis) and then ask them to make claims related to their observations. They then identify support for their claims that is based on things they see, feel, and know. They then ask a question about their claims—what isn't explained or what's left hanging. These questions point them to areas of experimentation.
Technology Applications	Though no technology applications directly apply to truth routines, any number of media can be used effectively to visualize and document the processes. These include, but are not limited to, video, digital photos, concept-mapping software, and SmartBoards.
Resources	Truth routines from Ritchart and Perkins (2008) are available at *www.pz.harvard.edu/vt*.

Instructional Tool 2.2 (continued)

Visible Thinking: Fairness Routines	Visible Thinking is a method that deepens students' subject matter understandings, increases interactions with peers, and cultivates dispositions toward thinking (Ritchart and Perkins 2008). Mini-strategies called "fairness routines" (see them at the Visible Thinking website, *www.pz.harvard.edu/vt*) are designed to help students explore diverse perspectives, consider present and past attitudes and judgments, separate fact and feeling, and explore the complexity of dilemmas. These strategies align with critical thinking as they relate to open-mindedness and sensitivity to others' feelings.
The Research	• The Visible Thinking website is based on years of research about thinking and learning, as well as research and development in classrooms. In all cases, it was found that skills and abilities are not enough; thinking and attitudes toward thinking and learning (dispositions) are as important. All strategies shared on the site were developed in classrooms and revised multiple times to ensure applicability in the classroom as well as promotion of student thinking and engagement. • These strategies allow students with disabilities and general education students to show what they know, provide gifted and talented students ways to explore ideas at a deeper level, and give teachers windows into their students' thinking, allowing them to provide targeted and differentiated instruction (Ritchart and Perkins n.d.). • Visible Thinking changes the nature of classroom discussions, making them more open, student-directed, and inclusive (Ritchart and Perkins n.d.).
Classroom Implications	• Visible Thinking routines are easy to use and designed for easy infusion of various content areas (Perkins 2003). • The "Circle of Viewpoints" strategy can be used to begin discussions about dilemmas and controversial issues. • "Here Now/There Then" is a strategy that helps students see how perspectives change through time, and it might be used when including the history of science (HOS) in a science lesson. • "Reporters Notebook" is a strategy that helps students separate fact from feeling. It can be used when teaching science concepts that conflict with students' beliefs and feelings and when clarifying the nature of science (NOS). • The website itself is rich with descriptions of various fairness routines and examples of those routines in action. We suggest you visit the site and explore it yourself.
Application Example	The "Circle of Viewpoints" strategy can be used for various controversial content issues. For instance, an ecology unit could begin with an issue such as deforestation or water pollution. The strategy requires students to brainstorm a list of perspectives related to the issue. Each student then selects a viewpoint, describes the topic from that viewpoint, and asks a question from that viewpoint. Finally, students consider new ideas and questions they have about the topic.
Technology Applications	Though no technology applications directly apply to fairness routines, any number of media can be used effectively to visualize and document the processes. These include, but are not limited to, video, digital photos, concept mapping software, and SmartBoards.
Resources	Fairness routines from Ritchart and Perkins (2008) are available at *www.pz.harvard.edu/vt*.

Graphic Organizers	See Instructional Tools 2.11 and 2.12. Although these organizers support critical thinking, their use in this book is promoted primarily for sense making.

Instructional Tool 2.2 *(continued)*

Sense Making: Socratic Dialogue	Socratic dialogue is the conversation that results from the Socratic method, a discussion process during which a facilitator promotes independent, reflective, and critical thinking. The process begins with a concrete question based on students' concrete experiences. Students' responses verify their understanding of the question and provide possible answers to it (drawing on personal experience). Students' responses determine subsidiary questions, and each question is explored until consensus is reached. Based on these responses, resolution is then reached on the initial question. (*Note:* Variations include Socratic Seminars and Socratic Circles.)
The Research	• Socratic dialogue reinforces critical and creative thinking (Marzano 1992). • White-boarding is strongly associated with Socratic dialogue and can promote conceptual understanding, encourage alternative representations of knowledge, improve classroom discourse, and increase student motivation (Wenning 2005). • It is difficult to engage students as the leaders of dialogues, even when traditional guidelines for dialogues are followed (Wenning, Holbrook, and Stankevitz 2006).
Classroom Implications	• Student-centered discussions can be promoted using text (text-based discussions). Examination and discussion of text promotes "the skills and habits of reading analytically, listening carefully, citing evidence, disagreeing respectfully, and being open-minded" (Hale and City 2006, p. 4). • White-boarding and Socratic dialogue should focus initially on evidence students have collected. All students should be held accountable, either for presenting and defending their work and conclusions or analyzing the work of others. Subsidiary questions that arise are then addressed, and consensus on the original question is reached (Wenning 2005). • White-boarding and the modeling method of instruction are used concurrently; this method has been recognized as an exemplary program in K–12 science education (Wenning 2005). • A typology of questions (Rhodes 1995) to use during Socratic dialogue includes the following question categories: information, interpretational, explanatory, procedural, relational, verificational, heuristic, and evaluational. For sample questions, refer to Wenning, Holbrook, and Stankevitz (2006). • Ways to promote student engagement in questioning (rather than just teacher questioning) include (1) allow students to talk without interruption during the initial whiteboard presentation; (2) encourage peer questioning, respect student conclusions when correct, and, when incorrect, ask further questions rather than directly critiquing; (3) get students to agree (first focusing on those things on which they all agree, move forward for further agreement, and suggest further experimentation if necessary); (4) establish a positive classroom atmosphere; (5) let students think through things themselves by asking questions and summarizing their thinking; and (6) acknowledge a job well done (Wenning, Holbrook, and Stankevitz 2006).
Application Example	To practice Socratic questioning, choose a complex issue for students to discuss. Use the fishbowl technique, with one group of students in the "inside circle" discussing the issue and the others in a circle around them, listening and taking notes about the inner-circle discussion. After the inner-circle discussion is complete, the teacher facilitates a discussion of the discussion, involving both groups of students. The focus should be on the implementation of Socratic questioning by the inner circle. Follow this up with a practice white-boarding session, conducted by a student with the teacher modeling Socratic questioning. The teacher should use a think-aloud approach to make this modeling explicit.
Technology Applications	• Social networking sites can be used for scientific discussion. Ning (*http://ning.com*) is one example of a free social networking platform that can be customized and made private to invited participants. • Online white-boarding (e.g., SMARTTHINKING, Inc.'s white-boarding environment) is also a possibility.
Resources	• Information and samples of white-boarding and Socratic dialogue, including links to Wenning (2005) and Wenning, Holbrook, and Stankevitz (2006) are found at *www.phy.ilstu.edu/ programs/ptefiles/311content/questioning/questioning.html*. In addition, this website has links to the Rhodes typology of questions and much more. • For further information on text-based Socratic seminars, see *Leading Student-Centered Discussions* (Hale and City 2006).

Instructional Tool 2.3

Strategies That Support Creative Thinking and Learning (Metacognitive Approaches)

Brainstorming Webs	See Instructional Tool 2.10. Although brainstorming webs actively engage and facilitate creative thinking—specifically mental fluency, flexibility, and curiosity—their use in this book is primarily explained as a form of nonlinguistic representation.

Creativity Routines	Visible Thinking is a method that deepens students' subject matter understandings, increases interactions with peers, and cultivates dispositions toward thinking (Ritchart and Perkins 2008). Visual Thinking routines are more than strategies because, once learned by students, they become part of the classroom culture. Creativity routines are one set of routines used to make thinking visible; these routines look at purposes and audiences, consider generating and transforming creative questions, think creatively about options, explore creative decision-making, and consider perspectives.
The Research	<ul><li>The Visible Thinking website (*www.pz.harvard.edu/vt*) is based on years of research about thinking and learning, as well as research and development in classrooms. In all cases, it was found that skills and abilities are not enough; thinking and attitudes toward thinking and learning (dispositions) are as important. All strategies shared on the site were developed in classrooms and revised multiple times to ensure applicability in the classroom as well as promotion of student thinking and engagement.</li><li>These strategies allow students with disabilities and general education students to show what they know, provide gifted and talented students ways to explore ideas at a deeper level, and give teachers windows into their students' thinking, allowing them to provide targeted and differentiated instruction (Ritchart and Perkins n.d.).</li><li>Visible Thinking changes the nature of classroom discussions, making them more open, student-directed, and inclusive (Ritchart and Perkins n.d.).</li></ul>
Classroom Implications	These easy-to-learn routines can be incorporated into any classroom. The teacher brings the content to the routine. Consider strategies chosen from the sense-making tools and then select a routine that aligns well with content goals.
Application Example	A great routine to use in a situation of decision making is "Options Diamond." Perhaps students are engaged in a case involving an environmental impact decision or an ethical decision about genetic engineering. This routine requires them to identify options and make a diamond diagram (with trade-off options at the corners of the left and right of the diamond). They brainstorm one to three solutions for each corner of the diamond with (1) solutions at the right and left aligning with that trade-off, (2) a compromise between them at the bottom point, and (3) a clever solution that combines what seem to be the opposites from the right and left corners. Students then reflect on the diagram to determine what they learned.
Technology Applications	Though no technology applications directly apply to creativity routines discussed here, any number of media can be used effectively to visualize and document the processes. These include, but are not limited to, video, digital photos, concept mapping software, and SmartBoards.
Resources	Creativity routines to make thinking visible (Ritchart and Perkins 2008) are found at *www.pz.harvard.edu/vt*.

Instructional Tool 2.3 (continued)

Self-Evaluation	Students self-evaluate when they judge the quality of their work based on evidence and explicit criteria. The purpose is to do better work in the future.
The Research	• Self-evaluation enhances self-efficacy and increases intrinsic motivation (Rolheiser and Ross n.d.). • When students set criteria, self-assess, and reset criteria, they better understand assessment and the language of assessment. This gives them a clearer image of what they need to learn, where they are in relationship to that, and how they might take steps to get there (Davies 2003).
Classroom Implications	• We move students toward self-evaluation by providing guided self-evaluation through individual conferences and use of checklists that focus on thinking processes. We then slowly allow students to complete this process more independently (Blakey and Spence 1990). • We should constantly encourage students to compare their current thinking with their original thinking and to determine what helped them achieve their current understandings. Various graphic organizers support this type of thinking. • Rolheiser and Ross (n.d.) suggest a four-stage process: (1) Involve students in defining the criteria used to evaluate performance, (2) teach students how to apply the criteria to their work, (3) give students feedback on their self-evaluations, and (4) help students develop goals and action plans. • Simple checklists can help students with self-evaluation
Application Example	As a means of practicing self-evaluation, give students time in class to keep journals.
Technology Applications	VoiceThread (*http://voicethread.com*) is appropriate.
Resources	*Science Formative Assessment: 75 Practical Strategies for Linking Assessment, Instruction, and Learning* (Keeley 2008) includes numerous strategies for self- and peer assessment.

Socratic Dialogue	See Instructional Tool 2.2, page 35.

Instructional Tool 2.4

Strategies That Support Self-Regulated Thinking and Learning (Metacognitive Approaches)

Identify What You Know and Don't Know*	At the beginning of an activity, students identify both what they know and what they don't know about a content topic. As they continue their research and learning about the topic, they verify, clarify, expand, or replace their original thinking (Blakey and Spence 1990).
The Research	• Concept mapping has been shown to benefit students' metacognitive abilities (Stow 1997). • Concept cartoons help learners be more aware of their own ideas (Keogh and Naylor 1996). • Personal goals are important since we all need to plan, manage resources, and so forth (Marzano 1992).
Classroom Implications	• Concept mapping coupled with interviews provides a frame of reference for students to analyze their own thinking, identify their strengths and weaknesses, and set learning targets (Stow 1997). • 3-2-1 Bridge and Generate, Sort, Connect, Elaborate: Concept Maps are visible thinking routines that help activate prior knowledge and make connections (Ritchart and Perkins 2008). • Graphic organizers generally require students to begin with identification of what they know and questions they have (KWL is probably the most common example).
Application Example	See Chapters 4 and 5 for examples of the use of concept cartoons. Another example is to start a lesson on just about any concept with a probing question. Have students respond to that question using either mapping tool or KWL charts. Then have students reflect on their individual charts or maps and identify personal learning goals for the lesson.
Technology Applications	Inspiration software can be used to generate initial ideas and questions. To capture unfamiliar concepts and terms or to note questions there are several simple ways to flag and annotate areas of digital resource or documents. These include digital sticky notes (Google for multiple links), highlighting and commenting tools in Word or Acrobat, as well as smart highlighters (http://firedoodle.com) and bookmarking tools (http://diigo.com) for web resources. In addition, scanner pens can capture and store text for transfer to computers on the same website that offers dictionaries and translators (www.wizcomtech.com).
Resources	• Consider the various books developed by Keeley that help probe student thinking (Keeley, Eberle, and Farrin 2005; Keeley, Eberle, and Dorsey 2008; Keeley, Eberle, and Farrin 2005; Keeley, Eberle, and Tugel 2007; Keeley and Eberle 2008). • Ritchart and Perkins' (2008) thinking routines are found at www.pz.harvard.edu/vt.

*Strategies outlined by Blakey and Spence (1990).

Instructional Tool 2.4 (continued)

Talk About Thinking*	Students externalize their thinking by thinking out loud. By verbalizing their thinking, students gain awareness and control over their problem solving and acquire a fresh perspective on their thoughts (Hartman and Glasgow 2002).
The Research	Concept mapping used throughout a lesson has been shown to benefit students' metacognitive abilities. Mapping coupled with interviews provides a frame of reference for students to analyze their own thinking, identify their strengths and weaknesses, and set learning targets (Stow 1997).
Classroom Implications	• Talking about their thinking helps students develop the language of thinking (Blakey and Spence 1990). • To help students recognize thinking processes, teachers can use modeling and discussion, as well as labeling thinking processes when students use them (Blakey and Spence 1990). • Paired problem-solving formalizes this process. In paired problem-solving a student talks through a problem, describing his or her thinking while a partner listens and asks questions to clarify thinking (Blakey and Spence 1990). This process makes problems more engaging, promotes self-monitoring and self-evaluation, and gives students feedback on their thinking. It also improves collaboration and communication. Teachers need to monitor the progress of each pair and provide them with feedback (Hartman and Glasgow 2002). • Reciprocal teaching is another strategy that formalizes the thinking process. In this case, small groups of students take on the role of teacher, asking questions, clarifying, and summarizing (see Resources, below).
Application Example	A student pair has just completed working through a simulation. They are trying to develop an explanation of the simulation, based on their current understandings. One student verbalizes all the thoughts she has as she thinks through what happened in the simulation. The other student actively listens. He also points out what might be perceived as errors, examines the accuracy of the statements, and probes the "thinker" to continue voicing her thinking. They can then change roles, and the second student voices his thoughts about the simulation and the first student actively listens and probes. At the end of this activity, they can prepare a written summary of their explanations.
Technology Applications	There are very simple voice annotations in PowerPoint, as well as VoiceThread, a much more powerful and collaborative tool at *http://voicethread.com*.
Resources	• Ritchart and Perkins' (2008) thinking routines are found at *www.pz.harvard.edu/vt*. • A brief overview of reciprocal teaching can be found at the North Central Regional Educational Laboratory website (*www.ncrel.org/sdrs/areas/issues/students/atrisk/at6lk38.htm*).

Keep a Thinking Journal or Learning Log*	The terms *learning log* and *science notebook* are often used interchangeably. However, learning logs are a less-structured way for students to maintain written records of their observations and thinking. They are a more free-form type of writing in which students can express feelings and observations.

Instructional Tool 2.4 (continued)

The Research	• The vast majority of writing in science has historically been, and still tends to be, writing for the "teacher-as-examiner" instead of a pupil–teacher dialogue. Writing is rarely for the student themselves or for their peers as an audience. This limited range of writing might well limit student opportunities in both science and reading literacy (Rangahau 2002). • Writing clarifies ideas in and about science (Hipkins et al. 2002; Rangahau 2002). • Writing assignments, especially journaling and on microthemes, promotes student personalization and understanding of biology (Ambron 1987). • Students who used learning diaries knowing that teachers would act on them and provide support were better able to identify their learning difficulties and overcome them than were students without that expectation (Rangahau 2002). • Extended writing sequences can be used for metacognitive reflection about conceptual, procedural, and NOS understandings (Baker 2004, Rangahau 2002). • Open-ended questions as writing prompts assess student understanding of content as well as thinking skills. They especially assess students' abilities to analyze, evaluate, and solve problems (Freedman 1994).
Classroom Implications	• Journals or learning logs allow students to reflect on their thinking in a diary format. It lets them make notes about their awareness of difficulties and comment on steps they've taken to deal with these difficulties (Blakey and Spence 1990). • Learning logs integrate content, process, and personal feelings and help students learn *from* their writing as opposed to writing about what they learn (Costa 2000). • It is important to use a variety of extended writing tasks, but it also important that the tasks do not lead to misleading NOS outcomes (Rangahau 2002). • Students should practice and write logical sequences of ideas, including writing as explanation or argument (Rowell 1997). • Learning logs can engage student thinking about a topic since they require students to focus on content in their writing, rather than on personal feelings (Barton and Jordan 2001). • Open-ended questions (probes) can be used to assess students' thinking and content understanding.
Application Example	Use Chapter 4 as an example. Students enter their responses to the prompt for an annotated drawing into their learning logs or journals. This, of course, involves annotated drawings as well as written descriptions. The teacher reviews the journals and provides written responses that encourage students to think further—both about the content and their own thinking about the content.
Technology Applications	• Students can keep electronic learning logs and share them with other students and the teacher. The logs allow students to reflect on their own thinking as well as defend their viewpoints and react to those of others (Baker 2004). • Blogs and vlogs are very appropriate to use here.
Resources	See *Open-Ended Questioning: A Handbook for Educators* (Freedman 1994) and the various NSTA publications on formative assessment probes (Keeley 2008; Keeley, Eberle, and Farrin 2005; Keeley, Eberle, and Farrin 2007).

Instructional Tool 2.4 (continued)

Plan and Self-Regulate*	Planning and self-regulating include estimating time requirements, organizing materials, scheduling procedures required to complete an activity, and developing criteria for evaluation (Blakey and Spence 1990).
The Research	• For students to become self-directed, they must take on increasingly more responsibility for planning and regulating their learning (Blakey and Spence 1990). • Contractual agreements with students in which they set goals and subgoals (within the context of teacher goals) have a positive impact (Marzano, Pickering, and Pollack 2001). • Some graphic organizers scaffold student-planning processes, providing thinking tools and memory support systems. They help students to bring prior knowledge to their awareness and later can be used to mark progress and compare/contrast what was known and what is currently known (Lipton and Wellman 1998).
Classroom Implications	• Peel the Fruit is a tool to make thinking visible and to plan and track over time the exploration of a topic (Ritchart and Perkins 2008). This routine allows the entire class, small groups, or individuals to track progress on a long-term project. Further information can be found at *www.pz.harvard.edu/vt*. • Setting goals is an important part of planning and self-regulation. Students should be encouraged to personalize the goals established by the instructor and adapt them to their personal needs. Teacher goals should be general enough to allow this flexibility (Marzano, Pickering, and Pollock 2001). • It is effective for students to track their effort and its impact on achievement using rubrics (Marzano, Pickering, and Pollack 2001).
Application Example	Students may be working on a long-term research project, studying a local habitat. They use group charts of a planning map (e.g., Peel the Fruit) to track progress and plan. They use Peel the Fruit initially to map their work, assign tasks, and make initial research plans. They periodically revisit the map, choose next steps, and monitor progress. They can map this progress on chart paper or electronically.
Technology Applications	NoteStar is an online tool that helps students to develop and write research papers. It lets students create subtopics for research, assign topics to group members, take notes, track source information, and organize notes and sources. It can be found online at *http://notestar.4teachers.org*. It can be used alone or in conjunction with ThinkTank (*http://thinktank.4teachers.org*). ThinkTank is another tool at *4Teachers.org* that helps students develop a research organizer for refining a subject to make it more manageable for online research.
Resources	• Ritchart and Perkins (2008) thinking routines, including Peel the Fruit, are found at *www.pz.harvard.edu/vt*. The actual understanding map is at *www.pz.harvard.edu/vt/VisibleThinking_html_files/03_ThinkingRoutines/ 03d_UnderstandingRoutines/PeelTheFruit/ PeelTheFruit_Routine.html*. • Information on monitoring and time management is found at *www.muskingum.edu/~cal/database/general*.

Instructional Tool 2.4 (continued)

Debrief the Thinking Process*	Debriefing includes activities that help students bring closure to and focus discussion on their work with thinking processes.
The Research	• These activities allow students the opportunity to develop their awareness of how the strategies might be applied in other situations (Blakey and Spence 1990). • When student groups have conversations about learning, they can check their thinking and performances, gain deeper understandings of their learning, and use better strategies for planning and monitoring. Experiences like these also prepare students for the risk-taking required of learning (Davies 2003). • When students share their work and organize evidence of their learning to share, they learn more about what they have learned, what they need to learn, and the support that will be required for them to learn more. The presence of other people encourages reflection—that is, thinking about and assessing what has been learned (Davies 2003).
Classroom Implications	• Blakey and Spence (1990) recommend a three-step process. First, the teacher facilitates a review of the activity, eliciting student responses on thinking processes and feelings. Second, students classify related ideas and identify the thinking strategies used. Third, they evaluate their success, identify helpful strategies, and eliminate unproductive strategies. • Reflection helps students develop the metacognitive skills they need to monitor their own learning.
Application Example	Student groups complete a complex online modeling activity and summarize their thinking about the concept in a formal, written explanation to share. They also complete an entry in their personal thinking journals about what challenged their thinking in the simulation, what clarified their thinking, and why. Finally, the group talks about the thinking process they used and whether or not it was effective. This discussion leads them to modify their group approach when they revisit the simulation.
Technology Applications	Use of VoiceThread (*http://voicethread.com*) is appropriate.
Resources	N/A

Self-Evaluate*	See Instructional Tool 2.3.

Instructional Tool 2.5

Standards-Based Approaches for Inquiry

Engage in Scientifically Oriented Questions	"Broadly, questions in science are associated with looking for patterns in nature and developing and using theories and models that explain phenomena in nature" (Milne 2008, p. 102). Scientifically oriented questions in the classroom center on core concepts, are meaningful to students, and can be answered by student observations and scientific information gleaned from reliable sources (NRC 2000).
The Research	• Question generation by students is linked to retention of content, higher conceptual achievement, and improvement of problem-solving abilities (Colbert, Olson, and Clough 2007). • To create an environment that encourages question posing, we need to establish a "question focus," not the "answer focus" typical of traditional instruction that concentrates on the products of inquiry (Milne 2008). • Students who are used to highly structured activities may require structured support as they begin their inquiry investigations (Hipkins et al. 2002). • Web-based discussion boards have been effective at increasing student-generated questions and interactions about content (Colbert, Olson, and Clough 2007). • Teachers can improve student questioning by providing examples of testable questions (Krajicek, Brown, and Bertram 1998), materials that stimulate questions (Chin et al. 2002; Harlen 2001), opportunities to explore information related to their questions (Krajicek et al. 1998), and feedback and the opportunity to change factual questions into testable questions or to generate new questions (Harlen 2001; Krajicek et al. 1998). • Teachers can improve student questioning by encouraging students to formulate their own questions and by responding positively to students' spontaneous questions (Harlen 2001).
Classroom Implications	• Student-generated questions probe students' understandings, guide inquiries, and develop conceptual understanding. Wonderment questions are questions that promote discussion and frame inquiry (Wright and Bilica 2007). • Question posing (question generation and evaluation) is essential to scientific inquiry. If we want students to pose questions, we must let them interact with phenomena and create situations where question posing is required (Milne 2008). • Question-generating activities engage students in phenomena and ask that they generate a list of possible questions that are derived from their prior knowledge and the experiences. Possible activities include laboratory explorations, demonstrations, reading scientific studies, and making observations in the community. Regardless of what the teacher uses as a starter, the goal is to generate a range of questions. • Posed questions are not all investigable. Some are too broad to investigate and some are too narrow and can be quickly answered by using reference materials (Milne 2008). "Why" questions are common but often not investigable; "how" questions, on the other hand, lend themselves to scientific inquiry (NRC 2000). • A questioning tree that helps students generate engaging and investigable questions is found at the Southwest Center for Education and the Natural Environment (SCENE) website (http://scene.asu.edu/habitat/inquiry.html#4). Questions are sorted first by unanswerable questions (why) and answerable questions (how, what, when, who, and which), then by interesting and uninteresting, next by comparative and noncomparative, and finally by manipulative or observational (Southwest Center for Education and the Natural Environment 2004).

Instructional Tool 2.5 (continued)

Classroom Implications (cont.)	• Once students generate a group of questions (perhaps using a mapping activity), they identify the types of questions that result and determine methods to answer the questions. The methods vary according to the type of question. The first type is *definition questions*, which result in answers accepted in science and are often shared prior to an investigation. Even though these confirm known ideas, students should investigate them to construct their own understanding and because they might lead to further questions. *Experimental questions* result in explorations of the empirical relationships between variables; answers describe cause-and-effect relationships. These questions help students develop explanations supported by evidence that results from designed experiments. Finally, *observational questions* don't manipulate nature, and observations serve as the source of information. Observations lead to questions that may require further observations, and the conclusions describe patterns (correlations and classifications). Each type of question leads to different inquiries (Milne 2008). • The Visible Thinking website (*www.pz.harvard.edu/vt*) includes a thinking routine called Think/Puzzle/Explore that activates prior knowledge, generates ideas and curiosity, and sets the stage for inquiry. The routine can be used with the whole class to generate possible ideas for inquiry. Students write down their own ideas and then share them, while the teacher generates a visible list of student ideas. The teacher poses questions such as, What do you *think* about this topic? What questions or puzzles do you have? What does the topic make you want to *explore*?
Application Examples	Have students interact with materials related to the content you are teaching. Examples could range from the study of osmosis (various stations with specific activities to complete) to the observation of animals. Set up organized stations at which students can complete set interactions with materials designed to explore various aspects of the content. Have students observe and generate questions. Then, work with students to identify which questions are investigable, which are not, and which might be changed to make them investigable (e.g., they can change why questions into how questions, or broad questions can be narrowed and made easier to control).
Technology Applications	• Inspiration software can be used to brainstorm/generate questions related to content investigations. Coupled with an analysis of each question using the questioning tree (see Resources, below), students quickly generate questions and then prune the questions to a set that are engaging and investigable. In addition, those questions that are informative and perhaps foundational to the content, but not investigable, might be answered via a web search. This can be done individually, in small groups, or as a whole class. • E-mail, web conferencing, or blogging with scientists and other students could be used to generate questions. • Microblogging, like Twitter (*http://twitter.com*) can be used to capture students' questions.
Resources	The SCENE website (*http://scene.asu.edu/habitat/inquiry.html#4*) offers a nice overview of a questioning cycle in inquiry and a questioning tree (Figure 3) that guides thinking about questions that are both engaging and investigable.

Give Priority to Evidence in Responding to Questions	Because science, unlike other disciplines, relies on empirical evidence to explain how the natural world works, student work should reflect that use of empirical evidence. Evidence includes data and measurements from observation of phenomena in natural settings. Senses and specialized instruments are used to collect data. Sometimes conditions can be controlled and other times they cannot. Data are verified for accuracy by checking measurements, repeating observations, and gathering various data about the same phenomenon. Evidence can be further questioned and investigated. Students can engage in all of these actions that give priority to evidence in responding to questions (NRC 2000).

Instructional Tool 2.5 (continued)

The Research	• Generating and testing hypotheses have a profound effect on student learning, with an average effect size of .61 (Marzano, Pickering, and Pollock 2001).
	• Generation and testing of hypotheses can be inductive or deductive. Inductive techniques require that students first discover the principle and then generate hypotheses, while in a deductive approach the teacher first presents the principles and then asks students to generate and test hypotheses. Although both approaches work well, deductive approaches tend to have better results. The effect size for deductive approaches is .60 compared to .39 for inductive approaches (Marzano, Pickering, and Pollock 2001).
	• It is beneficial to have students explain the principles on which their hypotheses are based, the hypotheses themselves, and why these hypotheses make sense to them. There is even greater benefit if students write down these explanations. It appears that these explanations better help students to understand the applied principles (Marzano, Pickering, and Pollock 2001).
Classroom Implications	• Inductive approaches might be more difficult to implement effectively because they require a very well organized set of experiences for students that infer the principles from which hypotheses are generated. Without experience in this type of instructional orchestration, the deductive approach might be better (Marzano, Pickering, and Pollock 2001). However, open inquiry requires students to have inductive approach experiences.
	• With an inductive approach, students write explanations of the logic underlying observations, as well as how their observations support their hypotheses, how their experiments test these hypothesis, and how the results confirm or reject them. If a deductive approach is used, observations are not involved (Marzano, Pickering, and Pollock 2001).
	• Generation and testing of hypotheses can be conducted in ways other than the traditional "scientific method." For instance, when studying a system (e.g., ecosystems), students can be asked to hypothesize what happens if a component of the system is removed. In problem solving, students can be asked to predict the impact of potential solutions (Marzano, Pickering, and Pollock 2001).
Application Example	• The Visible Thinking website (*www.pz.harvard.edu/vt*) includes a thinking routine called "What Makes You Say That?" It is a flexible thinking routine that asks students to describe something and then asks them to support their interpretations with evidence. It can be used to make scientific observations and hypotheses. (Go to "thinking routines" on the website.)
Technology Applications	• Free graphing software, including *http://nces.ed.gov/nceskids/creatagraph*, is now available. The Computations Science Education Reference Desk (*www.shodor.org/refdesk*) is a wonderful resource for (1) tools for creating graphs, (2) calculators that plot changes between dependent variables, (3) lots of simulations and computational models, and (4) software for creating computational models—all free!
	• Haury (n.d.) suggests two strategies to engage with data via the web: (1) access data sets built by science projects or agencies and (2) collaborate with other school groups to generate data.
	• InspireData, developed by Inspiration Software, Inc., lets students explore and analyze data using a variety of tools. Databases are available in the software, but you can also create databases using the InspireData e-Survey tool or import internet databases. Information is found at *www.inspiration.com/productinfo/inspiredata/index.cfm*.
Resources	• The Visible Thinking website is at *www.pz.harvard.edu/vt*.
	• Teaching Science through Inquiry with Archived Data (Haury 1996) shares two strategies for engaging with data via the Web to extend inquiry and includes links to sites with archived data. This ERIC Educational Report can be found at *http://findarticles.com/p/articles/mi_pric/is_200112/ai_1912240294*.

Instructional Tool 2.5 (continued)

Formulate Explanations From Evidence	"Although similar to the previous [inquiry] feature, [formulating explanations from evidence] emphasizes the path from evidence to explanation rather than the criteria for and characteristics of the evidence" (NRC 2000, p. 26). Explanation includes three components: making a claim, supporting the claim with appropriate and sufficient evidence, and reasoning, which links the claim with the evidences and explains why the data serve as evidence to support the claim (McNeill and Krajcik 2008). Cognitive processes used in formulating explanations include classification, analysis, inference, and prediction. In addition, formulating explanation requires the use of general processes such as critical reasoning and logic (NRC 2000).
The Research	<ul><li>Content learning increases when students think about whether evidence does or does not support their personal theories (Hipkins et al. 2002).</li><li>Some historical models of argumentation, especially the extremely logical Aristotelian style, are not as effective in classrooms as is a more relaxed style of argumentation when students feel comfortable to listen, question, introduce ideas, and modify ideas to build common understandings from evidence (Hipkins et al. 2002). The framework provided by McNeill and Krajcik (2008) is a bit more relaxed and directly related to the expectations of the standards.</li><li>Producing new science knowledge requires a balance of interpretation and argumentation that includes the following strategies: (1) conjectures are made [or presented, as in concept cartoons], (2) relevance of facts and information is judged, (3) evidence and counterevidence is found for each conjecture, and (4) the sufficiency and coherence of evidence is assessed (Norris et al. 2008).</li><li>Teachers cannot assume that students know how to write explanations; teachers should, instead, provide explicit instruction on writing explanations. While students have less difficulty with writing a claim, they struggle more with evidence and reasoning (McNeill and Krajcik 2008).</li><li>Concept cartoons can focus argumentation, provide a safe environment, focus the discussion, and sharpen the conceptual and metacognitive focus during argumentation (Keogh and Naylor 1999; Keogh and Naylor 2007). (See Instructional Tool 2.14 for further information on concept cartoons.)</li><li>Five general strategies that help in the formulation of explanations are (1) making the framework (claim, evidence, and reasoning) explicit, (2) modeling and critiquing explanations, (3) providing a rationale for creating explanations, (4) connecting scientific explanations to everyday explanations (e.g., how a student might convince a parent that he or she needs a higher allowance), and (5) assessing and providing feedback to students (McNeill and Krajcik 2008).</li></ul>

Instructional Tool 2.5 (continued)

Classroom Implications	• Since explanations are "ways to learn about what is unfamiliar by relating what is observed to what is already known" (NRC 2000, p. 26), they require students to build new ideas on current understandings. • Strategies to support that building include written and verbal discourse, small-group investigations, evaluation of evidence, and formulating explanations (Moreno and Tharp 2006). • Even when full inquiries are not conducted, students can improve their abilities of this feature of inquiry if they are provided raw data and primary sources from which they develop explanations. Reading, discussion, and research are also beneficial (Krueger and Sutton 2001). • The framework must be made explicit if teachers want students to formulate explanations. Teachers should provide specific definitions and examples of what is meant by *claim* and *evidence*. Student discussion of what they think evidence means is a productive strategy, especially since students struggle more with the concept of evidence than of claim (McNeill and Krajcik 2008). • It is important to model and critique explanations, either in written or verbal form. Strong student examples are beneficial; weak student examples can highlight misconceptions or difficulties students have with evidence (McNeill and Krajcik 2008).
Application Examples	Students are designing an experiment around a particular hypothesis. They begin the design process by diagramming what evidence would be necessary to confirm their prediction and what evidence would refute it. They also state what types and amounts of data would need to be generated to provide that evidence. They gather the appropriate data and, using it as evidence, formulate their explanations.
Technology Applications	• InspireData, developed by Inspiration Software, Inc., lets students explore and analyze data using various tools. Databases are available in the software, but you can also create databases using the InspireData e-Survey tool or import internet databases. Information is found at *www.inspiration.com/productinfo/inspiredata/index.cfm*. • Haury (1996) suggests two strategies to engage with data via the web: (1) access data sets built by science projects or agencies and (2) collaborate with other school groups to generate data. He provides a list of available resources as well (see Resources, below). • Digital libraries are good tools for finding scientific data sets. One example is the Science Education Resource Center's Using Data in the Classroom portal (*http://serc.carleton.edu/usingdata/index.html*), which has some good resources including data-set-integrated lessons. • Students can put georeferenced data that they generate into GoogleEarth, a good data visualization exercise. • Wikis can be used to record and analyze data.
Resources	*Teaching Science through Inquiry with Archived Data* (Haury 1996) shares two strategies for engaging with data via the web to extend inquiry and includes links to sites with archived data. This ERIC Educational Report can be found at *http://findarticles.com/p/articles/mi_pric/is_200112/ai_1912240294*.

Connect Explanations to Scientific Knowledge	Explanation includes three components: making a claim, supporting the claim with appropriate and sufficient evidence, and reasoning, which links the claim with the evidences and explains why the data serve as evidence to support the claim (McNeill and Krajcik 2008). The third of these components is what is done to connect explanations to scientific knowledge (principles).
The Research	Well-structured materials that make evidence for scientific theories apparent are necessary if students are expected to make assertions based on evidence (Hipkins et al. 2002).

Instructional Tool 2.5 (continued)

Classroom Implications	• "Alternative explanations may be reviewed as students engage in dialogues, compare results, or check their results with those proposed by the teacher or instructional materials" (NRC 2000, p. 27). It is important to make sure students connect their results with currently accepted scientific knowledge appropriate to their developmental level. • The framework must be made explicit if teachers want students to connect explanations to scientific knowledge. Teachers should provide specific definitions and examples of what is meant by *reasoning*. It is important to hold specific discussions that help students understand that they need to write the *underlying scientific principle* that they use to select their evidence (McNeill and Krajcik 2008). • It is important to model and critique explanations, either in written or verbal form. Strong student examples are beneficial; weak student examples can highlight misconceptions or difficulties students have with evidence (McNeill and Krajcik 2008).
Application Example	Studying the development of plate tectonics theory provides a good example of how the convergence of multiple lines of evidence (in this case, geophysical, geochemical, paleontological, biological, and other data) strengthens the validity of a scientific theory.
Technology Applications	• Digital libraries are rich sources. • Online research and electronic communication with science experts support this feature of inquiry, as do many organizations, such as the Globe Program. It is a premier program and actually supports each of the features of inquiry. Information can be found at *www.globe.gov*.
Resources	Newton's Ask a Scientists website is a good resource for students (*www.newton.dep.anl.gov/ aasquesv.htm*).

Communicate and Justify Explanations	Just as scientists do, students should clearly communicate their explanations in such a way that the work can be replicated. This requires communication of the question researched, procedures followed, evidence gathered, explanation proposed, and review of possible alternative explanations. These explanations are open to review.
The Research	Sharing explanations helps students question and/or reinforce their understandings about evidence, scientific knowledge, and their explanations (NRC 2000).
Classroom Implications	• Students should share explanations, and peers should "ask questions, examine evidence, identify faulty reasoning, point out statements that go beyond the evidence, and suggest alternative explanations for the same observations" (NRC 2000, p. 27). This helps students make connections among evidence, scientific knowledge, and their explanations. • An authentic argument includes (1) a potential explanation, (2) the data that supports the explanation, (3) a summary of other possible explanations, and (4) if required, an explanation of how the initial model proposed changed considering the evidence (Windschitl 2008).
Application Example	Students groups give poster presentations that summarize long-term environmental research in a habitat near their school. The groups give presentations to their fellow students, communicating and justifying their explanations. They are critiqued by their peers and provided time to finalize their posters and, as necessary, reconsider their explanations. They then present their results at a community forum that includes scientists, parents, and community members. They once again present their findings, sharing alternative explanations, and justifying their own explanation.
Technology Applications	Numerous technology applications can be used to support students in their communication and justification of explanations. These include blogs and presentation software such as PowerPoint.
Resources	A good general source would be *Inquiry and the National Science Education Standards* (NRC 2000).

Instructional Tool 2.6

Standards-Based Approaches: History of Science (HOS)

Demonstration Experiments	This approach entails repeating historical experiments so that students struggle with the same concepts that scientists did.
The Research	Student misconceptions often reflect historical explanations derived from earlier research by scientists. Using the HOS in lessons helps students construct understandings of science concepts and those related to NOS. They do this by assuming the problem-solving role of scientists, thus gaining some ownership of the concepts themselves (Rudge and Howe 2004).
Classroom Implications	• Teachers' choices of misconceptions that they want to address will help them select appropriate historical episodes (Rudge and Howe 2004). • Primary resources (original research papers) are ideal to use to help students confront misconceptions. Students should be asked to provide an explanation (make a claim) based on the data. Textbook accounts or brief summaries of history can also be used to provide the context (Rudge and Howe 2004). • Classroom discussions about historical experiments can not only review the content but also reveal the NOS.
Application Example	Students design an experiment that replicates van Helmont's experiment, using only specified materials. They then improve upon his procedure and consider the importance of various factors on plant growth.
Technology Applications	Virtual labs, such as those from ChemCollective (*www.chemcollective.org*), can be used. Open courseware and iTunes/YouTube videos also offer demonstration experiments.
Resources	• See history of science resources at the SciEd.ca website: *http://sci-ed.org/HOS.htm* • Also see history of science on the web: *www.ou.edu/cas/hsci/rel-site.htm*.

Reading and Narratives	Narrative pedagogy includes teachers' traditional use of stories related to science concepts. Stories used in science can include stories in everyday contexts, those related to the history of science, and those drawn from different cultural views of the world. They can be used to develop understandings about the history of science, the nature of science, and science conceptual understandings. To help students learn about the history of science, teachers can use narratives such as biographies and manuscripts from historical studies.
The Research	• Including science history and biography in class activities provides images of science and scientists in action. It also promotes interest, provides role models, and portrays a more accurate image of the NOS. It also draws students into the underlying science concepts (McKinney and Michalovic 2004). • Historical theories about photosynthesis in conjunction with the generative teaching model have been used to help students wrestle with the ideas of contemporary photosynthesis theory. That approach was found to be more effective than guided discovery experiences in which students participated in teacher-contrived experiments (Barker 1985; Barker 1986).

Instructional Tool 2.6 (continued)

Classroom Implications	• HOS infusion into lessons reinforces the multicultural nature of science and provides role models for students who might otherwise not consider the option of science as a career. • Narratives (telling stories) about the history of science help students understand the role of creativity in science as well as the complexity of science ideas.
Application Examples	Students use MendelWeb for guided studies. They conduct genetic experiments and use the website as a guided review of Mendel's work. They then compare their results and reasoning with those of Mendel.
Technology Applications	Digital libraries are good sources for archived source documents. Examples include the National Science Digital Library (NSDL), the Library of Congress, the Chemical Heritage Foundation, the U.S. Patent Office, and the Alsos Digital Library for Nuclear Issues. NSDL has a new initiative called Classic Articles in Context that has scientists comment on the impact of seminal scholarly works (*http://nsdl.org/pd/?pager=classic_articles*).
Resources	• See the history of science resources at the SciEd.ca website: *http://sci-ed.org/HOS.htm*. • See the history of science on the web: *www.ou.edu/cas/hsci/rel-site.htm*. • Go to MendelWeb at *www.mendelweb.org*.

Instructional Tool 2.7

Standards-Based Approaches: Nature of Science (NOS)

Formal Introduction of NOS	These are specific activities designed to introduce the aspects of NOS. Examples are detailed in the "classroom implications" section of this Instructional Tool.
The Research	• Teachers should model theory/evidence interactions so they link conceptual, procedural, and NOS understandings (Rangahau 2002). • Key features of NOS should be made visible to students so they can metacognitively compare their theorizing with scientific theorizing (Rangahau 2002).
Classroom Implications	• The card-exchange activity described by Clough and Olson (2004) can be very effective. • Use puzzle-solving activities (e.g., the black box activity) that have students solve problems and then discuss in a whole group how solving these puzzles is like doing science (Clough and Olson 2004). • Pictorial gestalt images (e.g., rabbit/duck and old lady/young lady) are good ways to show that observations are not as objective as we think but are dependent on prior knowledge. This can show how different explanations can be based on the same data (Clough and Olson 2004). • Infusion of historical and contemporary stories and manuscripts of science episodes can be used to formally introduce the NOS because they portray how science works. The resource list for the HOS includes websites with links to appropriate video. • Develop and implement a quiz that poses common misconceptions about the NOS. This type of quiz can be used at the beginning and end of lessons. See Chiappetta and Koballa's (2004, p. 59) "Myths of Science" quiz.
Application Examples	Details for a mini-lesson (Theory, Theory, Who's Got the Theory) that focuses on the scientific meaning of the word *theory* are found at *www.indiana.edu/~ensiweb/lessons/theory.html*. Groups are assigned different scenarios that describe a "theory" about how diverse life came into existence. They use a theory evaluation form and share findings for their "theory." The discussion clarifies the difference between the use of the word *theory* in science and in the vernacular.
Technology Applications	• To infuse historical stories and manuscripts, digital libraries are good sources for archived source documents. Examples include the National Science Digital Library (NSDL), the Library of Congress, the Chemical Heritage Foundation, the U.S. Patent Office, and the Alsos Digital Library for Nuclear Issues. NSDL has a new initiative called Classic Articles in Context that has scientists comment on the impact of seminal scholarly works (*http://nsdl.org/pd/?pager+classic_articles*). • Science is moving increasingly toward open, collaborative online and networked processes. There are many labs and researchers who are good about documenting their work, sharing virtual expeditions to the field, and offering citizen science opportunities in which students can participate.
Resources	*The Science Teacher* special focus issue on the NOS (November 2004) is helpful on this topic.

Instructional Tool 2.7 (continued)

Careful Attention to Language	Accurate portrayal of the NOS in the language we use when teaching content is essential. Students should be made aware of the way that certain words are used in science.
The Research	• Teachers should pay special attention to the use of words such as *law, theory, prove,* and *true* (Clough and Olson 2004). • Teachers should avoid use of the phrase "what do the data show?" because data do not tell us what to think. Instead we use data to provide evidence for our explanations (Clough and Olson 2004). • Teachers should model theory and evidence interactions, linking conceptual, procedural, and NOS understandings (Rangahau 2002).
Classroom Implications	• Teacher "think-alouds" model for students the interaction of theory and evidence as well as appropriate use of language. • It can be beneficial for a teacher to videotape his or her classroom instruction to determine how he or she is using language. • Students can analyze textbook segments for the portrayal of the NOS and use of language. They can look specifically for text usage of words such as *law, hypothesis, theory,* and *prove* (Clough and Olson 2004). Students can also analyze popular media for use of the same terms.
Application Example	The teacher identifies various text segments from the textbook, scientific writings (both current and historical), and from popular media and uses the texts during a lesson on natural selection. A sample text is used by the teacher who uses a "think-aloud" to model analysis of the text for appropriate use of language. Student groups each analyze a different text segment. Each group then shares its analysis with the class and the teacher facilitates a discussion based on student responses.
Technology Applications	N/A
Resources	*The Science Teacher* special focus issue on the NOS (November 2004) is helpful on this topic.

Questions and Discussion	Purposefully designed questions by the teacher that target aspects of the NOS can be used effectively in conjunction with laboratories and other classroom activities to promote discussion. This allows concurrent instruction about content, inquiry, and the NOS.
The Research	• Discussion and argumentation can be used to critically examine the relationships among conceptual, procedural, and NOS outcomes (Rangahau 2002). • Key features of the NOS should be made visible to students so they can metacognitively compare their theorizing with scientific theorizing (Rangahau 2002).
Classroom Implications	• Prepare questions that align with the aspects of the NOS that you want to stress in your lesson (e.g., observation and inference and the tentativeness of science). Thoughtful questions prepared to ask students during laboratory experiences can highlight the aspects of the NOS. • Explicitly point out aspects of the NOS at the conclusion of activities. As students learn more, they should be able to do this independently or in small groups. • Assessments should include questions on the NOS for full implementation. • Historical stories (e.g., news articles, biographies of scientists, magazine articles) can set the stage for student reflection on and discussion about the stories with a focus on the NOS. They can be used to teach both NOS and scientific inquiry. Short one-to-three page readings as homework set the stage for whole-class or small-group discussions that the teacher facilitates to develop NOS understandings (Kirchhoff 2008).

Instructional Tool 2.7 (continued)

Application Example	Kirchhoff (2008) used an article about sightings of a mysterious creature the article called a "river dinosaur." None had ever been found, but the newspaper article discussed eyewitness accounts of the creature in a southwestern town. Students were required to develop and support an argument using evidence from the article. She used the article as the foundation of a discussion about evidence and the difference between scientific and nonscientific evidence.
Technology Applications	• Voice annotations in PowerPoint are simple applications. More power and collaborative options are available with VoiceThread (*http://voicethread.com*). • Social networking sites can be used for scientific discussion. Ning (*http://ning.com*) is one example of a free social networking platform that can be customized and made private for invited participants.
Resources	Colburn (2004) provides specific questions that the teacher can use to target the NOS.

Focusing Labs on NOS	This strategy uses inquiry-based rather than cookbook laboratories and focuses during the labs on the NOS. The primary intent is to dispel the misconception that there is a single "scientific method" that all scientists follow during investigations.
The Research	• It is best to develop students' content knowledge, procedural knowledge, and knowledge about the nature of science at the same time, rather than separately (Rangahau 2002). • The teacher should model theory and evidence interactions to link conceptual, procedural, and NOS outcomes. Explicit attention to this relationship improves scientific reasoning, conceptual understanding, and opportunities for students to understand the NOS (Rangahau 2002).
Classroom Implications	• Cookbook labs imply that scientists are absolutely objective and follow research in a series of set steps, conclusions absolutely follow from data, and science is not creative. Such labs lead students to think that there is absolute knowledge. More open-ended inquiry provides extensive opportunity to explicitly address the NOS (Colburn 2004). • A student in each lab group can record in a journal everything the group says, does, or thinks. This does not preclude independent lab reports. Students can later compare the journal entries to their lab reports. The thoughts in the journals that were not in the lab reports can be shared with the class and the teacher can use these thoughts to illustrate the NOS (Colburn 2004). • Specific questions that the teacher asks can shape student experiences to promote the NOS (see previous "Questions and Discussion" section. • Always be on the lookout for opportunities to stress the NOS (i.e., varied lab results are not "wrong" but reflect varied results and the importance of evidence, accurate lab notebooks, and so forth).
Application Example	Colburn (2004) shares an example using chromatography. This example allows students to experiment with various ink sources (he includes indelible ink, which does not separate at all during chromatography). One student in each laboratory group records everything the group says, does, or thinks. The teacher facilitates group activity with focused questions. If testable questions arise, the teacher facilitates group predictions and testing of explanations. Students prepare lab reports and, the following day, they compare the lab reports to the previous day's journal entry that recorded group activity. In a discussion, they highlight what was not included in the report, and the teacher lists class omissions and facilitates a discussion around these omissions. The points made during discussion focus on the tentativeness of science and its openness to revision (no single method; messy and untidy; often leads to dead-ends; judgment involved in interpreting data; assumptions underlie the work; and science is a social process).

Instructional Tool 2.7 (continued)

Technology Applications	• Refer to many of the technology applications in Instructional Tool 2.6. The resources listed with each of the essential features of inquiry can also be used to focus on the NOS. • Many networked research projects can also support students' understanding of NOS. Some examples are the Microbial Life project, the GLOBE project, myPlantIT, Cornell Lab of Ornithology's "Research Citizen Science Conservation Education," North American Amphibian Monitoring Program, and Frogwatch USA.
Resources	The Colburn (2004) article provides examples in addition to the "Application Example" above. He also provides specific questions that the teacher can use to target the NOS.

Instructional Tool 2.8

Sense-Making Approaches: Linguistic Representations

Writing to Learn: Learning Logs	See Instructional Tool 2.4 (the section titled "Keep a Thinking Journal or Learning Log").

Writing to Learn: Science Notebooks	Science notebooks are a fixed location for students' work, a record of the information that students value, and a window into their mental activities. They are a link between science and literacy; writing, graphs, tables, and drawings all help students to make meaning of science learning experiences. Student reflections, questions, and decisions also help to build that link (Klentschy and Molina-De La Torre 2004). Science notebooks focus on the more structured writing of science while science journals and learning logs are more free-form. Although both types of writing are important, science journals and science notebooks should be separately maintained (Hargrove and Nesbit 2003).
The Research	• The vast majority of writing in science classes has traditionally been, and still tends to be, writing for the teacher-as-examiner rather than for a pupil–teacher dialogue. Such writing is rarely is done for the students themselves or for their peers as an audience. This limited range of writing might well limit student opportunities in both science and reading literacy (Rangahau 2002). • Writing clarifies ideas in and about science (Hipkins et al. 2002; Rangahau 2002). • Extended writing sequences can be used for metacognitive reflection about conceptual, procedural, and NOS understandings (Baker 2004; Rangahau 2002). • The first goal of writing in science should be *understanding* because writing is a tool with which to think. When students use their science notebooks during discussions, it helps them construct meaning from the science phenomena they observe (Harlen 2001; Klentschy and Molina-De La Torre 2004). • Active science learning that includes science notebooks is useful for assessment when (1) most of the work in the notebook is narrative and centered around authentic science tasks, (2) the notebook work is purposeful, with students investigating their own questions, (3) "right" answers or conclusions are uncommon, and (4) the notebook provides information not only to the teacher but also to the student and possibly to parents (Hargrove and Nesbit 2003). • Science notebooks focus on making sense of phenomena under investigation and give priority to evidence in responding to questions. They also require students to take responsibility for their learning in the content area, promoting metacognition (DeFronzo 2006). • One model for using science notebooks has seven parts: focus question, prediction/hypothesis, planning, data, claims and evidence, making-meaning conference, and conclusion/reflection (DeFronzo 2006).
Classroom Implications	• When students use their science notebooks during classroom discussions it helps them construct meaning from the science phenomena they observe (Harlen 2001). • Active science learning that includes science notebooks is useful for assessment when (1) most of the work in the notebook is narrative and centered around authentic science tasks, (2) the notebook work is purposeful with students investigating their own questions, (3) "right" answers or conclusions are uncommon, and (4) the notebook provides information not only to the teacher but also to the student and possibly to parents (Hargrove and Nesbit 2003).

Instructional Tool 2.8 (continued)

Application Example	Students maintain science notebooks/field journals during their fieldwork (see Chapter 7) that compare/contrast a local habitat and the adjacent schoolyard. Initial observations, resulting questions and predictions, data collection plans, data (e.g., observations, data, charts, graphs, drawings), claims, evidence, and conclusions are all recorded in the notebooks/field journals
Technology Applications	Blogs, wikis, and online lab notebooks are good applications.
Resources	Go online to *www.sciencenotebooks.org* and *www.ebecri.org/custom/toolkit.html.*

Writing to Learn: Writing Scientific Explanations	Scientific explanations address a combination of the goals of (a) explanation (how and why something happens) and (b) argumentation (written or oral social activity that justifies or defends a standpoint for an audience). Students justify their explanations of phenomena by making claims and supporting those claims with appropriate evidence and reasoning (McNeill and Krajcik 2006).
The Research	• Writing clarifies ideas in and about science (Hipkins et al. 2002; Rangahau 2002). • Extended writing sequences can be used for metacognitive reflection about conceptual, procedural and NOS understandings (Baker 2004; Rangahau 2002). • The transmissive style of writing limits students' use of writing to develop NOS outcomes. It constrains their use of writing to outline evidence for an argument and the reasoning behind planning decisions (Rowell 1997). • Supporting students in the construction of explanations results in improved student understandings about inquiry, science content, and science literacy (McNeill and Krajcik 2008; Sutherland, McNeill, and Krajcik 2006). • It is difficult for students to learn how to construct explanations in the context of learning content so teacher support is essential (Sutherland, McNeill, and Krajcik 2006). • Context-specific scaffolds are more effective than generic explanation scaffolds in promoting students' abilities to write scientific explanations and to understand science content (McNeill and Krajcik 2006)
Classroom Implications	• Because it is difficult for students to learn how to construct explanations, it is helpful to provide a framework and guidelines. One framework for writing scientific explanations has three components: (1) make a claim, (2) provide evidence for the claim, and (3) provide reasoning that links the claim to the evidence (Sutherland, McNeill, and Krajcik 2006). • Supporting actions to help students construct scientific explanations include (1) accessing students' prior knowledge about explanations, (2) generating criteria for explanations, (3) making the framework explicit, (4) modeling the construction of explanations, (5) providing students with practice opportunities, (6) practicing the critique of explanations, (7) providing feedback to students, and (8) providing opportunities to revise (Sutherland, McNeill, and Krajcik 2006). • Students should practice writing scientific explanations for phenomena with which they are already familiar and for which their content knowledge is well formed before advancing to writing scientific explanations related to their own investigations.

Instructional Tool 2.8 (continued)

Application Example	One way to support students' practice in writing explanations is to have them use a summary frame before they develop explanations on their own. Summary frames are a series of questions that are centered on a specific type of information. The questions highlight the important elements of that type of information and are intended to be used to help students write written summaries of the information (Marzano, Pickering, and Pollack 2001). For example, the teacher might use the "argumentation pattern," using text that tries to support a claim. The argumentation pattern contains four elements: evidence, claim, support, and qualifier (restriction on the claim or evidence that counters the claim). Specific questions in the summary frame might be (1) What information is provided (in the text) that leads to the claim? (2) What claim does the author make about the problem/situation? (3) What examples does the author use to support the claim? (4) What concessions does the author make about the claim? (For further information and examples of summary frames, see Marzano, Pickering, and Pollock's (2001) chapter on summarizing and note taking.)
Technology Applications	Blogs, wikis, and online lab notebooks are good applications.
Resources	See Chapter 3 in *Classroom Instruction That Works: Research-Based Strategies for Increasing Student Achievement* (Marzano, Pickering, and Pollock 2001).

Writing to Learn: Science Writing Heuristic	A science-writing heuristic (SWH) is a more structured approach than those discussed above. It combines guided inquiry, collaborative group work, and writing-to-learn activities. "The SWH provides an alternate format for students to guide their peer discussions and their thinking and writing about how hands-on guided inquiry activities relate to their own prior knowledge via beginning questions, claims and evidence, and final reflections" (Burke et al. 2005b, p. 2).
The Research	• Use of the SWH independently and in connection with textbook strategies had a positive impact on student conceptual understanding and metacognition (Wallace et al. 2004). • "Reformulating conceptual understandings in writing, such as a textbook explanation, can improve learning" (Wallace et al. 2004, p. 366). • The SWH process has been used in a variety of classrooms across grade levels (preK–postsecondary) and science disciplines. Productive integration of the SWH has had a positive impact on student learning gains (Burke et al. 2005a).
Classroom Implications	• Instructor preparation is essential for successful integration of the SWH and its impact on student learning (Burke et al. 2005a). • The SWH process involves students in activities such as the following: activities to identify pre-instructional ideas, prelaboratory activities to begin thinking about the concepts, the laboratory activity itself, small-group sharing and comparing of data, comparison of ideas with those of textbooks or other print resources, individual reflection and writing, and exploration of postinstruction understanding. These components are each essential and require attention by the teacher (Hand 2006). See the SWH homepage (*http://avogadro.chem.iastate.edu/SWH/homepage.htm*) for further information. Note that the SWH is a complex process that entails the use of multiple strategies from the Instructional Tools in this chapter.
Example in Application	The best example can be viewed at the SWH homepage, where video sequences illustrate the process. These videos are found at *http://avogadro.chem.iastate.edu/SWH/View_Video.htm*.
Technology Applications	Blogs, wikis, and online lab notebooks are good applications.
Resources	See the SWH homepage: *http://avogadro.chem.iastate.edu/SWH/homepage.htm*. This site includes a resource page that can be downloaded for more detailed information about the SWH.

Instructional Tool 2.8 (continued)

Reading to Learn: Vocabulary Development	These strategies help students understand the specialized vocabulary that is unique to science and the vocabulary terms that have different meanings in science than in everyday use.
The Research	• Vocabulary knowledge advances text comprehension; this finding is consistent across ages and populations (Magnusson and Palinscar 2004). Coaching in the language features of science, such as vocabulary, can simultaneously support reading and science literacy. However, specialized vocabulary should only be introduced after students understand the conceptual foundation of the topic (Hipkins et al. 2002). • Coaching in the language of science (vocabulary and grammar) can support both reading and science literacy (Rangahau 2002). • Words with dual meanings cause more problems than words with single meanings (Rangahau 2002). • Words used for hypothesizing, comparing, and other aspects of science reasoning (e.g., *frequently, simultaneously*) cause difficulty in the classroom. Student practice with argumentation, written and oral, helps build understandings of these words (logical connectives) (Rangahau 2002). • Often in science, nouns can be substituted for verbs or an entire sequence of events (e.g., *evaporation*), and nouns can be used as adjectives. Explicit coaching about these grammatical features of science enhances reading literacy and science literacy (Rangahau 2002). • Use of models and analogies builds shared meanings that facilitate the communication of individual understandings of technical science vocabulary (Rangahau 2002). • The context in which vocabulary is learned is important; therefore, a good portion of vocabulary learning should occur as students learn subject matter (Magnusson and Palinscar 2004). • Learning vocabulary is important for students so that they can learn the discourse of science. By embedding the language of science in guided-inquiry experiences, the teacher models how science language is used (Magnusson and Palinscar 2004).
Classroom Implications	• Vocabulary instruction not only prepares students to read and understand science text but also develops students' conceptual understanding so they can communicate these ideas. It is a challenge for teachers to prepare for vocabulary instruction. Four steps that help in this process are (1) identify learning goals, (2) develop a vocabulary list based on the goals, (3) determine required levels of understanding for the terms, and (4) select appropriate strategies (Barton and Jordan 2001). • One strategy that helps students with terms that don't require in-depth understanding is the Student VOC Strategy. Strategies that work better for terms that require deeper exploration include concept definition mapping, the Frayer model, and semantic feature analysis. These strategies can be used throughout a unit, modifying them as understanding grows (Barton and Jordan 2001). The Just Read Now website (*www.justreadnow.com/content/science/index.htm*) explores all these strategies. • It is important to give students multiple opportunities to learn terms in context, to provide some instruction on new concepts prior to reading, to help students connect an image to a term, and to focus only on those terms critical to learning the new content (Barton and Jordan 2001).

Instructional Tool 2.8 (continued)

Application Example	In Chapter 3 we use semantic feature analysis with three different sets of essential terms: (1) *mitosis* and *meiosis*, (2) *replication* and *division*, and (3) *recombination, variation,* and *mutational variation.* However, the chapter also includes words that we suggest be pruned from lessons on these topics (unless they are required by the school district. If the words are required, we suggest using the Student VOC Strategy. If a school district does not require the terms, they could be used in extension activities for students who have already mastered the essential terms and associated concepts).
Technology Applications	Inspiration software can be used for semantic mapping.
Resources	• See "Reading in the Sciences" at the Just Read Now website: *www.justreadnow.com/content/ science/index.htm* • Go to the Think Literacy website: *www.edu.gov.on.ca/eng/studentsuccess/thinkliteracy/files/ ThinkLitScienceReading.pdf.* • See "Reading Comprehension Strategies" in the Learning Strategies Database: *www. muskingum.edu/~cal/database/general/reading.html.* • See Barton, M. L., and D. L. Jordan. 2001. *Teaching Reading in Science: A Supplement to Teaching Reading in the Content Areas. Teacher's Manual.* 2nd ed. Aurora, CO: McREL.

Reading to Learn: Informational Text Strategies	Informational text strategies help students better understand text structure (organization and presentation), text coherence, and audience appropriateness. As a result, these strategies impact student learning of science.
The Research	• Students' reading and comprehension skills are often challenged in science because of science's specialist language and grammatical features. This may require significant teacher support (Rangahau 2002). • Teachers should help students recognize the role of prior knowledge and teach them how to use that knowledge when they learn science through reading (Barton and Jordan 2001). • Hands-on activities stimulate student questioning. Searching for answers in textbooks or other science materials provides meaning to reading and offers frames of reference for constructing meaning from text (Nelson-Herber 1986). • Use of text in inquiry-based science instruction is important because learning from text is an authentic science practice and is a way to promote both text comprehension and science instruction (Magnusson and Palinscar 2004). • Reading and inquiry both require that learners are aware of and use the appropriate discourse structures, can coordinate information across texts, and can interpret multiple representations in texts (Magnusson and Palinscar 2004). • Explicit instruction about recognizing and representing common text structures significantly improves student learning, as does familiarizing students with text presentation (Barton and Jordan 2001).

Instructional Tool 2.8 (continued)

Classroom Implications	• Reading strategies that can be applied across disciplines include discussion strategies (e.g., creative debate, discussion webs, Question-Answer Relationships [QAR], and think-pair-share), active reading strategies (e.g., anticipation guides, KWL, and reciprocal teaching), and organization strategies (concept diagrams, graphic organizers, and two-column notes). • Several of these strategies also help to identify student preconceptions for teacher planning. When students learn what their preconceptions are, they can grapple with their own thinking. • Text structures often used in science with which students should be familiar include comparison/contrast, concept definition, description, generalization/principle, and process/cause-effect. Teachers should scaffold students' learning about each structure when students begin to learn a skill or concept and use text that covers the content that is the focus of instruction (Barton and Jordan 2001). • It is helpful to work with students at the beginning of the year so they understand text presentation (how the material is laid out, its visual textual clues, and its illustrations and graphs), and to model for students how to predict text content based on presentation clues (e.g., headings) (Barton and Jordan 2001). • Teachers should assess the text used in the classroom for coherence. If there are limitations in the presentation, the teacher needs to pre-identify main ideas and make certain that students understand how concepts in paragraphs are related (Barton and Jordan 2001). • Many science textbooks are not audience appropriate. If that is the case, the teacher can use alternative text until appropriate text is adopted (Barton and Jordan 2001). • Anticipation guides, Directed Reading Thinking Activity (DRTA), various graphic organizers, Group Summarizing, KWL, PLAN, Problematic Situation, Proposition/Support Outline, Reciprocal Teaching, and think-alouds are all effective informational text strategies (Barton and Jordan 2001). Many of these strategies are explained and modeled at the Just Read Now website (*www.justreadnow.com/content/science/index.htm*).
Application Example	Students compare several types of informational text from different sources on a given topic—for example, explanatory signage from a local nature trail that describes the floral and fauna, a guidebook that includes that area, and a textbook chapter that describes the particular biome. Students discuss how the audience and the medium for informational text create expectations for writing style and how they can use this knowledge for clues to interpreting text from different sources. (*Note*: For additional examples, see Barton and Jordan 2001.)
Technology Applications	Connotea is a bookmarking tool that saves references in the proper bibliographic formats (*www.connotea.org*).
Resources	• Visit *www.mcrel.org* to find sites with science resource suggestions that supplement text. • NSTA annually publishes a compendium called *Outstanding Science Trade Books for Children*. Go to *www.nsta.org/publications/ostb*. • Barton and Jordan (2001) provide a list of questions to use as you determine whether alternative text sources are appropriate. They also provide information on and samples of numerous guides and organizers that serve as informational text strategies. • Go to "Reading in the Sciences" at the Just Read Now website: *www.justreadnow.com/content/science/index.htm* • Go to the Think Literacy website: *www.edu.gov.on.ca/eng/studentsuccess/thinkliteracy/files/ThinkLitScienceReading.pdf*.

Instructional Tool 2.8 (continued)

Reading to Learn: Reflection Strategies	Reflection strategies develop students' metacognitive abilities and help students to become effective readers. Specific strategies can be used to promote reflection on reading in science.
The Research	Reflection strategies that enhance metacognition related to reading in science do the following: (1) help students to better understand science text, science reading, and science reading strategies; (2) improve the skills students need to read science text and use science reading strategies; and (3) help students to understand why and when to use particular strategies.
Classroom Implications	• Reflective questioning, reflective writing, and discussion enhance students metacognition as related to learning science (including reading science) and enhance their understanding of science content. • Various reflection strategies include Creative Debate, Discussion Webs, Learning Logs, Question-Answer Relationship (QAR), Questioning the Author (QtA), Role/Audience, Format/Topic (RAFT), and Scored Discussion (Barton and Jordan 2001). See Resources, below, for where to go to learn more about these strategies.
Application Examples	Students read about global warming. The teacher uses a Discussion Web to facilitate class discussion. Students are asked, "Can we really control global warming?" Small groups record this question in the middle of a discussion web and then record as many "yes" or "no" reasons as they can, in a given amount of time, related to the question. These go on the right and left of the web. They discuss their responses and reach a consensus "yes" or "no" response, recording it in the conclusion box. Groups share responses and the teacher facilitates a discussion related to the question.
Technology Applications	Students can implement online journals and discussions. Social networking sites can be used for scientific discussion. Ning (*http://ning.com*) is one example of a free social networking platform that can be customized and made available only to invited participants.
Resources	• See Barton, M. L., and D. L. Jordan. 2001. *Teaching Reading in Science: A Supplement to Teaching Reading in the Content Areas. Teacher's Manual.* 2nd ed. Aurora, CO: McREL. • Go to "Reading in the Sciences" at the Just Read Now website: *www.justreadnow.com/content/science/index.htm.*

Reading to Learn: Thinking-Process Maps	Thinking-process maps can be used by students to read and interpret information. They are helpful in reading and writing, content-specific learning, and interdisciplinary learning. For further information, see Instructional Tool 2.12 and visit Thinking Maps, Inc., at *www.thinkingmaps.com/htthinkmap.php3.*

Instructional Tool 2.8 (continued)

Speaking to Learn: Large- and Small-Group Discourse	Classroom discourse is used to make sense of science learning experiences. The teacher and students explore ideas, pose questions, and listen to multiple points of view to establish understanding (Mortimer and Scott 2003). These discussions help students learn science concepts and better understand the nature of science.
The Research	• Discourse is beneficial to student learning, teacher-student rapport, equity and expectations, and formative assessment (ASCD 2008). Students enjoy and engage freely in focused talk in science without having to learn rules, conventions, structures, or vocabulary. Realistic and authentic problems provide focus for student discussion. Sense of purpose can be created using strategies such as concept cartoons that present authentic problems, focus on scientific issues, and lead to productive follow-up activities (Keogh and Naylor 2007).
	• Large- and small-group discourse can promote learning about concepts, metacognition, and the NOS as well as promote positive attitudes (Hipkins et al. 2002).
	• "Accountable talk" deepens conversation and understanding of the topic studied (ASCD 2008).
	• Norms and skills for "accountable talk" must be explicitly taught (Winokur and Worth 2006).
	• To promote "accountable talk," we should encourage our students to expect their peers to clarify, explain, and justify statements; to recognize and challenge misconceptions; and to demand evidence for claims and arguments (ASCD 2008).
	• Student-centered discussions can be promoted using text (text-based discussions). Examination and discussion of text promotes "the skills and habits of reading analytically, listening carefully, citing evidence, disagreeing respectfully, and being open-minded" (Hale and City 2006, p. 4).
	• Discussion is enhanced when students discern several plausible viewpoints. When only one viewpoint is presented, there is no reason for discussion. In science lessons, alternative viewpoints can be effectively presented via concept cartoons or puppets, both of which promote creative cognitive conflict. Discussion of alternatives consistently results in students' determining their own theories (Keogh and Naylor 2007).
	• Whole-class discussion works best in the context of an activity and when the focus of the discussion is shared student experiences. It is essential that students reflect on and discuss their current understanding of ideas as they develop them in order to enhance their conceptual understanding (Hipkins et al. 2002).
	• Small-group discourse allows students to build on each other's ideas as they generate explanations. Whole-class discourse has higher standards for clarity and explanatory power of students' products, and it more greatly challenges students' ideas. If students are aware of the purposes of the two types of discourse (small group and whole class), they are more likely to develop the ability to share understandings (Woodruff and Meyer 1997).
	• There should be a balance between whole-class and small-group discussions. These two modes reflect the two types of scientific discourse, one within the laboratory and one among laboratories working on similar research (Cartier 2000; Hipkins et al. 2002).

Instructional Tool 2.8 (continued)

Classroom Implications	• Discussion has multiple purposes within an inquiry environment—for example, eliciting and considering ideas, planning investigations, and developing conceptual understanding (Winokur and Worth 2006).
	• Survey activities allow us to assess students' initial ideas, and questions can serve as probes to determine students' pre-instructional ideas (Hartman and Glasgow 2002).
	• The teacher's role is critical, even in small-group discourse. For effective discussion, teachers must require students to produce an outcome as the result of discussion and provide students with carefully selected materials to focus discussion and decision-making. Teachers must also require students to operate at high cognitive levels and to allow everyone a chance to speak (Hipkins et al. 2002).
	• Students need time and space to work productively without teacher intrusion on small-group discussion. Teacher presence reduces pupil talk (Keogh and Naylor 2007). However, teacher questioning is important to discourse in the classroom. Questions that elicit factual recall tend to stop discussion while questions that probe student thinking tend to build problem-solving steps, encourage participation, and sequence conversation (ASCD 2008; Hipkins et al. 2002).
	• When the class is addressing a topic that requires thought and deduction, questions are essential. They should include cognitive, speculative, affective, and management questions. Within each category, questions can be asked at various levels (Hartman and Glasgow 2002).
	• Some research indicates that homogeneous grouping promotes more effective discussion in small groups. Role allocation in mixed-gender groups promotes more conceptual dialogue while role allocation is less necessary in same-gender groups (Hipkins et al. 2002).
	• We can promote "accountable talk" by pushing students to do the following: (1) clarify and explain, (2) provide justification for their proposals, (3) recognize and challenge misconceptions, (4) demand evidence from peers for claims and arguments, and (5) interpret and use each other's statements (ASCD 2008).
	• Student-generated questions, open-ended questions, student choice of inquiry topics, and more time for student research and exploration encourage deeper discussion and investigation (ASCD 2008).
	• Productive talk engages students. Some strategies shown to be effective in promoting this engagement include card sorts, concept cartoons, odd-one-out, and graphic organizers. These strategies promote student self-motivation and self-sustaining conversation. Concept cartoons can provide a safe environment, focus the discussion, and sharpen the conceptual and metacognitive aspects of argumentation (Keogh and Naylor 1999; Keogh and Naylor 2007). (See Instructional Tool 2.14 for further information on concept cartoons.)
	• Students should be able to talk in the way they would normally talk in a social situation rather than attempting a more formal and structured way of talking (Keogh and Naylor 2007).
	• Individual student worksheets often prevent student talk. Instead, given a worksheet, they immediately complete the worksheet and discussion stops (Keogh and Naylor 2007).
Application Example	On a rotating basis, all students in a class are assigned responsibilities for facilitating both large- and small-group discussions. The discussions should have a variety of goals and outcomes and occur at multiple points in the learning cycle.
Technology Applications	Voice annotations in PowerPoint are simple applications. More powerful and collaborative options are available with VoiceThread (http://voicethread.com).

Instructional Tool 2.8 (continued)

Resources	• The chapter "Talk in the Science Classroom" (Winokur and Worth 2006) in the NSTA Press book *Linking Science & Literacy in the K–8 Classroom* describes characteristics of talk that serves various purposes in the science classroom. The chapter also provides prompts and questions. • Two excellent resources on questioning are *Quality Questioning: Research-Based Practice to Engage Every Learner* (Walsh and Sattes 2005) and *Open-Ended Questioning: A Handbook for Educators* (Freedman 1994) • An additional resource is *Leading Student-Centered Discussions: Talking About Texts in the Classroom* (Hale and City 2006).

Speaking to Learn: Student Questioning	Student questioning should include not only questioning during small- and large-group discourse but also questioning as an essential feature of inquiry.
The Research	• See Instructional Tool 2.6, "Standards-Based Approaches: History of Science." • Student-generated questions, open-ended questions, student choice of inquiry topics, and more time for student research and exploration encourage deeper discussion and investigation (ASCD 2008). • Formulating questions is the key to metacognitive knowledge, which includes strategic knowledge, knowledge about cognitive tasks, and self-knowledge (Walsh and Sattes 2005). • Making students aware of what a good question really is helps them to become better learners and improves their questioning abilities (Hartmans and Glasgow 2002).
Classroom Implications	• See Instructional Tool 2.6. • Teachers should provide students with models of good questions and discuss effective questioning strategies. They should also provide students with opportunities to practice questioning and provide them with feedback on their questions (Hartman and Glasgow 2002; Walsh and Sattes 2005). • Reciprocal teaching and paired-problem-solving strategies require students to ask and answer questions. This promotes students' questioning abilities and metacognitive knowledge (Walsh and Sattes 2005).
Application Example	Students generate questions prior to a class discussion, based on their current understandings about the content. They share questions in small groups, and peers critique the questions based on previously learned criteria. Each group then shares a single question with the class, and the teacher facilitates a class critique of the questions.
Technology Applications	• Inspiration software—as well as use of the questioning tree (see Resources, below)—can be used to generate questions related to content investigations. Students can then prune the questions to a set that is engaging and investigable. In addition, those questions that are informative and perhaps foundational to the content, but not investigable, might be answered via a web search. This can be done individually, in small groups, or as a whole class. • E-mail/web conferencing/blogging with scientists and other students could be used to generate questions. • Microblogs, like Twitter (*http://twitter.com*), can be used to capture students' questions.

Instructional Tool 2.8 (continued)

Resources	• The SCENE website (*http://scene.asu.edu/habitat/inquiry.html#4*) offers a nice overview of a questioning cycle in inquiry and a questioning tree (Figure 3) that guides thinking about questions that are both engaging and investigable.
	• Two excellent teacher resources on questioning are *Quality Questioning: Research-Based Practice to Engage Every Learner* (Walsh and Sattes 2005) and *Open-Ended Questioning: A Handbook for Educators* (Freedman 1994). Walsh and Sattes include a chapter with specific suggestions on how to teach students to generate questions.

Speaking to Learn: Socratic Dialogue	See Instructional Tool 2.2.

Instructional Tool 2.9

Sense-Making Approaches: Nonlinguistic Representations—Models

Mental Models	A model is a representation of an idea, object, event, process, or system. "Mental models" are cognitive constructions that help explain phenomena we can't directly experience (Hipkins et al. 2002). Scientific models are sets of ideas that describe natural processes (Cartier 2000).
The Research	• When students have trouble with models, it is generally because they (1) learn the model instead of the concept, (2) lack awareness of the boundary between the model and reality, (3) are confused by unshared attributes, (4) lack the necessary visual imagery, (5) find it difficult to apply the model in contexts other than the one in which it was taught, or (5) are mixing up different models (Hipkins et al. 2002). • Conceptual development is enhanced if students construct and critique their own models (Hipkins et al. 2002). • Authentic inquiry engages students in the construction, revision, and assessment of their own models and leads to a richer understanding of genetics (Cartier 2000). • Students who receive instructions and guiding questions along with a model better understood molecular genetics than those who do not receive that support (Rotbain, Marbach-Ad, and Stavy 2005). • "Students display misconceptions when they apply their mental model to a problem and reach an inappropriate answer. The difficulty may be related to the model they have constructed or in the way in which they have applied the model" (Modell, Michael, and Wenderoth 2005, p. 22).
Classroom Implications	• Teachers must recognize whether a student's errors are due to his or her mental model or the way in which the model was applied to the problem. Student explanations help in this analysis (Modell, Michael, and Wenderoff 2005). • Teachers should inform students about the basis of mental models, about scientists' constructions that are generated to explain data, and about model processes and behavior (Hipkins et al. 2002). • A think-aloud approach can be used to share the teacher's mental models with students. This would entail the teacher thinking out loud through problem-solving steps during a problem-solving activity. The teacher thereby demonstrates to students how he or she thinks about a problem and plans an approach to solving it (Hartman and Glasgow 2002). • Don't always model "error-free" thinking when modeling a think-aloud for students. As you make "errors," think out loud about your errors, modeling for students that scientists are not always "correct." Make deliberate errors and model how you self-monitor and recover (Hartman and Glasgow 2002). • Pedagogies that use various modes of modeling produce the best content outcomes and NOS outcomes if students reflect on and discuss both their own models and those of scientists (Hipkins et al. 2002). • Peer discussion provides students with alternative models and introduces criteria and evidence by which to distinguish among scientific models (Hipkins et al. 2002). • Students' conceptual models include their images, and memories, which may be different from the teacher's or those of scientists. These models evolve through experience and thinking. If we provide students with experiences and both examples and nonexamples, their conceptual models become richer (Gilbert and Ireton 2003).

Instructional Tool 2.9 (continued)

Application Example	Because students can arrive at the same answer but for different reasons (Hartman and Glasgow 2002), teachers should ask students to explain their thinking and how they arrived at their answers. Several students can share their thinking, and then the teacher can reflect on these explanations of thinking, using a think-aloud strategy.
Technology Applications	N/A
Resources	See *Understanding Models in Earth and Space Science* (Gilbert and Ireton 2003).

Physical Models	"Expressed" models are mental models expressed in public. They are expressed in either two dimensions (e.g., those found in textbooks) or three dimensions (e.g., working models and scaled models).
The Research	• Expressed models are simplified from a mental model and exist somewhere between reality and the mental model. All models are "wrong" in some way because they concentrate on specific aspects to try to explain something unfamiliar in terms of something familiar and are based on incomplete understandings about how the world works. Thus, models have limitations in pragmatic use. Understanding this fact constitutes one difference between science experts and novices. Students often hold very different views on the nature of mental models than do scientists and their teachers. Students need to learn to be metacognitive about their use of models (Hipkins et al. 2002). • Student practice in construction, critique, and use of their own models enhances conceptual development (Hipkins et al. 2002). • As students work with physical models, their attitudes will improve if the teacher links conceptual and metacognitive learning (Hipkins et al. 2002). • Making physical models enhances nonlinguistic representations in the minds of students and, as a result, enhances their understanding of the content (Marzano, Pickering, and Pollock 2001). • Generating a concrete representation creates an "image" of the knowledge in a student's mind (Marzano, Pickering, and Pollock 2001). • Developed models can be shared and critiqued, help students see connections between ideas, changed as students learn more, and help teachers recognize gaps in student understanding (Windschitl 2008).
Classroom Implications	Students who receive instructions and guiding questions along with a model (e.g., a physical model of beads and illustrations from a textbook) understand molecular genetics better than students who do not receive a physical model. The physical model of beads is more effective than the illustration activity or traditional teaching because it helps students visualize abstract concepts (Rotbain, Marbach-Ad, and Stavy 2005).
Application Example	Bottle Biology TerrAqua Columns (Ingram 1993) are one of many physical models for ecosystems. Use these models in the classroom prior to and/or in conjunction with fieldwork. Be certain to discuss with students the strengths and deficiencies of the models as contrasted to an actual ecosystem.
Technology Applications	N/A
Resources	See *Understanding Models in Earth and Space Science* (Gilbert and Ireton 2003).

Instructional Tool 2.9 (continued)

Verbal Models: Analogies	"Expressed" models are mental models expressed in the public and include visual and verbal metaphors and analogies (Hipkins et al. 2002). Creating analogies as a process identifies relationships between pairs of concepts, identifying relationships between relationships (Marzano, Pickering, and Pollock 2001).
The Research	• Analogies help students construct more accurate conceptions of complex ideas (Hartman and Glasgow 2002), especially when students have alternative conceptions (Calwetti 1999). • They help familiarize students with concepts that are outside their previous experience (Calwetti 1999). They help students see that what seem to be dissimilar things are similar, and therefore increase understanding of new information (Marzano, Pickering, and Pollock 2001). • Creating analogies is an effective way to identify similarities and differences, a strategy shown effective at increasing student achievement (Marzano, Pickering, and Pollock 2001). • Studies have shown that in biology instruction some students, when skilled in the use of multiple analogies, develop a more scientific understanding of the concept studied. "Use of multiple analogies in a bridging sequence has been successful in helping students make sense of initially counter-intuitive ideas" (Cawelti 1999). • Use of analogies may be motivational to students as they provoke interest (Calwetti 1999).
Classroom Implications	• In order to be effective, the analogies must be familiar to students so they can determine if their features and functions are congruent with the targeted concept. Students should spend time in discussions about the similarities and differences between the analogy and the target. To fully understand the effectiveness of an analogy, it can be helpful to compare multiple analogies to a single target (Cawelti 1999). • Identifying similarities and differences, which can be accomplished through creating analogies, is effective both when explicitly guided by the teacher and when created independently by the student. If there are very specific similarities and differences on which the students should focus, then direct instruction is more effective. On the other hand, if divergence is student thinking is the goal, independent student work is more effective (Marzano, Pickering, and Pollock 2001). • Discussion of analogies helps students build understanding (Cawelti 1999). You might provide students an analogy to a concept and have them discuss it, including its relevance and limitations (Hartman and Glasgow 2002). • Finding analogies to develop conceptual understanding in science might be difficult when relationships are abstract. Ideas can be made more concrete by helping students form concrete mental images based on personal life experiences and then having them create their own analogies (Hartman and Glasgow 2002). • Care must be taken because students often have trouble fitting new ideas into existing frameworks. The framework used for an analogy must be familiar to students for them to understand the analogy. Otherwise, the analogy can be biased socially, experientially, or culturally (e.g., the analogy of cell to city certainly makes more sense to students who are city dwellers).

Instructional Tool 2.9 (continued)

Application Example	Marzano, Pickering, and Pollock (2001) share a teacher-directed analogy, which provides structure to students as they learn to use analogies. They share the analogy "thermometer is to temperature as odometer is to distance" (Marzano, Pickering, and Pollock 2001, p. 26). They then suggest that the teacher asks the student to explain how the two relationships are similar. Try this in your classroom. After helping students with several additional analogies, have students use an analog graphic organizer to develop analogies related to cell structure, the current topic of study in the classroom. Make sure to discuss the strengths and weaknesses of developed analogies.
Technology Applications	If the analogy is supported by images, standard graphics programs can be used.
Resources	• *Using Analogies in Middle and Secondary Science Classrooms: The FAR Guide–An Interesting Way to Teach with Analogies* (Harrison and Coll 2008). • *Understanding Models in Earth and Space Science* (Gilbert and Ireton 2003). • The Just Read Now website (*www.justreadnow.com/strategies/analogy.htm*) describes and gives examples of word analogies.

Verbal Models: Metaphors	"Expressed" models are mental models expressed in the public and include visual and verbal metaphors and analogies (Hipkins et al. 2002). Creating metaphors is a process that identifies a general or basic pattern in a topic and finds another topic that seems different but has the same general pattern. However, the relationship between the two items in the metaphor is abstract (Marzano, Pickering, and Pollock 2001).
The Research	Creating metaphors is an effective way to identify similarities and differences, a strategy shown effective at increasing student achievement (Marzano, Pickering, and Pollock 2001).
Classroom Implications	• Identifying similarities and differences, which can be accomplished through creating metaphors, is effective both when explicitly guided by the teacher and when created independently by the student. If there are very specific similarities and differences on which the students should focus, then direct instruction is more effective. On the other hand, if divergence in student thinking is the goal, independent student work is more effective (Marzano, Pickering, and Pollock 2001). • In teacher-directed metaphors, the teacher provides the first element and the abstract relationship, which scaffolds the student's construction of the metaphor. Once students become familiar with these abstract relationships, they can be given the first portion of the metaphor and develop the second component, as well as identify the relationship (Marzano, Pickering, and Pollock 2001). • Because the relationship in a metaphor is abstract, it is important that instructional strategies that involve metaphors address this abstract relationship (Marzano, Pickering, and Pollack 2001).
Application Example	Return to the example in the previous section on analogies. There, students developed analogies for cell parts. Now they can be provided the first element of a metaphor (the cell) and provide the second element as the relationship.
Technology Applications	N/A
Resources	*Understanding Models in Earth and Space Science* (Gilbert and Ireton 2003).

Instructional Tool 2.9 (continued)

Visual Models: Graphs, Pictures, and Diagrams	Visual models include images of actual objects (photographs), or graphics of objects, graphs, and or other two-dimensional representations of ideas or data. Different visual models are more or less effective for different purposes and yield different understandings (e.g., photographs to capture images and graphs to display relationships).
The Research	• Graphic models can be used to determine students' preconceptions. Presenting a graph, table or figure and asking students to describe/interpret the image allows you to determine what they know and/or misunderstand about the represented ideas. This can be done individually or in small groups (Wright and Bilica 2007). • Developed models can be shared and critiqued, help students see connections between ideas, change as students learn more, and help teachers recognize gaps in student understanding (Windschitl 2008).
Classroom Implications	• In a small group, this presents alternative explanations from the student group, allowing students to confront their preconceptions and those of their peers. • Student development of figures, graphs, and charts during experimentation serve as part of and help explicate students' mental models.
Application Example	See the use of graphic models to elicit student preconceptions in Learning Target #1 of Chapter 7.
Technology Applications	• Free graphing software is available, including *http://nces.ed.gov/nceskids/creatagraph*. The Computations Science Education Reference Desk (*http://www.shodor.org/refdesk*) is a wonderful resource for free tools for creating graphs, calculators that plot changes between dependent variables, lots of simulations and computational models, and software for creating computational models. • There are free programs for 3-D modeling such as Google's SketchUp (*http://sketchup.google.com*), though it is a bit advanced.
Resources	The BioSciEdNet (the digital library portal for teaching and learning in the biological sciences) provides access to numerous slides, images, and diagrams that can be accessed and used. Go to *www.biosciednet.org/portal/index.php*.

Dynamic Models	These are visualization and analysis tools that help students detect patterns and understand data. They include simulations, computer-based models, geographical information systems, and animations.
The Research	• Computer simulations can enhance students' conceptual understandings, as well as improve achievement on complex concepts more quickly than traditional instruction (Calwetti 1999). • Simulations are more effective when used by students individually or in small groups, resulting in better conceptual understanding. It also appears to increase problem-solving and process skills (Cawelti 1999). • "[A]dvances in molecular modeling and visualization enable students to manipulate a variety of visual representations of abstract concepts, explore these concepts, and therefore, bring the study of science closer to the doing of science" (Trunfio et al. 2003, p. 1). • Molecular modeling and visualization help simulate the behavior of complex systems, helping students see the connection between what happens at the submicroscopic world with the macroscopic properties of matter (Trunfio et al. 2003). • A combination of computer modeling and hands-on laboratories was shown more effective than either strategy alone in promoting students' understanding of the gas law (relationship between temperature and pressure) (Liu 2006). • An interactive dynamic model used with scaffolding improved students' abilities to explain human inheritance and evolutionary phenomena, connecting ideas about phenotypes, chromosomes, and gametes (Schwendimann 2008). • Molecular models are effective tools for teaching genetics at the high school level (Fink 1990). • Animation with or without narrative is more effective than static graphics to learn protein synthesis (O'Day 2008).

Instructional Tool 2.9 (continued)

Classroom Implications	• Computer simulations are helpful when instruction involves scientific models that are difficult or impossible to observe. They also can simplify complex systems (Calwetti 1999).
	• The Science Writing Heuristic process suggests that simulations are effective to probe students' pre-instructional ideas (Hand 2006).
	• One of the areas in which students could benefit is modern genetics. Computer simulations (computer-based bioinformatics tools) used in guided inquiry can provide students with experiences similar to those of scientists as they explore authentic problems using authentic tools. This addresses a major misconception and helps students connect genotype and phenotype (Gelbart and Yarden 2008).
	• "By supporting guided student explorations of interactive, dynamic models, students can get a deep conceptual understanding of atomic-scale phenomena and their relationship to macroscopic phenomena" (Trunfio et al. 2003, p. 4). (*Note*: This was quoted in relationship to use of the Concord Consortium's Molecular Workbench Project.)
	• Simulations can be used in whole-class, small-group, and individual instruction, though they are most effective in small groups or when used by individual students (Cawelti 1999).
	• Use of simulations can promote misconceptions unless the teacher explicitly works with students to identify limitations of the simulated model (Cawelti 1999).
	• Students who receive instructions and guiding questions along with a computer simulation better understood molecular genetics; the simulation is more effective than a textbook illustration activity or traditional teaching as it helps students visualize the abstract concepts (Rotbain et al. 2005).
	• In laboratories that lack expensive equipment, virtual manipulatives allow students experiences they might otherwise not have (Hartman and Glasgow 2002).
Application Example	If you do not live near a forest and want students to learn about forest ecosystems, visit SimForest web site at *http://ddc.hampshire.edu/simforest/index.html*. This site is developed by NSF and available for use. Students can plant trees from a pool of more than 30 New England species, set environmental parameters such as rainfall, temperature, and soil conditions, and watch the forest plot grow and evolve over many years. Graphing and analysis tools are provided within the programs for collection of hard copy data. The site includes access to software, lesson ideas, and more.
Technology Applications	• STELLA software allows online systems diagramming (modeling). However, this is quite sophisticated software
	• Model It, developed at the University of Wisconsin, is designed specifically to make systems diagramming and modeling software accessible to precollege students. Information and research about modeling in general and Model It in particular are available at *http://hi-ce.org/modelit/index.html*.
Resources	Visit *http://biology.merlot.org* for tips on teaching biology with technology, learning materials, and more. Numerous virtual manipulatives are available including virtual microscope, simulations, and animations.

Instructional Tool 2.10

Sense-Making Approaches: Nonlinguistic Representations—Brainstorming Webs

Clustering	This is a nonlinear activity using ovals and words to generate ideas, images, and feelings around a stimulus word. Clustering lets you begin without clear ideas, and explores ideas as they come to you.
The Research	There is a strong link between associative thinking, drawing, creativity and fluency of thinking when using clustering as a prewriting strategy (Rico 2000).
Classroom Implications	• Clustering techniques require no drawing abilities and are a good starting point to develop mental fluency. • Clustering may be a class, small-group, or individual activity. • Begin with an idea, write a phrase or word in the central oval, branch out to other ovals and add words, and extend these ovals by adding details or new ideas. This is not a structured organization of ideas but, instead, a network of associations. • These clusters can serve as a foundation to develop more focused webs that lead to greater clarity of thinking and writing.
Application Example	In a biology classroom this strategy can be used as a prewriting activity in which you want students to freely associate what they know about a topic.
Technology Applications	• The Rapid Fire tool in Inspiration software can be used for student brainstorming (See Resources). • Open source clustering software is also available (see Resources).
Resources	• For a visual image of clustering go to www.sdcoe.k12.ca.us/SCORE/actbank/tcluster.htm. • Open source clustering software is found at http://bonsai.ims.u-tokyo.ac.jp/~mdehoon/software/cluster/software.htm. • Information on Rapid Fire in Inspiration is found at www.inspiration.com.

Mind Mapping	This more specific webbing technique allows students to represent relationships and conceptual knowledge, using both words and images. This supports creativity and memory because it deepens the links of logical operations and creative functions. Though similar in some ways to concept mapping, this approach and its inclusion of images depends on both the right and left sides of the brain (Hyerle 2000).
The Research	• Mind mapping connects brain hemispheres, drawing on creativity and logic in their development (Hyerle 2000). • It draws from students' prior knowledge and allows them to connect new information to their map. Drawing on past knowledge is essential for students to transfer information to new contexts (Hyerle 2000). • It supports memory and depth of understanding (Hyerle 2000).

Instructional Tool 2.10 (continued)

Classroom Implications	• Mind mapping allows "think time" to students to show what they know in an interconnected way (Hyerle 2000). • This strategy can be used in many ways. It can determine prior knowledge but can also be used during the course of study about a concept (Hyerle 2000). • It is useful when studying content-area textbooks, as students can take notes that show both the big picture and details, and shows interrelationships among concepts over the course of a text. Mind mapping is also a good strategy to use for note taking (Hyerle 2000). • Students start in the middle of the page with a word or drawing for a concept, write on arched lines to build connections between ideas, and draw connections among different parts of the map. They use both words and images.
Application Example	In a lesson on behavior, begin with a mind-mapping activity. Have students work individually, beginning with the word *behavior* in the center of a blank page. Remind them to use only one word on each branch, building as many branches and ideas as they can. Then ask students to use their map to describe their thinking about *behavior* to a partner, and then have students reverse roles. Finally, have the student pairs generate a map together, merging their current thinking about behavior. Hold a class discussion of key ideas. Revisit these maps during the course of your unit on behavior, asking students to reflect on changes they would make to their maps.
Technology Applications	• Multiple mind-mapping software applications are available. The mapping software developed by Buzan, the originator of mind mapping, is called iMindMap and can be found at Buzan's iMindMap website: *www.imindmap.com*. • Open-source software, FreeMind, is found at *http://freemind.sourceforge.net/wiki/index.php/Main_Page*. • Content Clips is an NSDL project that provides for import of photos and video, and then provides tools for sorting and conceptual organizing (*www.contentclips.com*). • Regardless of software used, SmartBoards are always an option for sharing and interacting.
Resources	A quick, easy introduction to mind mapping provided by Tony Buzan (the originator) is found at YouTube at *http://www.youtube.com/watch?v=MlabrWv25qQ*. Additional videos also provide examples. Finally, any of Buzan's books on mind mapping are valuable resources.

Circle Maps	Circle maps help students focus thinking and make connections among ideas. They help students focus on a topic and brainstorm related ideas, while framing them in context. This helps them better understand their own and other students' points of view. They are easy to use, yet help students make connections between ideas.
The Research	Circle maps purposefully make no connections, leaving the brain free to brainstorm and later make connections (Hyerle 2000).

Instructional Tool 2.10 (continued)

Classroom Implications	• Circle maps are best used in small groups of three or four students, using chart paper. Generating a group circle map enhances accountability and shared ownership (Lipton and Wellman 1998). • Circle maps consists of a circle within a circle on a sheet of paper. Students place a word, symbol, or picture that represents a concept or idea being studied in the center circle. In the outer circle they list words and phrases that relate to that concept or idea. This lets us know the context of the students' current thinking. Hyerle (2000) suggests that outside the circle the students write information about their lives that provides the context for their ideas. • Lipton and Wellman (1998) suggest that in the upper-right-hand corner, students list categories of ideas they have generated so far. And in the lower-left-hand corner they list their frames of reference. • To help students list frames of reference you can ask questions like "what types of thing influence your point of view—for example, prior knowledge, personal influences, cultural influences, or student role (student, daughter, musician)" (Lipton and Wellman 1998).
Application Example	Use circle maps to determine students' thinking about proteins. Student groups of three or four begin with the word *protein* in the center of the map. They then brainstorm, adding words, phrases, and/or pictures in the outer circle. They then write, in the upper-right-hand corner of their chart paper, categories for the words they listed in the outer circle. This provides you with ideas about their prior knowledge. It also helps launch a lesson on protein. You can use the student charts, specifically their generated categories, to begin a lesson on proteins and their importance.
Technology Applications	Thinking Map software is available (see Resources, below).
Resources	The "Thinking Maps" website developed by David Hyerle describes software that implements eight thinking maps, including circle maps. See *www.thinkingmaps.com/htthinkmap.php3*.

Instructional Tool 2.11

Sense-Making Approaches: Nonlinguistic Representations—Task-Specific Organizers

Descriptive Organizers	These describe persons, places, events, and things. They have a main idea at the center with subcategories or properties radiating out from the center (Marzano, Pickering, and Pollock 2001; Gregory and Hammerman 2008).
The Research	• Because task-specific graphic organizers are "highly structured, they directly facilitate several habits of mind: persistence, self-control (managing impulsivity), accuracy, and precision of language and thinking" (Hyerle 2000, p. 61). • Task-specific organizers guide students through steps, providing a concrete system and model for progressing through a problem on which students might otherwise give up, providing the students with a global view of the process as well as an end-point (Hyerle 2000).
Classroom Implications	These are simple visual representations of key concepts and related terms/ideas. They let students see relationships among ideas and how they link together. They also help students represent abstract ideas, show relationships, and organize ideas for storage and recall.
Application Example	Students use the organizer to make sense of initial ideas they have about populations. The word *population* is placed in the center of a sheet of paper. From there, they web out ideas, including definitions. This can be used to elicit student preconceptions but also modified during the course of study as students learn more.
Technology Applications	• Regardless of software and/or strategy used, SmartBoards are always an option for sharing and interacting. • Inspiration is appropriate software.
Resources	• See "describing" in the matrix at *www.graphic.org/goindex.html.* • Online graphic organizer generators are found at *www.teach-nology.com/web_tools/graphic_org/.*

Sequential Organizers	These organize events in a sequential pattern and include flowcharts, timelines, and cycle diagrams.
The Research	• Because task-specific graphic organizers are "highly structured, they directly facilitate several habits of mind: persistence, self-control (managing impulsivity), accuracy, and precision of language and thinking" (Hyerle 2000, p. 61). • Task-specific organizers guide students through steps, providing a concrete system and model for progressing through a problem on which students might otherwise give up, providing the students with a global view of the process as well as an end-point (Hyerle 2000). • Timeline note-taking is effective for students with disabilities. Flowcharts are useful when teaching a process with several steps (Gore 2004). • Flowcharts can represent simple one-way processes (e.g., simple experiment), more complex scientific processes with loops and decision points, or cause and effect (Gore 2004).

Instructional Tool 2.11 (continued)

Classroom Implications	• Flowcharts are useful when teaching a process with several steps. They can represent simple one-way processes (e.g. simple experiment), more complex scientific processes with loops and decision points, or cause and effect (Gore 2004). • Timelines can also be used to help students understand cause and effect (Gore 2004). • Flowcharts are useful when teaching a process with several steps. They can represent simple one-way processes (e.g. simple experiment), more complex scientific processes with loops and decision points, or cause and effect (Gore 2004).
Application Example	Introduce students to one of the organizers. Flowcharts are nicely applied to lessons about various organic processes, as well as lessons related to events in nature. Cycle diagrams clearly apply to cycles in nature, as well as stages and phases in organisms.
Technology Applications	• Regardless of software and/or strategy used, Smartboards are always an option for sharing and interacting. • Various sequential organizer templates are found at www.educationoasis.com/curriculum/GO/sequence.htm and at http://edhelper.com/teachers/Sequencing_graphic_organizers.htm.
Resources	• See "chain of events" at www.sdcoe.k12.ca.us/score/actbank/torganiz.htm and "sequencing" at www.graphic.org/goindex.html. • Online graphic organizer generators are found at www.teach-nology.com/web_tools/graphic_org.

Process/ Cause-Effect Organizers	These show either cause-and-effect relationships or a sequence of causal events. They describe how events affect one another in a process. The student has to identify and analyze the cause(s) and effect(s) of an event or process.
The Research	• Because task-specific graphic organizers are "highly structured, they directly facilitate several habits of mind: persistence, self-control (managing impulsivity), accuracy, and precision of language and thinking" (Hyerle 2000, p. 61). • Task-specific organizers guide students through steps, providing a concrete system and model for progressing through a problem on which students might otherwise give up, providing the students with a global view of the process as well as an end-point (Hyerle 2000).
Classroom Implications	There are many different types of cause-and-effect organizers. Select the organizer that best fits the content studied. Some types of organizers include disjointed events, one cause leading to multiple events, multiple causes leading to one event, and chain of events.
Application Example	Use a fishbone diagram to study the multiple causes of diminishing species diversity in a local habitat.
Technology Applications	Regardless of software and/or strategy used, SmartBoards are always an option for sharing and interacting.
Resources	• Various templates for cause-and-effect organizers are found at www.enchantedlearning.com/graphicorganizers/causeandeffect and also at www.educationoasis.com/curriculum/GO/cause_effect.htm. • Fishbone diagrams (www.sdcoe.k12.ca.us/score/actbank/torganiz.htm) are useful for multiple causes/effects. • Online graphic organizer generators are found at www.teach-nology.com/web_tools/graphic_org.

Categorical Organizers	These are used for classification and have a horizontal or vertical tree-like organization. Network trees display hierarchical ideas.

Instructional Tool 2.11 (continued)

The Research	• Because task-specific graphic organizers are "highly structured, they directly facilitate several habits of mind: persistence, self-control (managing impulsivity), accuracy, and precision of language and thinking" (Hyerle 2000, p. 61). • Task-specific organizers guide students through steps, providing a concrete system and model for progressing through a problem on which students might otherwise give up, providing the students with a global view of the process as well as an end-point (Hyerle 2000).
Classroom Implications	• Network trees support classifying and categorizing. They are used to show causal information, hierarchies, or branching procedures. Key considerations during construction include the superordinate and subordinate categories, how they are related, and how many levels there are. • They can be used to show a system of things ranked one above another or left to right. • They can be used at the beginning of a project to visually arrange interrelated and sequentially ordered sections within a whole. • Projects, term papers, and study of organizations or systems all work well with hierarchical organizers.
Application Example	Students are asked to create a graphic that summarizes all life they found in a studied ecosystem. To organize their thinking, the teacher asks them to begin by completing a network tree. The tree is to summarize all of the organisms they found during their study. They also can research to identify other typical organisms not found in the immediate environment but typical of it, and add them to the tree. The focus is on the types of organisms, not their interrelationships.
Technology Applications	Regardless of software and/or strategy used, SmartBoards are always an option for sharing and interacting.
Resources	• See "classifying" at *www.graphic.org/goindex.html*. • Online graphic organizer generators are found at *http://www.teach-nology.com/web_tools/ graphic_org*.

Comparison or Relational Organizers	These identify similarities and differences or comparisons among objects, events, etc. They include Venn diagrams and Euler diagrams and compare and contrast matrices.
The Research	• Because task-specific graphic organizers are "highly structured, they directly facilitate several habits of mind: persistence, self-control (managing impulsivity), accuracy, and precision of language and thinking" (Hyerle 2000, p. 61). • Task-specific organizers guide students through steps, providing a concrete system and model for progressing through a problem on which students might otherwise give up, providing the students with a global view of the process as well as an end-point (Hyerle 2000). • Venn diagrams and Euler diagrams help students acquire the skill to compare and contrast because the abstract is made visible, supporting reasoning (Gore 2004).
Classroom Implications	• Venn diagrams and Euler diagrams are used to compare and contrast (when they overlap). They can also help develop logic, deductive reasoning, and cognitive processes, by looking at various relationships among classes such as circles within circles, circles outside of circles, etc. (Gore 2004). • When we compare and contrast more than two things, matrices are helpful (Gore 2004). Matrices are used to show similarities and differences among things.

Instructional Tool 2.11 *(continued)*

Application Example	Use Venn diagrams to compare and contrast ecosystems.
Technology Applications	Regardless of software and/or strategy used, SmartBoards are always an option for sharing and interacting.
Resources	• Various compare and contrast organizer templates are found at *www.educationoasis.com/ curriculum/GO/compare_contrast.htm.* Also see Compare/Contrast and Venn diagram at *www.sdcoe.k12.ca.us/score/actbank/torganiz.htm* and "comparing/contrasting" at *www. graphic.org/goindex.html.* • Online graphic organizer generators are found at *www.teach-nology.com/web_tools/ graphic_org.*

Problem–Solution Organizers	These identify a problem and possible solutions. They show the problem-solving process by defining the parts of the problem and attempted solutions.
The Research	• Because task-specific graphic organizers are "highly structured, they directly facilitate several habits of mind: persistence, self-control (managing impulsivity), accuracy, and precision of language and thinking" (Hyerle 2000, p. 61). • Task-specific organizers guide students through steps, providing a concrete system and model for progressing through a problem on which students might otherwise give up, providing the students with a global view of the process as well as an end-point (Hyerle 2000). • Problem–solution organizers help identify goals and conditions when working through a problem (Hyerle 2000).
Classroom Implications	The organizers structure a process to identify a problem, identify a goal and possible ways to perceive the goal, identify constraints and effects on the problem context, and generate solutions and text alternatives. The organizer "gives a flow of possible solutions and pathways back when a solution is not immediately apparent" (Hyerle 2000, pp. 71 and 74).
Application Example	Students are studying water use and the multiple demands on water, including irrigation, wildlife habitat, recreation, and water supply. They use a problem–solution organizer to determine possible solutions to the problem that demand exceeds supply and that some of the demands pollute the water. As groups complete their organizer, the teacher facilitates a class discussion about the possible solutions and leads the class to consensus on the "best" solution.
Technology Applications	Regardless of software and/or strategy used, SmartBoards are always an option for sharing and interacting.
Resources	• See graphic organizers at the SCORE website: *www.sdcoe.k12.ca.us/score/actbank/torganiz. htm.* Also see problem/solution at *www.sdcoe.k12.ca.us/score/actbank/torganiz.htm.* • Online graphic organizer generators are found at *www.teach-nology.com/web_tools/graphic_org.*

Instructional Tool 2.12

Sense-Making Approaches: Nonlinguistic Representations—Thinking-Process Maps

Concept Mapping	Concept mapping is not only a tool but also symbolic language (Hyerle 2000). It is a schematic diagram or network that reflects hierarchical relationships and interrelationships (Cawelti 1999). Concept maps show relationships between concepts and through these relationships help concepts derive meaning (Novak 1996).
The Research	• Concept maps help people learn how to learn, differentiate misconceptions from accurate conceptions, decrease anxiety, and improve self-confidence (Hartman and Glasgow 2002).
• "The curriculum focus of science instruction at all levels should be on the core concepts and concept relationships (i.e., principles) within the areas of science to be taught and learning (consistent with the conceptual organization of experts and representing the logic of the discipline" (Vitale and Romance 2006, p. 339).
• Concept mapping has positive effects on both student attitudes and achievement (Horton et al. 1993 in Cawelti 1999). Classes involved with group concept mapping outperform classes where maps are created individually or not at all (Brown 2003).
• Concept maps are useful for assessment, and help determine changes in understandings of concepts and connections among them (Cawelti 1999).
• There appears to be no difference in achievement when the maps are made by teachers or by students. However, greater achievement is demonstrated if students supply the key words in concept map construction (Cawelti 1999).
• Concept mapping promotes metacognitive abilities. Mapping couples with interviews provide a frame of reference for students to analyze their own thinking, identify their strengths and weaknesses, and set learning targets. Mapping also increases student motivation (Stow 1997).
• Concept maps are especially effective when working with concept-rich units such as photosynthesis (Brown 2003).
• "Mapping tools have in common the expression of perceived relationships among concepts, and so are uniquely qualified to elucidate the differences between alternative conceptions and the scientific conception" (Fisher et al. 2000, p. 69).

Instructional Tool 2.12 (continued)

Classroom Implications	• The process should be modeled for students. Cooperative learning lets students model the techniques for others (Hartman and Glasgow 2002). • Concept maps can be made by the teacher, the student, or groups of students (Calweti 1999). • Maps can be used to help students recognize and overcome misconceptions, especially if used in small-group settings. If students work individually on maps and then work collectively to merge their maps into a more comprehensive group map, it provokes dialogue and debate and keeps students more on task during collaborative efforts (Novak 1996). • Group construction of concept maps makes evident some students' misunderstandings and allows students to correct each other's mistakes. Joint map creation allows some students to address peers' misunderstandings and develop deeper understanding of themselves (Brown 2003). • Questioning is important to the effectiveness of concept maps. A good focus question leads to a richer map and teacher questioning during construction is important to probe student thinking and to guide instruction (Cañas and Novak 2006). • Maps can be used at the beginning, during, or at the end of a unit. They are effective evaluation tools because they require high levels of synthesis and evaluation. The teacher can use the maps to guide curriculum development (Novak 1996). In our model, this occurs during the *responsive phase*.
Application Example	"If students are provided with 10 to 20 concepts to map for a given topic of study, they must evaluate which concepts are the most significant superordinate concepts and also determine the subordinate concepts and appropriate linking words to describe the concept relationships. This requires successive efforts at synthesis and evaluation, as well as knowledge of the specific concepts and their definitions. If students are also asked to add to their maps several more concepts that are related to the concepts given, the challenge of recall, synthesis, and evaluation is strengthened further" (Novak 1996, p. 39).
Technology Applications	• Inspiration mapping software can be used in a variety of ways. Information can be found at the Inspiration Software, Inc. website: *www.inspiration.com*. • Content Clips is an NSDL project that provides for import of photos and video, and then provides tools for sorting and conceptual organizing (*www.contentclips.com*). • Regardless of software used, SmartBoards are always an option for sharing and interacting.
Resources	Novak, J. D. 1998. *Learning, Creating, and Using Knowledge: Concept Maps as Facilitative Tools in Schools and Corporations*. Mahwah, NJ: Lawrence Erlbaum.

Systems Diagrams	Systems diagrams are used to represent ideas about complex situations and help us make sense of the world. They usually are used to describe either a structure or process, but not both. They are great tools for systems thinking. Systems diagrams have many forms and uses, but when studying a system they can be considered a "model" (Mind Tools n.d.).
The Research	• For most people, it is easier to interpret and remember images than text, and drawing a diagram shows the linkages among concepts or variables better than text. Connecting new information to existing knowledge, using diagrams, helps stimulate thinking about the situation (ICRA n.d.). • Constructing diagrams as a group aids brainstorming, analysis, communication, and understanding (ICRA n.d.). • Diagramming can overcome language barriers (ICRA n.d.).

Instructional Tool 2.12 (continued)

Classroom Implications	• Systems diagrams can be used for brainstorming. But they are also extremely helpful as we try to understand connectivity in a system. They can also be used to diagnose, plan and implement, and communicate (Mind Tools n.d.). • Simple diagrams with 5–10 elements are best, but it is difficult to keep a diagram to these few elements. Include only essential elements and use single words and short phrases. • A variety of systems diagrams are available, each with different purposes (see Resources, below).
Application Example	Students make a diagram that models the cell as a system.
Technology Applications	• STELLA software allows online systems diagramming (modeling). However, this is quite sophisticated software. • Model It, developed at the University of Wisconsin, is designed specifically to make systems diagramming and modeling software accessible to precollege students. Information and research about modeling in general and Model It in particular are available at *http://hice.org/ modelit/index.html*. • Regardless of software used, SmartBoards are always an option for sharing and interacting.
Resources	An excellent tutorial that will help you learn about various systems diagrams, their uses, and their construction is found at *http://systems.open.ac.uk/materials/t552/index.htm*. A full open-learning tutorial on systems diagramming is available at *http://openlearn.open.ac.uk/course/view. php?id=1290&topic=all*. Finally, guidelines for systems diagrams are found at *www.icra.edu.org/ objects/anglolearn/Systems_Diagrams-Guidelines1.pdf*.

Thinking Maps	These maps, developed by Hyerle, are often highly structured and are, in that way, like task-specific organizers. However, they are different in that they also help students see the big picture because they analytically organize material. They are, in many ways, a synthesis of brainstorming webs and graphic organizers. The eight different maps focus students' thinking on the map but also on what influences the creation of the map. Implementation requires use of recurrent thinking patterns and reflective questioning (Hyerle 2000).
The Research	Thinking maps "focus explicitly on different forms of concept development and reflection, facilitating four habits of mind: questioning, multi-sensory learning, metacognition, and empathic listening" (Hyerle 2000, p. 82).
Classroom Implications	• When using the maps, students ask themselves these metacognitive questions: "How am I perceiving this system? What sense or inputs am I using? What thinking skills am I using? What frame of reference (or mental model) is influencing how I am patterning this information? What are some other ways of seeing this patterns? Where are my blind spots?" (Hyerle 2000, p. 82). • The eight thinking maps are found at *www.thinkingmaps.com/htthinkmap.php3*. They can be used individually or in concert, and include circle maps (define context), tree maps (classify/ group), bubble maps (describing with adjectives), double bubble maps (compare/contrast), flow maps (sequence and order), multi-flow maps (analyze cause and effect), brace maps (identify part/whole relationships) and bridge maps (seeing analogies). Implementation is by a school or school system.
Application Example	Use a bridge map to help develop analogies for homeostasis.

Instructional Tool 2.12 (continued)

Technology Applications	• There are free online versions of cognitive mapping tools such as bubbl.us (*http://bubbl.us*) and Mind Meister (*www.mindmeister.com*). • ThinkingMaps software is also available (see Resources, below). • Regardless of software used, SMART boards are always an option for sharing and interacting.
Resources	• *A Field Guide to Using Visual Tools* by David Hyerle (2000) includes a full chapter (Chapter 6) on thinking maps. • The "Thinking Maps" website developed by David Hyerle shows the eight thinking maps. These include circle maps for defining context, tree maps for classifying and groups, bubble maps for describing with adjectives, double bubble maps for comparing and contrasting, flow maps for sequencing and ordering, multi-flow maps for analyzing causes and effects, brace maps for identifying part/whole relationships, and bridge maps for seeing analogies. The website describes each of the maps, the differences between thinking maps and graphic organizers, and a description of the ThinkingMaps software. This website can be found at *www.thinkingmaps.com/htthinkmap.php3*. • The *ThinkingMaps.org* website includes a video introduction to thinking maps by Pat Wolfe, examples of maps, and podcasts to help you use the maps. This website can be found at *www.opencourtresources.com/thinking_maps*.

Instructional Tool 2.13

Sense-Making Approaches: Nonlinguistic Representations—Drawing Out Thinking

Drawings and Annotated Drawings	Drawing uses the right brain to visualize and solve problems and allows thinking in a visual language. Drawings can be used to assess science concept knowledge, observational skills, and ability to reason. They also allow students to explore their own understanding about a concept.
The Research	• 80–90% of the information the brain receives is visual. Drawing frees the expression of much of this information (Hyerle 2000). • Student-created drawings provide assessment of conceptual knowledge, observational skills, and the ability to reason. They reveal how the student perceives an object and the degree to which he or she perceives and represents details (McNair and Stein 2001). • Drawing tasks and annotated illustrations support selection, organization and integration, and cognitive processes necessary for meaningful learning (Edens and Potter 2003). • Drawing enhances nonlinguistic representations in students' minds, as well as their content understanding (Marzano 2001). • Descriptive drawing is a viable way to promote conceptual change. Significant differences resulted between students who generated descriptive drawings and those who wrote in a science log (Edens and Potter 2003). • Student-created drawings provide teachers with information that helps determine activities that will best serve students' learning needs (Stein and McNair 2002). • They can provide information about specific misconceptions, help students grapple with their own ideas and questions, and provide information that shows development of ideas over time (Stein and McNair 2002). • The process of drawing elicits questions and encourages clarification (McNair and Stein 2001). • Drawings are considered more fair (less biased) because students can choose what they draw and because drawings are related to a student's own experiences (McNair and Stein 2001). • The effectiveness of drawings may depend on the level of a student's prior understandings (Edens and Potter 2003). • Drawing activities coupled with interviews help explore students' ideas about abstract concepts (Köse 2008).

Instructional Tool 2.13 (continued)

Classroom Implications	• Mental models and scientific thinking are typically presented verbally to students. Drawings are a viable alternative to explore students' thinking and should be used more often (Edens and Potter 2003). • Annotated drawings are an alternative form of expression that allow students who may understand, but find it difficult to express themselves in words, to express themselves (Atkinson and Bannister 1998). • A combination of verbal and visual representation allows the teacher to match for correspondence and allows students to elaborate on their understandings (Edens and Potter 2003). • Because annotated drawings are flexible in terms of a student's form of expression, they allow students to reveal understandings that might not otherwise be uncovered (Atkinson and Bannister 1998). • Teachers should use drawings along with discussion about the drawings to address misconceptions (Edens and Potter 2003). • Students can revisit drawings, reconstruct earlier concepts, and use drawings to rethink an idea (McNair and Stein 2001). • Because drawings are based on a student's own experiences, teachers can be responsive to students' interests, background knowledge, and emerging skills (McNair and Stein 2001). • Visual-based strategies may be best used when teaching nonobservable science concepts (Edens and Potter 2003).
Application Example	"Talking drawings" translate mental images into simple drawings (McConnell 1993). Students are asked to (1) create a mental image of their understanding of a topic prior to instruction, (2) draw a picture representing their mental images and label it, (3) draw another picture and label it after experiencing content instruction, and (4) write about how their drawings have changed. This strategy makes student construction of knowledge visible, allows them to check their own understandings, and lets them adjust their thinking and study habits (Scott and Weishaar 2008).
Technology Applications	Any graphics program or photo-editing program can be used. There are many free ones.
Resources	See *Science Formative Assessment: 75 Practical Strategies for Linking Assessment, Instruction, and Learning* (Keeley 2008)

Instructional Tool 2.13 (continued)

Concept Cartoons	Cartoon-style drawings present alternative conceptions in science, elicit students' ideas, and challenge their thinking to promote further development of their ideas.
The Research	• Concept cartoons have been shown to be effective in eliciting and addressing student misconceptions about photosynthesis (Ekici, Ekici, and Aydin 2007). • Concept cartoons enable concurrent or consecutive occurrence of elicitation of student ideas and restructuring of their thinking, making the learning process more continuous (Keogh and Naylor 1999). • They provide opportunity for students to discuss the causes of misconceptions and create an environment where all students participate during class discussion, activate them to support their ideas and, thus, remedy misconceptions (Ekici, Ekici, and Aydin 2007). • They require that students choose between alternative explanations, individually and/or in small groups, making the need for investigation evident. Students become responsible for choosing what is appropriate to investigate, lessening the need for teachers to respond to each student individually about his or her idea (Keogh and Naylor 1999). • They stimulate learners to focus attention on constructing explanations for situations in the drawings, thus promoting active engagement of the student in the learning process (Keogh and Naylor 1999). • Concept cartoons offer a strategy that works in variety of teaching situations and across grade levels (Keogh and Naylor 1999).
Classroom Implications	• They present cognitive conflict through the alternative explanations shown in the cartoon, providing motivation (Keogh and Naylor 1999). This conflict is important in challenging a students' misconceptions, a phase of our framework. • They can help students consider what they might want to investigate to clarify their understandings.
Application Example	See Chapter 4 on photosynthesis for an example in application. See the section on eliciting and confronting preconceptions.
Technology Applications	Consider using ComicLife (*http://plasq.com/comiclife-win*) or Comic Creator (*www.readwritethink.org/materials/comic*).
Resources	• Visit the Concept Cartoons website at *www.conceptcartoons.com*. • A rich set of evolution concept cartoons are available at *www.biologylessons.sdsu.edu/cartoons/concepts.html*. • See *Science Formative Assessment: 75 Practical Strategies for Linking Assessment, Instruction, and Learning* (Keeley 2008).

Instructional Tool 2.14

Sense-Making Approaches: Kinesthetic Strategies

Hands-on Experiments, Activities, and Manipulatives	This category involves movement required during a science learning experience. Examples include classroom experimentation that makes use of equipment/probeware and requires movement from one part of the lab to another, use of other manipulatives (e.g., physical models), excursions into the field, and projects that require construction of materials.
The Research	• Kinesthetic activity involves physical movement, and movement when associated with specific knowledge builds a mental image of that knowledge in the learner's mind (Marzano, Pickering, and Pollock 2001). • Concrete experiences engage more of the senses and activate multiple pathways to store and recall information (Wolfe 2001). • Hands-on activities engage students because they interact with materials and peers (Wolfe 2001). • Simply moving activates the brain; if you add the requirement of communication to this action, much more of the brain is involved in the learning experience (Lazear 1991).
Classroom Implications	• Almost any concept or idea can be transformed to involve physical movement. Consider each lesson and determine ways in which experimentation and other hands-on activities can replace lecture/demonstration approaches. • When students present research results, have them actively move. This movement can include demonstration of techniques used, samples gathered, and so forth.
Application Example	Begin a class period modeling the use of sampling materials that will be used in fieldwork. Have students practice using those materials. Then go out into the field to complete sampling. On return to the classroom, students sort and identify samples. They determine the best way to present their materials during a poster presentation. They prepare the poster and share in a round-robin session. Notice that each step in this series of activities involves students with movement and manipulation.
Technology Applications	Using probeware to collect data requires movement on the part of students.
Resources	Lesson Plans, Inc. (*www.lessonplansinc.com*) provides a variety of activities that make sure to address kinesthetic learners.

Physical Movement and Gestures	These kinesthetic activities include the use of gestures, hand signals, and arm motions, as well as acting and role-playing. These are not science-specific actions, but work across the curriculum to improve acquisition and retention of information.
The Research	• Kinesthetic activity involves physical movement, and movement when associated with specific knowledge builds a mental image of that knowledge in the learner's mind (Marzano, Pickering, and Pollock 2001). • Physical simulations and role-playing engage both physical activity and emotions, which helps with acquisition and retention of knowledge (Wolfe 2001). • Almost any concept or idea can be transformed to involve physical movement. • Changing location during a lesson enhances acquisition of information and memory (Jensen 1998). • Gestures associated with learning new information helps retain information (Jensen 1998). • Simply moving activates the brain, and if you add the requirement of communication to this action much more of the brain is involved in the learning experience (Lazear 1991).

Instructional Tool 2.14 (continued)

Classroom Implications	• Simple activities like Jigsaw activities require students to move around the room. Learning stations are another way to ensure movement. • Students can respond, indicating level of understanding (e.g., thumbs-up and thumbs-down). • Role-playing can be used to illustrate concepts, practice skills, stimulate interest, and make ideas more concrete for discussion (Hartman and Glasgow 2002).
Application Example	• Use Four Corner Synectics to determine students' preconceptions about almost any concept. This activity requires you to use four different metaphors for a concept, placing a label for each metaphor in each of the four corners of the room. Ask students to take a moment to personally reflect on and record which metaphor best reflects their current understanding of the concept. They then go to that corner and discuss with the other student(s) at the corner why they selected the metaphor. Students then share their thinking as a whole class. These multiple metaphors both provide the teacher a glimpse into the students' preconceptions and start a discussion around the concept. • Also, see examples of meiosis/mitosis role-playing in Chapter 3.
Technology Applications	Various educational games are available (see *www.supersmartgames.com/blogcategory/62/*), some for Wii. A very good role-playing science game is WolfQuest (*www.wolfquest.org*).
Resources	Lesson Plans, Inc. (*www.lessonplansinc.com*) provides a variety of activities that make sure to address kinesthetic learners.

Recommended Resources

Technology Applications and Websites

In the Instructional Tools in this chapter, you will find the URLs of websites that provide ideas and resources aligned with strategies in each tool. Here is a list of general strategy sites that also might be helpful to you:

- *www.middleweb.com/CurrStrategies.html*

- *www.newhorizons.org/strategies/front_strategies.html*

- *http://science.uniserve.edu.au/school/support/strategy.html*

- *www.muskingum.edu/~cal/database/general*

In addition to the Visible Thinking resources *(www.pz.harvard.edu/vt)* for critical and creative thinking, consider the following websites:

- *www.engin.umich.edu/~problemsolving/strategy/crit-n-creat.htm*

- *http://members.optusnet.com.au/~charles57/Creative/Techniques/index.htmlwww.mindtools.com/pages/main/newMN_CT.htm*

Consider these graphic organizer sites:

- Graphic Organizer Website (*www.graphic.org*),

- SCORE website (*www.sdcoe.k12.ca.us/SCORE/actbank/torganiz.htm*)

- Education Oasis website (*www.educationoasis.com/curriculum/graphic_organizers.htm*).

Build Your Library

Several books that address *instructional strategies* are

Gregory, G. H., and E. Hammerman. 2008. *Differentiated instructional strategies for science, grades K–8.* Thousand Oaks, CA: Corwin Press.

Hartman, H. J., and N. A. Glasgow. 2002. *Tips for the science teacher: Research-based strategies to help students learn.* Thousand Oaks, CA: Corwin Press.

Hyerle, D. 2000. *A field guide to using visual tools.* Alexandria, VA: Association for Supervision and Curriculum Development.

Marzano, R. J., D .J. Pickering, and J .E. Pollock. 2001. *Classroom instruction that works: Research-based strategies for increasing student achievement.* Alexandria, VA: Association for Supervision and Curriculum Development.

Resources on *inquiry* include

Llewellyn, D. 2005. *Teaching high school science through inquiry: A case study approach.* Thousand Oaks, CA: Corwin Press.

Luft, J., R. L. Bell, and J. Gess-Newsome, eds. 2008. *Science as inquiry in the secondary setting.* Arlington, VA: NSTA Press.

National Research Council (NRC). 2000. *Inquiry and the national science education standards.* Washington, DC: National Academy Press.

Our resource recommendations for *assessment* include

Black, P. J., and C. Harrison. 2004. *Science inside the black box: Assessment for learning in the science classroom.* London, UK: nferNelson Publishing Company.

Coffey, J. E., and J. M. Atkin, eds. 2003. *Everyday assessment in the science classroom.* Arlington, VA: NSTA Press.

Coffey, J. E., R. Douglas, and C. Stearns. 2008. *Assessing science learning: Perspectives from research and practice.* Arlington, VA: NSTA Press.

Keeley, P. 2008. *Science formative assessment: 75 practical strategies for linking assessment, instruction, and learning.* Thousand Oaks, CA: Corwin Press.

Keeley, P., F. Eberle, and L. Farrin. 2005. *Uncovering student ideas in science, Volume 1: 25 formative assessment probes.* Arlington, VA: NSTA Press.

Keeley, P., F. Eberle, and J. Tugel. 2007. *Uncovering student ideas in science, Volume 2: 25 more formative assessment probes.* Arlington, VA: NSTA Press.

Keeley, P., F. Eberle, and C. Dorsey. 2008. *Uncovering student ideas in science, Volume 3: Another 25 formative assessment probes.* Arlington, VA: NSTA Press.

Endnotes

1. We used extant research to develop Part I of this book, specifically in the creation of the 13 Instructional Tools presented in this chapter. Students' conceptual learning is informed by research related to three perspectives: (1) cognitive perspectives that focus on individual conceptual change, (2) sociocultural and social constructivist perspectives that recognize the importance of conceptual change but view the social context as central to the learning process, and (3) participative perspectives that view learning as a process best established through an apprenticeship model. For a more thorough discussion of each approach, their strengths and weaknesses, and ways in which each contribute to our thinking about learning science, see the chapter "Student Conceptions and Conceptual Learning in Science" (Scott, Asoko, and Leach 2007). Curriculum and instruction are likely informed to some degree by each of these perspectives (Carlsen 2007; Scott, Asoko, and Leach 2007).

Our agreement with this contention is evident in the strategies included in the tools. Our Instructional Planning Framework builds strongly on conceptual change research, but we also recognize the importance of social interaction using language (discourse) and other multiple resources (e.g., writing, visual images, actions) to mediate learning. Tools to facilitate social interaction are central to the sense-making approaches and Instructional Tools we include. We also recognize the importance of student participation in experiences that resemble those of scientists. This topic is further discussed in the section on standards-based approaches. As a result, the strategies included in this chapter both support our Instructional Planning Framework and reflect aspects of each of these three perspectives. This provides you with the flexibility to select tools that best fit both the context of your instruction and your personal teaching philosophy.

Our review of research yielded themes (underlined in the following text) that guided the design of Part I in this book. The Instructional Planning Framework discussed in Chapter 1 is partly built on two of these themes (in italics): the importance of *identifying essential topics* in a discipline and *focusing on these few topics in depth* (Bransford, Brown, and Cocking 1999; Masilla and Gardner 2008; Michaels, Shouse, and Schweingruber 2007; Vitale and Romance 2006). This thinking is core to the *predictive phase* of our framework, and implications are further explored in Chapter 3. Our selection of strategies and tool development were guided by the thinking that essential topics on which we focus should be *approached in multiple ways* (Masilla and Gardner 2008). Of course, all activities, assessments, and teaching strategies should be directly related to the selected core content. But the learning sequence should allow students to experience a variety of learning activities to develop meaningful understanding of the concepts and engage in a variety of application and problem-solving experiences after development of their initial understanding (Vitale and Romance 2006).

We also used the research base to determine the various approaches and specific strategies in this chapter. Five different research themes emerged that guided our selection of approaches and strategies. These five themes, a summary of the associated research, and how they inform book design, are as follows:

Learning to think and *thinking to learn*: These themes are essential to shape a "thought-filled" curriculum (Costa 2008). Learning is a consequence of thinking (Ritchart and Perkins 2008), and skillful thinking is best nurtured in the context of the content domain

(Costa 2008; Swartz 2008). Multiple researchers consider thinking skills and habits of mind to be essential to learning (Costa 2008; Marzano 1992; Ritchart and Perkins 2008; Swartz 2008). Based on this research, we developed Instructional Tools and selected strategies you will find in the sections on sense-making approaches and metacognitive approaches.

Thinking about our own thinking: Metacognition is strongly supported by the research community (Baird and White 1996; Costa 2008; Fisher et al. 2000; Gore 2004; Ritchart and Perkins 2008; Swartz 2008; Tanner and Allen 2005). "Productive habits of mind" (Marzano 1992) frame our thinking and tools for metacognitive approaches. This research drove our development of the metacognitive approaches.

Thinking together: The importance of social interaction to student learning is well recognized (Costa 2008; Fisher et al. 2000; Ritchart and Perkins 2008; Swartz 2008). In this book, we do not fully explore cooperative learning but, when possible, build connections.

Thinking big: This determines how learning contributes to "building more thoughtful classrooms, schools, and communities, and a more thoughtful work" (Costa 2008, p. 24) and considers learning experiences that promote respect for humans and the world in which we live. Authentic learning experiences and real-world research fill this need, and strategies are included that encourage big thinking.

Discipline-based thinking: For students to understand their world it is essential to understand a discipline's perspectives. Capacities to develop include understanding (1) the purpose of disciplinary expertise, (2) a discipline's essential knowledge base, (3) inquiry methods of the discipline, and (4) a discipline's forms of communication (Masilla and Gardner 2008). In addition, instructional approaches to facilitate conceptual change are essential to replace a resistant misconception with a scientific idea, and effective conceptual change strategies are consistent with inquiry-based science teaching (Wandersee, Mintzes, and Novak 1994). Inquiry-based teaching is effective at teaching for conceptual change since inquiry has students question their preconceptions and challenge their own knowledge, activities common to both conceptual change and scientific habits of mind (Tanner and Allen 2005). The section in this chapter on standards-based approaches focuses on inquiry, the nature of science (NOS) and the history of science (HOS) and explores the importance of scientific thinking and processes.

2. Dimension two (Marzano 1992), acquiring and interpreting knowledge, includes steps to develop understanding of declarative knowledge. These steps include "constructing meaning" that correlates to "perceiving and interpreting" for meaningful learning. Additional steps require "organizing and storing declarative knowledge," called "organizing and encoding information" in the meaningful learning model (Fisher, Wandersee, and Moody 2000). Dimension three (Marzano 1992), extending and refining knowledge, is referred to as "retrieving and applying information" in meaningful learning (Fisher, Wandersee, and Moody 2000). Dimension four (Marzano 1992), application of information, requires using knowledge meaningfully.

PART II
Toolbox Implementation: The Framework and Strategies in Practice

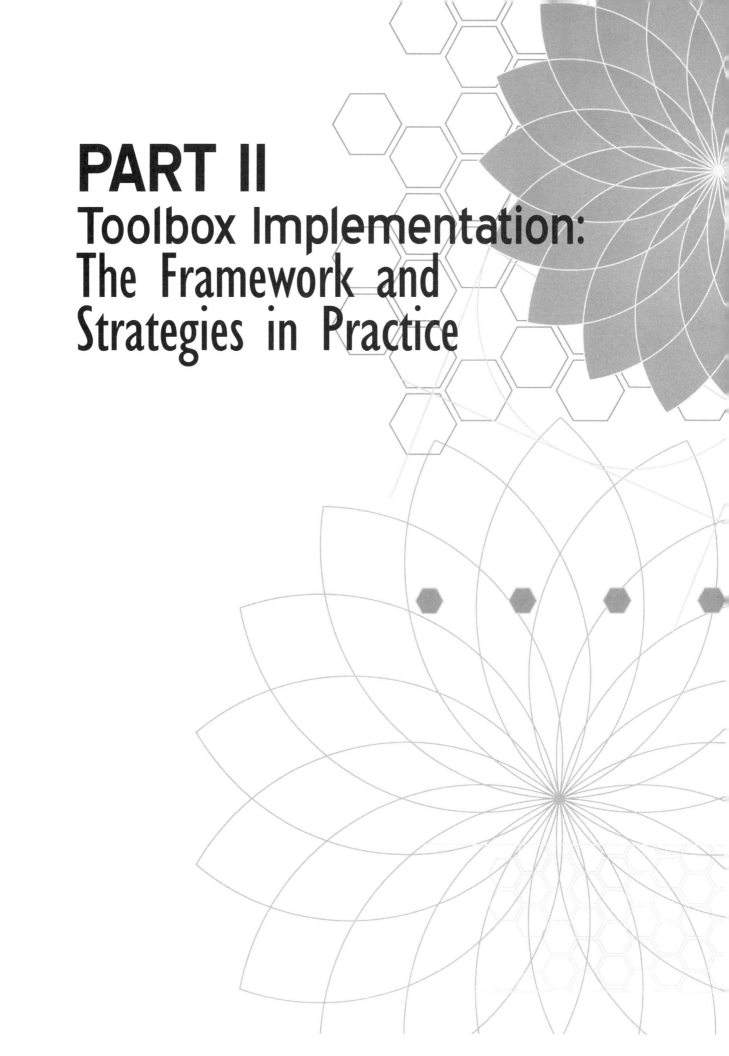

Instructional Planning Framework

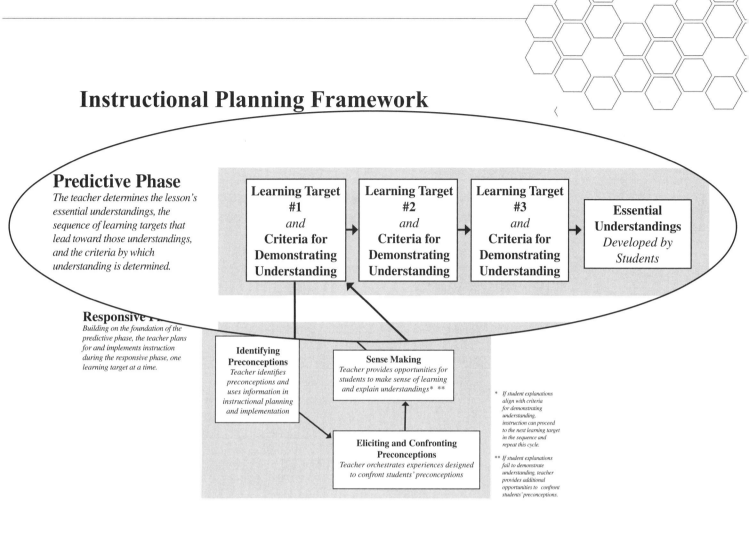

Predictive Phase
The teacher determines the lesson's essential understandings, the sequence of learning targets that lead toward those understandings, and the criteria by which understanding is determined.

Learning Target #1 *and* **Criteria for Demonstrating Understanding**	Learning Target #2 *and* **Criteria for Demonstrating Understanding**	Learning Target #3 *and* **Criteria for Demonstrating Understanding**	**Essential Understandings** *Developed by Students*

Responsive Phase
Building on the foundation of the predictive phase, the teacher plans for and implements instruction during the responsive phase, one learning target at a time.

Identifying Preconceptions
Teacher identifies preconceptions and uses information in instructional planning and implementation

Sense Making
Teacher provides opportunities for students to make sense of learning and explain understandings* **

Eliciting and Confronting Preconceptions
Teacher orchestrates experiences designed to confront students' preconceptions

* *If student explanations align with criteria for demonstrating understanding, instruction can proceed to the next learning target in the sequence and repeat this cycle.*

** *If student explanations fail to demonstrate understanding, teacher provides additional opportunities to confront students' preconceptions.*

Chapter 3

Reproduction: Meiosis and Variation

"Several studies, involving students of all ages, point to very persistent alternative conceptions about the source of variation. Students invariably attribute observable variation to environmental factors alone. Sexual reproduction is not recognized as the source of variation in a population."

—Driver et al. 1994, p. 52

Why This Topic?

Meiosis, the foundation for genetics, is considered to be an essential science topic in both the *Benchmarks of Science Literacy* (AAAS 1993) and the *National Science Education Standards* (NRC 1996). Genetics is also one of the most difficult topics for students (Bahar, Johnstone, and Hansell 1999; Mertens and Walker 1992), partly because of their incomplete understanding of meiosis. Students make little distinction between mitosis and meiosis, poorly understand their purposes and processes, and misunderstand the underlying chromosome behavior. Thus, they have a poor conceptual basis for genetics (Knippels, Waarlo, and Boersma 2005). In addition, the instructional separation of reproduction and meiosis from the occurrence of hereditary phenomena at the varied levels of biological organization contributes to learning problems (Kindfield 1994; Knippels 2002; Lewis and Wood-Robinson 2000). With a deep understanding of the meiotic process, students will be more likely to understand inheritance, an otherwise very difficult topic. In addition, as they begin their studies of evolution, their understanding of both the concepts of gene pool and the interaction of selection pressures and gene pool will be enhanced.

Overview

This lesson does not address all aspects of meiosis. Rather, it builds on middle grade instruction by clarifying the relationship between reproduction and meiosis, as well as the distinctions between mitosis and meiosis. The intent is to address students' major difficulties and misconceptions, providing the foundation for more detailed coverage that is required to understand genetics and evolution.

In this chapter, we use a case study approach to focus on the *predictive phase* of the Instructional Planning Framework (p. 6). We also briefly look at the *responsive phase* of the framework, waiting for later chapters to flesh out in detail how that phase can be applied to specific content. (*Note:* All tables are grouped together at the end of the chapter, beginning on p. 110. They are followed by Recommended Resources and Endnotes.)

Case Study: Setting the Stage

Before we explore the framework, we present the work context for Brenda, the teacher in our case study (Figure 3.1). Let's get familiar with her situation and consider how it might apply to yours.

Figure 3.1

Case Study: An Experienced Biology Teacher Faces a New Assignment

Brenda, a biology teacher for eight years, found out that her teaching assignment would change the following school year. Because of the school district's move to provide a two-year curriculum that addressed the state science standards, she would now teach the first year of the new two-year natural science course sequence. Furthermore, students ranging from those who had been identified as needing special education to those who had been identified as gifted and talented could now be placed in the same classrooms.

Although this new course would be a real challenge, Brenda felt lucky that one of the required topics in the course was genetics because it was one of her areas of strength. Indeed, she was confident in her biology content knowledge overall, but she had never had to teach biology to such a heterogeneous group.

Brenda thought about the genetics unit she currently taught and how she might change it to better suit her new teaching assignment. In the past, her students had been very engaged in the activities she provided. Yet a significant percentage of her current biology students did not demonstrate mastery on the district benchmark assessment. One difficulty was that the assessment included questions on meiosis that focused more on phases and vocabulary than it did on the underlying mechanisms and the importance of the process.

Although Brenda tried her best to focus on the underlying concepts during instruction, she also needed to make sure that students would demonstrate mastery on the assessment. She found that many students could distinguish between meiosis and mitosis, identify where in the reproductive cycle each process fit, distinguish the stages of meiosis, and knew the required vocabulary, but the majority were unable to explain why a reduction division was important in meiosis or why meiosis was a natural source of variation.

Brenda knew she should think very carefully about the learning targets for her new assignment and about what her students should know in order to understand the core biological concepts and to master the district assessment. The related district standard focused on the molecular basis of genetics; it began with cell reproduction to transfer genetic information from generation to generation and that genes determine the traits of living things. However, the detailed list of information to cover included sexual/asexual reproduction, mitosis, meiosis, genes, chromosomes, DNA/RNA, protein, protein synthesis, and mutations. She felt she should focus on the core concepts, yet vocabulary was essential to master the benchmark. Where should she begin?

Instructional Planning Framework: *Predictive Phase*

How do we use the *predictive phase* as we think about an appropriate lesson for Brenda? This phase of the framework addresses three major areas (Figure 3.2): (1) to clarify the conceptual target, (2) to establish a learning sequence, and (3) to identify criteria to demonstrate understanding. We use Brenda's case to model the *predictive phase* of our framework.

Figure 3.2

Instructional Planning Framework: Predictive Phase

Predictive Phase

The teacher determines the lesson's essential understandings, the sequence of learning targets that lead toward those understandings, and the criteria by which understanding is determined.

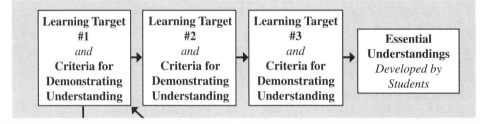

To instruct students in this hard-to-teach topic, where does a teacher start? Teachers are accountable for teaching to the science standards and benchmarks established by their districts and state departments of educations—and to their students who need to demonstrate mastery of these standards and benchmarks. In some cases, as in Brenda's, the required assessments focus on low-level cognitive knowledge rather than on essential concepts. How does a teacher move from very broad standards to quality instruction that promotes learning for each student?

What Is the Conceptual Target?

If you were working on Brenda's lesson, where would you start? We suggest that it is not only important to establish the conceptual target, but also to understand what experiences about the science concept your students are likely to have had prior to arriving in your classroom and what you want them to understand by the time they graduate and become adults in the community. Numerous resources are available that simplify this process. These include *Benchmarks for Science Literacy* (commonly known as the Benchmarks) (AAAS 1993), the *National Science Education Standards* (commonly known as the NSES) (NRC 1996), and *Science for All Americans* (AAAS 1989).[1]

Adult Science Literacy

We begin with what should constitute adult science literacy because, for many of our students, high school biology provides their last formal encounter with the discipline. Take a look at the *Science for All Americans* (AAAS 1989) summary of what adults should understand about reproduction (Figure 3.3).

Figure 3.3

Expectations of Adult Science Learning on the Topic of Reproduction

"Instructions for development are passed from parents to offspring in thousands of discrete genes, each of which is now known to be a segment of a molecule of DNA.... In sexual reproduction of plants and animals, a specialized cell from a female fuses with a specialized cell from a male. Each of these sex cells contains an unpredictable half of the parent's genetic information. When a particular male cell fuses with a particular female cell during fertilization, they form a cell with one complete set of paired genetic information, a combination of one half-set from each parent.... The sorting and combination of genes in sexual reproduction results in a great variety of gene combinations in the offspring of two parents. There are millions of different possible combinations of genes in the half apportioned into each separate sex cell, and there are also millions of possible combinations of each of those particular female and male sex cells." (AAAS 1989, pp. 61–62)

According to the summary in Figure 3.3, understanding meiosis does not require memorization of phases and labels. However, in Brenda's case, the district standards and assessment focused heavily on memorization. It is important to review both your district standards and the national standards to ensure that your lesson meets grade-level expectations. If your district standards do not reflect the NSES and Benchmarks, some corrections are in order, perhaps initiated by you!

Middle and High School Science Standards

The NSES stress that all too often, as teachers struggle to make choices about what to teach that will help students understand life science content, there is an emphasis on information rather than on conceptual understanding. Reflecting on Brenda's case, it seems possible that she overemphasized information at the cost of conceptual development. Her students' benchmark results demonstrated some mastery of the lower cognitive level content (phase names and vocabulary) but less so the important understanding that the meiotic process is a natural source of variation. The national standards should help Brenda target the big ideas and, perhaps, avoid this dilemma.

Let's consider how we prepare students for adult science literacy not only at the grade level we teach, but also at the previous grade levels, in order to identify the understandings our students should bring with them to our classrooms. Details about these learning expectations are provided in the Benchmarks and the NSES. The Benchmarks say, "Learning the genetic explanation for how traits are passed on from one generation to the next can begin in the middle years and carry into high school. The part played by DNA in the story should wait until students understand molecules" (AAAS 1993, p. 106). The Benchmarks also stress that during the middle years the passing on of traits could be handled as a natural part of the study of human reproduction.

The NSES also provide a listing of ideas to cover in the middle grades. The high school NSES and Benchmarks build on this middle level understanding and apply it to the role of meiosis in recombination and the resulting variation among individuals in a species.

Assuming that Brenda's students enter her class with mastery of middle grade standards and their underlying concepts, Brenda should focus on the high school standards as she begins to plan her lesson. We use a Teacher Work Template (Table 3.1, p. 110) to undertake the *predictive phase* of lesson development. (You will do the same thing when you broach other topics; Appendix A1 is a blank Teacher Work Template for your use.) This template corresponds to the Instructional Planning Framework outlined in Chapter 1 and we will visit it again in Chapters 4–7. We begin the template for this topic by including the appropriate NSES and Benchmarks (see "National Standards Addressed"), as well as the middle school Benchmarks and NSES (see "Previous Conceptual Learning" from both the Benchmarks and the NSES). We urge you to carefully review the standards in the template.

Digging Further Into the Standards

We now have a sense of adult science literacy expectations, the topics that should be covered in the middle grades, and expectations of learning in high school. But we need to further unpack the standards to explore the deeper meaning of these expectations and to provide Brenda with ideas for lesson focus and modification. What is core in these standards for student understanding? What should be stressed and what should be pruned? To answer these questions, we dig a bit deeper into the Benchmarks and the NSES and also review some additional sources, including the *Atlas of Science Literacy* (2001a) and the *NSTA Pathways to the Science Standards*—both the High School Edition (Texley and Wild 2004) and the Middle School Edition (Rakow 2000).[2][3]

According to these resources, students in the early-middle-school years explain inheritance entirely through physical traits—that is, easily observable features. Indeed, before students are introduced to the genetic explanation of heredity, they are asked to identify traits through observation, an appropriate middle school approach (Rakow 2000). It isn't until later middle school and high school that students begin to understand that these traits are connected to genetic information carried in chromosomes and translated by the cell; and it is essential that biology students have an understanding of the molecular basis of genetics (AAAS 2001a; Texley and Wild 2004). So Brenda should plan instruction to develop students' conceptual understanding of chromosomal behavior during meiosis in order to build a foundation for understanding genetics.

In addition, understanding meiosis addresses the sorting of genes referred to in the portion of the *Atlas of Science Literacy* (2001a, p. 71) Map for Heredity shown in Figure 3.4, which reads "sorting and recombination of genes in sexual reproduction results in a great variety of possible gene combinations in the offspring of any two parents." Note that this box of the map links directly to the middle school understanding of life cycles (5B/1 and 5B/2...) as well as to the 9–12 understanding about the genetic information coded in DNA molecules (5B/3 and 5B/4...).

Figure 3.4

Concept Map for *Heredity: "Variation in Inherited Characteristics"*

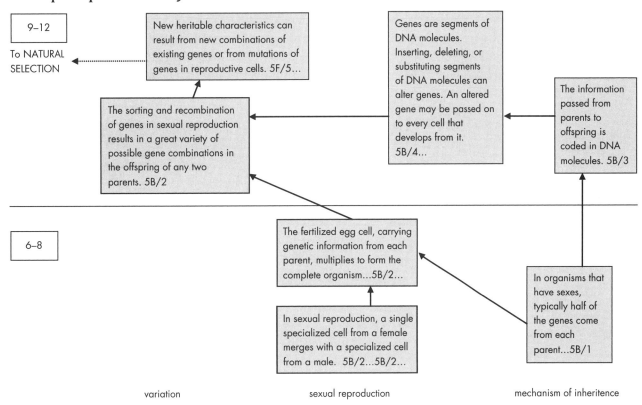

9–12

To NATURAL SELECTION

New heritable characteristics can result from new combinations of existing genes or from mutations of genes in reproductive cells. 5F/5…

Genes are segments of DNA molecules. Inserting, deleting, or substituting segments of DNA molecules can alter genes. An altered gene may be passed on to every cell that develops from it. 5B/4…

The information passed from parents to offspring is coded in DNA molecules. 5B/3

The sorting and recombination of genes in sexual reproduction results in a great variety of possible gene combinations in the offspring of any two parents. 5B/2

6–8

The fertilized egg cell, carrying genetic information from each parent, multiplies to form the complete organism…5B/2…

In organisms that have sexes, typically half of the genes come from each parent…5B/1

In sexual reproduction, a single specialized cell from a female merges with a specialized cell from a male. 5B/2…5B/2…

variation   sexual reproduction   mechanism of inheritence

Source: American Association for the Advancement of Science (AAAS). 2001. *Atlas of science literacy.* Washington, DC: AAAS, p. 71. Extract printed with permission

Abbreviations: 5B/1, 5B/2, 5B/3, 5B/4, and 5F/5 refer to the chapter, section, and number of the corresponding goal statement in *Benchmarks for Science Literacy.* American Association for the Advancement of Science (AAAS). New York: Oxford University Press, 1993.

Based on this information, it is critical that Brenda make sure that her students have these understandings and, if not, she should provide them the opportunity to gain them. She should make sure that (1) her students' prior understandings prepare them to connect, through the process of meiosis, their concrete middle school experiences with observable traits to both life cycles and the molecular basis of genetics and (2) her lesson targets the grade-level appropriate aspects of the standards in a conceptual ways without an overemphasis on phases and vocabulary. Later in the chapter we demonstrate how this might be done.

Fundamentally, Brenda wants her students to understand that continuity of life depends on reproduction and that meiosis is essential for continuity of life as well as for the variation within any sexually reproducing species. In addition, it is essential that she connect any new instruction to her students' middle school experiences. To begin to plan this lesson, she needs to ensure that students bring with them the following understandings from prior instruction:

- *Mitosis* is a process of cell division that produces new somatic (body) cells required for growth and repair and can be the primary way to increase populations for many species.
- *Meiosis*, followed by fertilization in the reproductive cycle, passes on genetic information that results in physical traits we can observe.

Consider Research on Learning Progressions

If you study research on learning progressions in genetics, you are likely to confirm what this book has covered so far. You will also deepen your thinking about instructional design—and, as a by-product, enhance your content understanding. The research identifies the ultimate learning goals for high school students as well how learning should progress if they are to reach these goals. We encourage your review of research on learning progressions, but we understand that this might be beyond the time and resources available to you. Also, research is incomplete on some topics in biology. But we will model use of the research here and include an optional step for your future use, since we consider this a rich resource.

But first, what are learning progressions? They are "descriptions of the successively more sophisticated ways of thinking about a topic that can follow one another as children learn about and investigate that topic over a broad span of time" (Duschl et al. 2007, p. 214) and are grounded in the findings of current research. There is a growing national research effort to establish learning progressions in science that can serve as a basis for both instruction and assessment. A review of research on a genetics learning progression helps lay the foundation for instructional progressions in biology courses before we sequence the learning activities for Brenda's lesson.

Roseman et al. (2006) recommend a learning progression that differs significantly from traditional instruction. Their recommendations also address the concerns we've stated previously about the need to make connections among the varied and complex level of organization in living things. They suggest that proteins should be emphasized before DNA and that DNA should be focused on before genes and chromosomes. Their rationale is based on the conceptual strand maps in *Atlas of Science Literacy* (2001a), which indicate that, in middle school, students should learn about the cell's work in carrying out the functions of organisms and in high school that learning should extend to understanding that proteins do this work and that an organism's traits reflect the action of its proteins. At this point, students' understandings of cells and protein molecules prepare students to learn about the link between proteins and DNA and, thus, between DNA and traits (Roseman et al. 2006). This learning progression is supported by additional research to help teachers determine the sequence of instruction in their own biology courses.[4]

Recall the detailed list of information Brenda was required to cover: sexual/asexual reproduction, mitosis, meiosis, genes, chromosomes, DNA/RNA, protein, protein synthesis, and mutations. The research suggests that all but meiosis and mutations should be covered prior to this lesson and that students should understand the following concepts as prerequisite knowledge for Brenda's lesson: Cells (and in particular proteins) do the work of organisms; DNA controls protein synthesis; and the functioning of these proteins results in an organism's traits. This requires that students understand cell structure and function and DNA structure and replication in addition to the facts that the gene is encoded in the DNA and part of the chromosome and that the genetic information guides protein synthesis. We can now add the conceptual learning from previous instruction in the biology class to the Teacher Work Template (refer to Table 3.1, p. 110, "previous conceptual learning from prior instruction in the biology course").

Pruning the Content

Now we need to ask, What are the concepts and skills students need to have to understand the standards in Table 3.1? How do we know what to include and what to exclude from our lessons? *Designs for Science Literacy* (2001b) helps us think further about "unburdening" the curriculum.[5] It is important to eliminate something from biology instruction for several reasons. Biology steadily grows as a discipline and, although we continue to add content to our courses, we rarely eliminate anything. There is only so much time in a school day, however, and it is critical that we spend our time on important content. It is also vital that we address this content in deep and meaningful ways, rather than superficially. Pruning or unburdening the curriculum is a good way to proceed.

What are our pruning recommendations related to meiosis? We suggest that the teacher prune the following topics when the class is studying growth and division: rates of cell growth, controls of cell growth, phases of mitosis, cytokinesis, chromatin, chromosome structure, and centriole and spindle. It is clear that much traditional instruction, including Brenda's lesson, is inappropriate. Technical terms sometimes suggested for omission include even the term *meiosis*! But, as in Brenda's case, a teacher might be required to ensure student mastery of some of the content that might more appropriately be pruned. Even though conceptual understanding of the meiotic process and its importance can be taught without teaching the term, the reality of the classroom might require the details. How should teachers balance quality instruction with accountability and the demands of high-stakes assessments?

We suggest that it is possible to begin the lesson conceptually and then layer on the facts and vocabulary that will be assessed. In other words, we consider the conceptual approach the ideal for an introductory biology course, but we recognize the demands placed on some teachers because of various accountability systems.

Topic: Meiosis
Go to: *www.scilinks.org*
Code: HTB001

Topic Mitosis and meiosis
Go to: *www.scilinks.org*
Code HTB002

Topic: Genetic variation
Go to: *www.scilinks.org*
Code: HTB003

We can now fill in the "knowledge and skills" section of the Teacher Work Template (Table 3.1, specifically p. 111). Notice that in this section, some concepts and some vocabulary are listed as "essential" and some as "may be pruned." If the concepts and vocabulary that may be pruned are necessary in your school district, then the essential components should be developed first and the "may be pruned" elements added later in instruction. We believe that these lesson additions are appropriate for developing conceptual understanding and that they will give Brenda's students the understanding they need to master the district assessment.

Reflection and Application

Let's take some time to reflect on Brenda's case, the steps we used to think through how she might begin her lesson planning, and how these steps might inform your own teaching. First review a summary of the process that we have used thus far in the *predictive phase* (Figure 3.5). Then respond to the three questions that follow the figure.

Figure 3.5

Planning in the Predictive Phase: *Identify Essential Understandings*

Identify the essential understandings for the lesson.
1. Begin with the descriptions of adult science literacy to determine an anchor goal.
2. Consider the middle school and high school standards and benchmarks.
3. Optional: Study existing research on learning progressions. A good resource (*www.project2061.org/publications/2061Connections/2007/2007-04a-resources.htm*) is found in the 2061 Connections online newsletter (AAAS 2007a).
4. Dig a bit deeper and think about the standards.
5. Decide what is essential and what can be pruned.

1. This process is one way to clearly identify the conceptual target for a lesson. What in this process would work well for you?
2. What challenges might you face in carrying out the process outlined in Figure 3.5 if you were beginning a new lesson? How would you overcome them?
3. Reflect on the implications of the five steps in Figure 3.5 for your own teaching. What ideas do you have about your own teaching of meiosis?

What Is a Logical Learning Sequence?

Still in the *predictive phase*, we now establish a learning sequence. Based on what we now know about the standards, what is a logical sequence of learning targets that will build the understandings called for in the standards? Let's think through a process we can use to make this determination.

Build on Middle School Experiences

In an ideal situation, high school biology teachers would have students in their classes who bring certain understandings about science with them from middle school. The teachers could then build on those understandings. But, in reality, not all students will have command of that knowledge and some might still carry with them misconceptions. It seems logical that teachers should begin with those understandings and formally introduce meiosis—not as a term, but as a concept. Teachers also know that middle school experiences are grounded in the concrete, and high school instruction must move to the abstract. Thus, we suggest beginning the lesson with a sexual life cycle, something with which students are familiar from their middle school instruction. The sexual life cycle becomes Learning Target #1 in our learning sequence:

Organisms that reproduce sexually have life cycles that include cell divisions where the chromosomes/DNA are exactly replicated in new cells and other cell divisions (reduction divisions) where the number of chromosomes is halved in new cells. These two types of cell division are similar yet distinctly different, each serving a different purpose. Reduction divisions are essential if genetic information from each parent is to be contributed to the offspring.

Tease Apart the Components of the High School Standards

Two major ideas about sexual reproduction are found in the Benchmarks and in the NSES. The Benchmarks say, "The sorting and recombination of genes in sexual reproduction results in a great variety of possible gene combinations from the offspring of any two parents" (AAAS 1993, p. 108). We know that students are introduced in middle school to the idea that sexually produced offspring are not identical to their parents. But they have not learned the reason for the variation. We therefore introduce this thinking in Learning Target #2:

The movement of chromosomes (and therefore genes) during these reduction divisions results in reproductive cells with varied genetic makeup. Chromosomes can exchange parts during this process, resulting in further variation. This exchange transfers genes/DNA between chromosome pairs. As a result, the genes that parents contribute to offspring can vary.

And the NSES say, "The fact that the human body is formed from cells that contain two copies of each chromosome—and therefore two copies of each gene—explains many features of human heredity, such as how variations that are hidden in one generation can be expressed in the next" (NRC 1996, p. 185). It is now time to connect thinking about the meiotic process as a source of variation to Mendelian genetics, so we identify Learning Target #3:

Additional variation is introduced through the random process of fertilization. The variation in genetic makeup introduced through meiosis and random fertilization can result in offspring with traits expressed or hidden in a particular generation.

Note: To ensure that students understand that variation is largely, but not only, the result of natural processes, we introduce the concept of mutation, which will be covered later in this chapter. Although we do not include a learning target for mutation, we should lay the foundation that not all variation arises from meiosis and random fertilization.

The learning sequence we just determined and how it leads to essential understandings is summarized in Figure 3.6.

We can now add this sequence of learning targets and the lesson's essential understandings to our Teacher Work Template (Table 3.1, "Learning Targets" and "Essential Understandings," p. 311).

Figure 3.6

Learning Sequence for "Sources of Natural Variation"

Target #1: Organisms that reproduce sexually have life cycles that include cell divisions where the chromosomes/DNA are exactly replicated in new cells and other cell divisions (reduction divisions) where the number of chromosomes is halved in new cells. These two types of cell division are similar yet distinctly different, each serving a different purpose. Reduction divisions are essential if genetic information from each parent is to be contributed to the offspring.	**Target #2:** The movement of chromosomes (and therefore genes) during these reduction divisions results in reproductive cells with varied genetic makeup. Chromosomes can exchange parts during this process, resulting in further variation. This exchange transfers genes/DNA between chromosome pairs. As a result, the genes that parents contribute to offspring can vary.	**Target #3:** Additional, natural variation is introduced through the random process of fertilization. The variation in genetic makeup introduced through meiosis and random fertilization can result in offspring with traits expressed or hidden in a particular generation.

Essential Understanding: The continuity of genetic information is assured when chromosomes and their DNA are replicated and passed on to other cells. Reduction divisions during meiosis in the reproductive cells are critical because they allow continuity from one generation of sexually reproducing organisms to the next. But it is also important as a source of variation among offspring. The ways in which chromosomes move during these divisions provide a source of natural variation. Coupled with random fertilization it results in offspring with a variety of traits that can be expressed or hidden in a particular generation.

What Criteria Should We Use to Determine Understanding?

We now move to the final planning step in the *predictive phase* of our planning model: establishing criteria to determine understanding. What will this understanding look like? What should students be able to do to demonstrate their conceptual understanding? We first must back up a bit and discuss the assessments that will undergird our establishment of criteria.

There are different reasons for us to assess student learning, using both formative and summative assessments. Summative assessments are cumulative assessments that try to capture what a student has learned and can be used for grading, placement, promotion, or accountability (NRC 2001a). However, this type of assessment is not the intent of the criteria-determination section of the Instructional Planning Framework. Instead, in this case, the planning process establishes criteria by which a student's understandings can be assessed. The exact form of assessment that teachers use to determine whether or not their students learn a lesson's fundamental understandings will depend on many aspects of their teaching situations. This process simply establishes the criteria by which teachers can measure understanding. As we stated in Chapter 2, it was not our intent to include detailed coverage of assessment, even though formative assessments are thoroughly embedded in the model and in the lessons outlined in this and the following chapters.

We now determine what students' understanding of the topic—meiosis as a source of variation—should "look like" at the end of instruction. Specifically, we determine the criteria teachers can use to decide whether their students have learned the content and processes that were the instructional focus. As we've said earlier in this chapter, we recommend that teachers focus on big ideas and conceptual understanding. However, if your school or district expects mastery of facts and vocabulary, you need to prepare your students for that as well.

How Do We Use the Term Criteria*?*

First, let's define what we mean by *criteria* to determine understanding. We follow the well-known "backward design" process as described in *Understanding by Design* (Wiggins and McTighe 1998). Criteria are what teachers should look for when they examine student products and performances to determine student success or acceptability of work. In other words, "[criteria are] the qualities that must be met for work to measure up to a standard (McTighe and Wiggins 1999, p. 275). What is most important in backwards design is that teachers consider these criteria *before* they begin to think about activities or even specific performance tasks.

McTighe and Wiggins (2004) also note that when using backwards design it is important to consider six facets of understanding: explanation, interpretation, application, perspective, empathy, and self-knowledge. Notice that the first three facets relate to our content learning targets and that the last three relate to the aspects of metacognition we outlined in Chapter 2 (particularly pp. 18 and 33–42).

How Are Criteria Determined?

The Instructional Planning Framework calls for the following three criteria:

- One criterion for each of the learning targets, so that the teacher focuses on what is most important to understand the topic.
- One criterion for the selected strategy for the standard-based approach (Inquiry, History of Science [HOS], or Nature of Science [NOS]) to ensure that the students' understanding (content) is assessed in the context of how science is, and was historically, carried out. (*Note:* We defer selection of the standards-based strategy—thus identification of this criterion—until our discussion of the *responsive phase*, when we look at the research on common misconceptions and we consider effective instruction related directly to the content [see Chapter 4].)
- One criterion for the selected strategy for the metacognitive approach so that the teacher can judge the degree to which his or her students "own" their learning as well as their understanding of the content. (We also defer the identification of this criterion until we begin the *responsive phase.*)

The teacher eventually develops these criteria into summative assessments that are appropriate in his or her context. (As we noted, we won't be discussing specific summative assessments or ways to expand these criteria into rubrics using traits. There are many resources available that can assist teachers on summative assessment and use of rubrics. We have outlined the foundational work (the criteria) to give teachers a start in the creation of summative assessments and rubrics.)

What does this discussion of criteria mean for this topic and for Brenda's lesson? For each of the learning targets, we select one of the "facets" (explanation, interpretation, or application) as identified by McTighe and Wiggins (2004). In general, because a lesson builds a student's understandings, we might expect the early aspects of a lesson to include explanation and later aspects to lean more toward interpretation or application. Consider, however, the various learning cycles approaches, including the 5E Learning Cycle (Bybee 1997). The phases of the 5E cycle are Engage, Explore, Explain, Extend, and Evaluate. In general, the lessons in this book build in a way similar to the 5E Learning Cycle. You will find that the early learning targets are more explanatory than interpretive or applicatory. And that is just the case for this lesson. Review the criteria for each of the learning targets established for Brenda's lesson and see how the facets were applied (Figure 3.7). We can now add these criteria to our Teacher Work Template (Table 3.1, p. 112, under "Criteria to Determine Understanding").

Figure 3.7

Criteria for Demonstrating Understanding About "Meiosis as a Source of Variation"

Learning Target #1: Conceptually clarify the primary differences between mitosis and meiosis and describe how these differences are important in relationship to the reproductive cycle and distribution of genes.

Learning Target #2: Model meiosis, highlight critical aspects, and interpret the importance of these aspects as sources of variation.

Learning Target #3: Interpret a pedigree and describe at the multiple levels of biological organization the variation among offspring in a particular generation.

Standards-Based Target: Formulate explanations from evidence.

Metacognitive Target (Self-regulated thinking): Demonstrate self-knowledge of what is known and not known about "meiosis as a source of variation" using concept mapping and peer interviews.

Figure 3.8

Planning in the Predictive Phase

1. Identify the essential understandings for the lesson.
   a. Begin with the descriptions of adult science literacy to determine an anchor goal.
   b. Consider the middle school and high school standards and benchmarks.
   c. *Optional:* Study existing research on learning progressions. A good resource (*www.project2061.org/publications/2061Connections/2007/2007-04a-resources.htm*) is found in the 2061 Connections online newsletter (AAAS 2007a).
   d. Dig a bit deeper and think about the concepts included in the standards.
   e. Decide what is essential and what can be pruned.
2. Develop a logical sequence of learning targets for the lesson.
   a. Consider first the middle school experiences students should have had.
   b. Outline the key ideas embedded in the high school standards and benchmarks.
   c. Sequence the key ideas in a way to build student understanding.
   d. Consider connections from one lesson to the next.
3. Identify the criteria for demonstrating understanding.
   a. Identify one criterion for each Learning Target. *(Note:* Steps b and c are completed later, after a review of research.)
   b. Identify one criterion for your selected standards-based strategy (Inquiry, HOS, or NOS).
   c. Identify one criterion for your selected metacognitive strategy.

Reflection and Application

Let's take some time again to reflect. Review the process (Figure 3.8) we used during the *predictive phase* of planning a lesson for Brenda. Consider how that process might inform your own teaching. Reflect on the following four questions.

1. Why do you think meiosis is hard to teach? Hard to learn?
2. In Figure 3.8, consider step # 2 and step #3. This process described in these steps involves sequencing learning targets, determining the essential understandings to which they lead, and establishing criteria to determine whether students reach these understandings. What in this process would work well for you?
3. What challenges might you face in these two steps if you were beginning a new lesson? How would you overcome them?
4. Reflect on the implications of this portion of the process to your own teaching. What ideas do you have about your own teaching of meiosis?

Instructional Planning Framework: *Responsive Phase*

Chapters 4–6 will describe the *responsive phase* in detail. Here, we examine it briefly and consider how it might impact Brenda's lesson (see Figure 3.9 for another look at the components of the *responsive phase*). (*Note*: In Chapter 7 we will work through the entire Instructional Planning Framework.)

Recall that the *responsive phase* is cyclical in nature, not linear. As a result, for each learning target we should (1) consider the common preconceptions (both our students' own preconceptions and the misconceptions identified in the research), (2) develop an initial plan for instruction ("eliciting and confronting preconceptions" and "sense making,) and (3) establish a formative assessment plan ("demonstrating understanding"). As the lesson progresses, formative assessments may change this plan. However, in this chapter, we discuss only a pre-instructional plan that we created based on our model, saving details on the iterative nature of the *responsive phase* for later chapters.

Once the conceptual target, the learning sequence, and the criteria for understanding for a lesson are identified, it is important to determine what the research says about students' typical understandings and misconceptions regarding the topic, as well as the preconceptions our own students bring to the classroom. The process used to identify common misconceptions that have been identified in the research is outlined in Chapter 4. At this point, we simply identify for you the misconceptions we found during our search. We have placed them by learning target in the second portion of the Teacher Work Template that focuses on the *responsive phase* (Table 3.2).

While we were conducting the search for the research in Table 3.2, we also found research on the subject of lesson design. The two key pieces that we held in mind as we completed Table 3.2 were (1) it is important to avoid focusing on vocabulary and "steps" without a broader conceptual focus that should make explicit connections to reproduction (Bahar, Johnstone, and Hansell 1999; Chattopadhyay 2005; Knippels, Waarlo, and

Figure 3.9

Instructional Planning Framework: **Responsive Phase**

Planning is based on the learning targets and the essential understandings established during the predictive phase.

Responsive Phase

Building on the foundation of the predictive phase, the teacher plans for and implements instruction during the responsive phase, one learning target at a time.

Identifying Preconceptions
Teacher identifies preconceptions and uses information in instructional planning and implementation

Eliciting and Confronting Preconceptions
Teacher orchestrates experiences designed to confront students' preconceptions

Sense Making
Teacher provides opportunities for students to make sense of learning and explain understandings* **

**If student explanations fail to demonstrate understanding, teacher provides additional opportunities to confront students' preconceptions.

*If student explanations align with criteria for demonstrating understanding, instruction can proceed to the next learning target in the sequence and repeat this cycle.

Boersma 2005; Longden 1982), and (2) it is important to provide concrete experiences to make sense of the abstract processes (Mertens and Walker 1992; Smith 1991).

In addition to being informed about research-identified misconceptions, it is important to be aware of the understandings each of your students brings to the table. This awareness allows you to determine the depth of instruction required, as well as ways to differentiate instruction. As you read in Chapter 2, many strategies can be used to identify your students' preconceptions. We suggest that you review these strategies in Instructional Tools 2.2–2.14 and determine which are best suited for you and your students. The strategies we selected for Brenda's lesson to identify her students' preconceptions were developed into an activity (identifying preconceptions), which is now added to the Teacher Work Template (Table 3.2, p. 112). You will learn more about the process of determining strategies in Chapter 4. For now, our work has been completed for each of the learning targets for meiosis. Remember, this is the prein-structional planning for the lesson, although the results of formative assessment might call for changes in instructional plans. Recall, too, that the Teacher Work Templates on the pages that follow are not full lesson plans. They do, however, provide outlines that you can flesh out to develop lesson plans, especially after learning the entire framework process.

Table 3.1

Teacher Work Template——Predictive Phase

Lesson Topic—Reproduction: Meiosis and Variation		
Conceptual Target Development	National Standard(s) Addressed	*From 9–12 NSES:* Transmission of genetic information to offspring occurs through egg and sperm cells that contain only one representative from each chromosome pair. An egg and a sperm unite to form a new individual. The fact that the human body is formed from cells that contain two copies of each chromosome—and therefore two copies of each gene—explains many features of human heredity, such as how variations that are hidden in one generation can be expressed in the next. (p. 185)	*From 9–12 Benchmarks:* The sorting and recombination of genes in sexual reproduction results in a great variety of possible gene combinations from the offspring of any two parents. (p. 108)
	Previous Conceptual Learning	*From middle grade NSES:* • Reproduction is a characteristic of all living systems; because no individual organism lives forever, reproduction is essential to the continuation of every species. Some organisms reproduce asexually. Other organisms reproduce sexually. • In many species, including humans, females produce eggs and males produce sperm. Plants also reproduce sexually—the egg and sperm are produced in the flowers of flowering plants. An egg and sperm unite to begin development of a new individual. That new individual receives genetic information from its mother (via the egg) and its father (via the sperm). Sexually produced offspring never are identical to either of their parents. • Every organism requires a set of instructions for specifying its traits. Heredity is the passage of these instructions from one generation to another. • Hereditary information is contained in genes, located in the chromosomes of each cell. Each gene carries a single unit of information. An inherited trait of an individual can be determined by one or by many genes, and a single gene can influence more than one trait. A human cell contains many thousands of different genes. • The characteristics of an organism can be described in terms of a combination of traits. Some traits are inherited and others result from interactions with the environment. (p. 56)	*From middle grade Benchmarks:* • In some kinds of organisms, all the genes come from a single parent, whereas in organisms that have sexes, typically half of the genes come from each parent. • In sexual reproduction, a single specialized cell from a female merges with a specialized cell from a male. As the fertilized egg, carrying genetic information from each parent, multiplies to form the complete organism with about a trillion cells, the same genetic information is copied in each cell. (p.108)
		From prior instruction in biology course: Cell structure and function, DNA structure and replication, the gene as encoded in the DNA and as part of the chromosome, protein synthesis and the role of proteins in determining traits

Table 3.1 (continued)

Conceptual Target Development (continued)	**Knowledge and Skills**	**Essential Knowledge:** See **Learning Targets #1–#3**, below, and unpack for embedded knowledge. **Subtopics that may be pruned:** • Identify the important stages in meiosis. • Distinguish between homologous and nonhomologous pairs of chromosomes. **Essential vocabulary (to apply and distinguish):** *replicating* and *dividing* (as terms apply to chromosomes), *recombination*, *variation*, and *mutational variation* **Vocabulary that may be pruned** (but if taught, should be applied and distinguished): *asexual* and *sexual reproduction*; *chromosomes, chromatids,* and *chromatin; haploid* and *diploid; homologous pairs* and *nonhomologous pairs; tetrad* and *"two pair of chromatids," centriole* and *centromere*
	Essential Understandings	The continuity of genetic information is ensured when chromosomes and their DNA are replicated and passed on to other cells. Reduction divisions during meiosis in the reproductive cells are critical because they allow continuity from one generation of sexually reproducing organisms to the next. But reduction divisions are also important as a source of variation among offspring. The ways in which chromosomes move during these divisions provide a source of natural variation. Coupled with random fertilization, reduction divisions result in offspring with a variety of traits that can be expressed or hidden in a particular generation.
	**Learning Sequence Targets**	
	Learning Target #1	Organisms that reproduce sexually have life cycles that include cell divisions during which the chromosomes/DNA are exactly replicated in new cells and other cell divisions (reduction divisions) during which the number of chromosomes is halved in new cells. These two types of cell division are similar yet distinctly different, each serving a different purpose. Reduction divisions are essential if genetic information from each parent is to be contributed to the offspring.
	Learning Target #2	The movement of chromosomes (and therefore genes) during these reduction divisions results in reproductive cells with varied genetic makeup. Chromosomes can exchange parts during this process, resulting in further variation. This exchange transfers genes/DNA between chromosome pairs. As a result, the genes that parents contribute to offspring can vary.
	Learning Target #3	Additional variation is introduced through the random process of fertilization. The variation in genetic makeup introduced through meiosis and random fertilization can result in offspring with traits expressed or hidden in a particular generation.
	Criteria to Determine Understanding	• Conceptually clarify the primary differences between mitosis and meiosis and how these differences are important in relationship to the reproductive cycle and distribution of genes. • Model meiosis, highlight critical aspects, and interpret the importance of these aspects as sources of variation. • Interpret a pedigree and describe at the multiple levels of biological organization the variation among offspring in a particular generation. • Formulate explanations from evidence (see Instructional Tool 2.5). • Use self-reflection to determine what is known/not known about meiosis and variation (metacognitive focus)

Table 3.2

Teacher Work Template—Responsive Phase

Lesson Topic—Reproduction: Meiosis and Variation	
Identifying Student Preconceptions	Use these essential questions as probes to which students provide individual written responses. • If the cell's machinery makes replicas of genetic information, why aren't we all the same? • Why do we look similar to but different from our brothers and sisters? • What might happen to a species if only mitosis occurred? Students share responses through paired discussion and then facilitated dialogue. The steps include the following: • Teacher uses essential questions as probes. • Students generate written responses. • Students exchange responses with partner and highlight two or three ideas they think are very important. • Partners discuss rationale for highlighting and select two ideas they think are most important. • Teacher selects student pairs to share ideas. • Teacher records key ideas and facilitates a whole-class discussion.

Learning Sequence Targets

Learning Target #1	Organisms that reproduce sexually have life cycles that include cell divisions during which the chromosomes/DNA are exactly replicated in new cells and other cell divisions (reduction divisions) during which the number of chromosomes is halved into new cells. These two types of cell division are similar yet distinctly different, each serving a different purpose. Reduction divisions are essential if genetic information from each parent is to be contributed to the offspring.

Research-Identified Misconceptions Addressed

Students have trouble distinguishing mitosis from meiosis (Longden 1982) and between somatic and germ lines (Lewis, Leach, and Wood-Robinson 2000). The lack of a precise concept distinguishing mitosis and meiosis appears to preclude an understanding of the origins of variation.

Initial Instructional Plan

Eliciting and Confronting Preconceptions: To activate students' prior knowledge about the roles of cell division in life cycles, use a human life cycle graphic (or a generic life cycle). The advantage of the human cycle is that it connects with students and makes the process more concrete. Based on the selected graphic, facilitate a brief whole-class discussion about the diagram, probing students' current understandings about the role of both mitosis and meiosis in the life cycle. Then ask students to complete a graphic organizer that categorizes their understandings of what happens to chromosome numbers, the degree of similarity of daughter cells to the parent cell, and whether the divisions occur in the somatic or germ lines.

Table 3.2 (continued)

Confronting Preconceptions and Sense Making: Students observe visuals that contrast the steps of mitosis and meiosis, looking for similarities and differences between the processes. We use "Cells Divide: Mitosis vs. Meiosis" (Groleau 2001), a resource available at Nova Online. Students need explicit instruction when they first begin to identify similarities and differences. Graphic organizers are helpful for comparisons (Marzano, Pickering, and Pollock 2001), so we use a specific recording format, "I notice/I wonder."

1. Students prepare a page in their science journals (I notice...I wonder).
2. Students record their observations in the left-hand column (I notice) that help them determine the similarities and differences between meiosis (on the right) and mitosis (on the left).
3. Step through the Flash interactive map, reminding students to record observations.
4. Instruct students to work with a partner, review their observations, and generate ideas and questions about their observations. These questions should be recorded in the right-hand column in their notebooks (I wonder).
5. Facilitate a class discussion, record questions, and keep them visible through the lesson.
6. Provide a brief interactive lecture (short segments of direct instruction with interspersed questioning) to revisit the life cycle, stressing changes from haploid to diploid (without using the terms) and the location in the body where each process occurs.
7. Have students summarize their current understandings in a journal entry or concept map.

Formative Assessment Plan (Demonstrating Understanding)

Informal methods include student dialogue during whole-class and small-group discussions and questions generated by the pairs. More formal methods include semantic feature analyses, I notice/I wonder charts, and final journal entries or concept maps.

Learning Target #2	The movement of chromosomes (and therefore genes) during these reduction divisions results in reproductive cells with varied genetic makeup. Chromosomes can exchange parts during this process, resulting in further variation. This exchange transfers genes/DNA between chromosome pairs. As a result, the genes that parents contribute to offspring can vary.

Research-Identified Misconceptions Addressed

- Students do not understand the role of chance in producing new heritable characteristics by forming new combinations of existing genes or by mutations of genes (AAAS 1993; Driver et al. 1994).
- Students often believe there is a blending of characteristics from the mother and father, with various ideas about either the mother or father having a stronger contribution and that girls inherit traits from mothers and boys from fathers (AAAS 1993; Driver et al. 1994).
- Though many students recognize the word *gene* and fewer the word *chromosome*, in general students do not appreciate the chemical basis of inheritance. In a study, half of adults responded that genes are responsible for similarities between parents and offspring but they could not explain the phenomenon. More important, people who had studied science were no more knowledgeable about this phenomenon than were people who had not studied science (AAAS 1993; Driver et al. 1994).
- Students often are unable to identify at what time reductional division occurs in the meiotic process, and they struggle with the relationship between replication and chromosome separation (Longden 1982).
- Several studies of students of all ages indicate that sexual reproduction is not recognized as a source of variation. Only 14% of 15-year-olds, some studying biology, mentioned sexual reproduction or natural variation when probed about sources of variation. These misconceptions are consistent among age groups (AAAS 1993; Driver et al. 1994).

Table 3.2 (continued)

Initial Instructional Plan

Eliciting and Confronting Preconceptions and Sense Making:

- We use role-playing experiences that engage students as "chromosomes" and require them to double (replicate), pair (synapsis), and separate (disjunction).[6] This role-play occurs without the use of names or phases or other extensive vocabulary (Chinnici 2006). It helps us *elicit and confront misconceptions* as well as begin *sense making*. The first role-play models reduction from diploid to haploid status (see endnote #6). During the role-play, the teacher makes specific connections to the life cycle diagram, takes care to indicate where in the human body this occurs, and stresses the importance of the change of ploidy status. The only vocabulary stressed is the difference between *replication* and *division* and names of appropriate cell parts (prior instruction). The teacher pauses for a sense-making discussion. He or she shows a graphic of meiosis that models the separation of homologues and facilitates student discussion about what students see and how it relates to the role-play activity.
- The second set of role-plays model independent assortment and how it leads to variation among gametes. Repeating enactments demonstrate varied results because different chromosomes (maternal/paternal indicated by whether the student is a male or female—see endnote #6) and different alleles likely result each time. The only vocabulary to be stressed is *variation* and *recombination*. Pause for another discussion, once again using a visual that stresses the separation of homologues and assortment of alleles, resulting in cells with varied genetic makeup.
- A third role-play models crossing over, but without a focus on vocabulary. Students exchange one set of their "allele" name tags to model the process. Your school, district, or state may or may not require this understanding, so this step is optional. Optional activities to teach phases and vocabulary can be inserted at this point.[7] Show images/video of cells going through meiosis. Facilitate a discussion that summarizes meiosis and demonstrates similarities and differences between the role-play model and the actual process. Students then individually apply their understandings, which are differentiated based on their learning styles or on the choice of activities.[8]

Formative Assessment Plan (Demonstrating Understanding)

Informal methods include student dialogue during class discussions, role playing, and peer questioning and feedback. More formal methods include role playing without teacher guidance and written products from the application activities

Learning Target #3	Additional variation is introduced through the random process of fertilization. The variation in genetic makeup introduced through meiosis and random fertilization can result in offspring with traits expressed or hidden in a particular generation.

Research-Identified Misconceptions Addressed

- Students do not understand the role of chance in producing new heritable characteristics by forming new combinations of existing genes or by mutations of genes (AAAS 1993; Driver et al. 1994).
- Students often believe there is a blending of characteristics from the mother and father, with ideas about either the mother or father having a stronger contribution and that girls inherit traits from mothers and boys from fathers (AAAS 1993; Driver et al. 1994).
- Though many students recognize the word *gene* and fewer the word *chromosome*, in general students do not appreciate the chemical basis of inheritance. In a study, half of adults responded that genes are responsible for similarities between parents and offspring but they could not explain the phenomenon. More important, people who had studied science were no more knowledgeable about this phenomenon than were people who had not studied science (AAAS 1993; Driver et al. 1994).

Table 3.2 (continued)

Initial Instructional Plan

This portion of the lesson, though brief, is very important. It makes the final connections among reproductive life cycles, meiosis, Mendelian genetics (prior instruction in middle school), and molecular genetics.

Eliciting and Confronting Preconceptions: Present a simple scenario that demonstrates the resulting offspring of two parents and their variation in alleles. Pairs of students discuss the variations and prepare a whiteboard presentation of why the two differ, using concepts related to life cycles, meiosis, Mendelian genetics, and molecular genetics (DNA structure, replication, protein synthesis, and the function of proteins). They share their thinking with the class.

Sense Making:
- Pose a problem, using a pedigree, to students that requires they explain how one child in a family has a particular genetic disorder (ruled by Mendelian inheritance) while another does not. They must build connections among reproductive life cycles, meiosis, Mendelian genetics, and molecular genetics for a thorough response. They will make a claim and support that claim through evidence.
- End the lesson with a brief "thinking ahead" activity. For instance, simply provide the following prompt and ask students to reflect on it: "Describe a way in which identical twins might end up with variations in their DNA."

Formative Assessment Plan (Demonstrating Understanding)

The major form of assessment for this learning target is the student work products. Each is analyzed for conceptual understanding and how accurately students provide evidence to support their claims as they build their arguments.

Recommended Resources

Technology Applications and Websites

- We used the Flash interactive available at the NOVA website called "How Cells Divide" (Groleaau 2001) to compare and contrast meiosis and mitosis (*www.pbs.org/ wgbh/nova/baby/ divide.html#*).

- Many other images, flash interactives, and animations are available at the Teacher's Domain website (*www.teachersdomain.org*). Free registration is available.

Build Your Library

The materials we used to support the *predictive phase* include the following:

- Both sets of national standards: *National Science Education Standards* (NRC 1996) and *Benchmarks for Science Literacy* (AAAS 1993).

- *Science for All Americans* (AAAS 1989) to determine expectations of adult science literacy.

- The *Atlas of Science Literacy* (AAAS 2001a) to help determine our learning target sequence. We also suggest that you examine the newer volume, *Atlas of Science Literacy, Volume 2* (AAAS 2007b).

- To dig deeper into the standards and to help determine our learning sequence: *NSTA Pathways to the Science Standards* (middle school edition) (Rakow 2000) *and NSTA Pathways to the Science Standards* (second high school edition) (Texley and Wild 2004). *Designs for Science Literacy* (AAAS 2001b) helped us determine what to prune from the lesson.

- Keeley's (2005) *Science Curriculum Topic Study* for help with the *predictive phase*. Keeley identifies specific pages in some of the resources listed above and in additional resources. This, of course, limits the amount of searching you need to do on your own.

Endnotes

1. These are good sources to begin with if you have them in your library. If you do not own these books, they are all available online. Links to both the *Benchmarks for Science Literacy* and *Science for All Americans* can be found at *www.project2061.org* and the NSES are available at *www. nap.edu/catalog.php?record_id=4962*. The process used to better understand teaching of meiosis as a source of variation can be applied to the instruction of any biological topic.

2. These resources are not available online. Selected maps from the Atlas can be accessed at *www.project2061.org/publications/atlas/default.htm*. The Atlas Volume 1 maps are all available at the National Science Digital Library (*http://strandmaps.nsdl.org*). The Pathways books are great additions to any library and help to clarify the standards.

3. The process to think through this content has recently been simplified by the addition of a wonderful book, *Science Curriculum Topic Study* (Keeley 2005). Keeley's book provides study guides for numerous topics in each of 11 science categories, walking readers through the steps of unpacking the standards. It also provides an introductory overview of the misconception research on each particular topic. Use of this book eases the process of researching the essentials of any science concept. (The resources we used to complete this first step in the Instructional Planning Framework are largely available online so it is not absolutely necessary to purchase the Keeley book for this aspect of your lesson development.)

4. Other research clarifies this thinking with two "big ideas" (Duncan, Rogat, and Yarden 2007, pp. 14–15).

- "All organisms have genetic information to specify the structure of proteins that carry out a multitude of functions and ultimately result in our phenotype. The genetic information is replicated in cell division and its expression is tightly regulated."

- "There are patterns of gene transfer across generations (Mendel's model of inheritance). Cellular mechanisms drive these patterns (meiosis) and result in genetic variation. The environment interacts with our genetic makeup leading to variation."

The implication of these statements is that the thinking in the first big idea should be prerequisite to, yet interrelated with, the second big idea. Brenda should ensure that students understand, prior to this lesson, that genes are nucleotide sequences in DNA, that DNA makes up the chromosomes, that cell division involves DNA replication, that DNA is essential to protein synthesis, and that proteins lead to an organism's traits (because of their particular three-dimensional shape). She should consistently connect the ideas in her lesson back to these ideas to ensure that students connect their thinking about the various levels of organization in organisms.

5. Chapter 7 of *Designs for Science Literacy*, which focuses on unburdening the curriculum, is available at *www.project2061.org/publications/designs/ch7intro.htm*. The link provides an overview

of the importance of pruning topics, subtopics, and technical vocabulary (click "Read More". This chapter also presents a rationale for and thinking about unburdening the curriculum.)

6. There are many different examples of role-playing activities for mitosis and/or meiosis. For many years, the first author has used a simple role-play. In it, 12 students are selected to act out the role-play, initially under the teacher's direction. An original group of 6 students (3 female and 3 male, representing maternal and paternal chromosomes) is selected. In the ideal, pairs of male and females of varying heights are chosen, to model the variations among chromosome lengths. Each pair holds a pair of genes (name tags labeled with selected alleles, possibly "A" for one student and "a" for the partner). Another 6 students (3 male and 3 female) are chosen as replicates (also given name tags), as the initial 6 students wander the nucleus. Rope is used as a nuclear membrane and is removed at the appropriate time. As "human chromosomes" replicate, the partner from the second set of 6 students hooks arms with the initial chromosome (modeling the centromere, even though the vocabulary is not stressed). Eventually replicated homologous pairs randomly line up opposite each other along the equator and split. The entire process plays out and the teacher facilitates a discussion of the random mix of maternal and paternal chromosomes in the potential gamete. This role-play is repeated several times to show the role of independent assortment as a source of variation.

We have also modeled random fertilization. Of the many role-play activities out there, we particularly like the work of Chinnici (2004). In one of his activities, a cap with a tag for another pair of alleles is added for each pair of student "chromosomes." The tag on the cap, toward the end of the chromosome (student's head), models the easier exchange of this allele during crossing over (again, vocabulary is not important) in contrast to the one on the student's shirt.

7. To reinforce phases of meiosis, teachers can have students sequence images of the phases of the process and identify the ploidy status of each image and the phase name of each step. Teacher questioning during small-group sequencing and then during a whole-class discussion can reinforce these concepts and the phase names. Specific attention should be paid to the placement of replication in interphase (not easily demonstrated in the role-play model) and the placement and significance of the reductional division. Students can also view prepared slides and identify phases. Role-plays can reinforce the vocabulary. To ensure that students understand the vocabulary, assign pairs of students with pairs or groups of terms as homework (see vocabulary in the Teacher Work Template, Table 3.1). In the next portion of the lesson, students work in groups to determine how the terms could be exemplified in the role-play or explain why they can't be demonstrated. This activity reinforces vocabulary already learned and applies new vocabulary.

8. There are various activities that address different learning modalities. A few include

Review Cells Alive—Students view "Animal Cell Meiosis" and respond to associated questions (see *www.cellsalive.com/meiosis.htm)*.

Bajema Strategy (Mertens, T., and J. Walker 1992)—Students use outline drawings of cells, proceeding through the stages of meiosis; they use colored pencils to draw two pair of chromosomes, place genes on them, and trace the sequence of events in meiosis. The cell's genetic information is summarized in a box beneath each cell.

Meiosis Model—Students model meiosis using traditional materials (pop beads, clay, or purchased manipulative model kits for meiosis/mitosis) and write summaries of how they modeled meiosis.

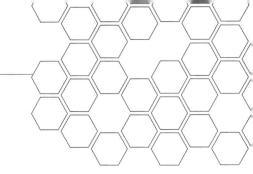

Instructional Planning Framework

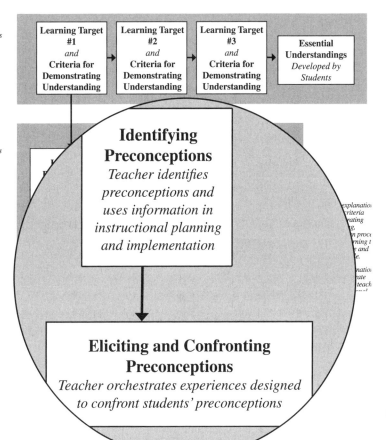

Predictive Phase
The teacher determines the lesson's essential understandings, the sequence of learning targets that lead toward those understandings, and the criteria by which understanding is determined.

| Learning Target #1 *and* Criteria for Demonstrating Understanding | Learning Target #2 *and* Criteria for Demonstrating Understanding | Learning Target #3 *and* Criteria for Demonstrating Understanding | Essential Understandings *Developed by Students* |

Responsive Phase
Building on the foundation of the predictive phase, the teacher plans for and implements instruction during the responsive phase, one learning target at a time.

Identifying Preconceptions
Teacher identifies preconceptions and uses information in instructional planning and implementation

Eliciting and Confronting Preconceptions
Teacher orchestrates experiences designed to confront students' preconceptions

Chapter 4

Flow of Energy and Matter: Photosynthesis

"It doesn't seem intuitive that you could add mass by taking in a gas."
—*Student speaking in the video* A Private Universe, Minds of Our Own, 1995

Why This Topic?

Photosynthesis is one of the most difficult topics to teach, partly because it is such a broad and conceptually complex topic. The cycling of matter and flow of energy occur at many levels of biological organization—molecules, cells, organs, organisms, and ecosystems—and crosses many disciplines (AAAS 1993; Russell, Netherwood, and Robinson 2004). It is hard for students to visualize the process because it is abstract and microscopic and plants grow so slowly that learners don't see immediate results (Russell, Netherwood, and Robinson 2004).

It is especially tricky because photosynthesis is often presented purely as a molecular process (Russell, Netherwood, and Robinson 2004) even though many biology students have a limited understanding of chemistry, specifically of matter and the atomic-molecular levels of interactions (Duschl, Schweingruber, and Shouse 2007; Ross, Tronson, and Ritchie 2006). Furthermore, students are often given only words and descriptions of processes for topics such as photosynthesis. As a result, students tend to develop shallow understandings of the processes and hold on to the preconceptions they brought with them to the class. Many of these preconceptions cross grade levels and even persist in adults who, like our students, find it hard to believe that much of the mass of plants comes from the air around them (Duschl, Schweingruber, and Shouse 2007). What can teachers do to make this concept more accessible? In our experience, the answer is to contextualize the process in the plant, helping students to visualize photosynthesis and providing the framework to add molecular details (Russell, Netherwood, and Robinson 2004). We elaborate on this process later in the chapter.

In the meantime, we ask you to consider a segment from the well-known video *A Private Universe: Minds of Our Own* (Harvard-Smithsonian Center for Astrophysics 1995). The video begins with interviews of Harvard and MIT graduates. The graduates are shown a seed and a log and are asked to imagine the seed planted in the ground and growing into a tree. They are then asked where they think all the "stuff" that makes up the tree came from. Responses include

- water and minerals in the soil;
- water, light, and soil; and
- minerals in the soil itself—the water and nutrients it absorbs.

Notice that none of the responses refer to carbon dioxide.

The graduates are further asked what they would say if someone told them that most of the weight came from carbon dioxide in the air. In each case they are disbelieving. One graduate says that she would disagree because the same volume of air could not weigh as much unless it were highly compressed. Another states that she would be very confused and wonders how that could happen. A third says it would be hard for him to believe since carbon dioxide is a gas, and it doesn't seem intuitive to him that mass could be increased by taking in a gas. These graduates, who are among those often considered our best and brightest, have the same basic misconception found among students across grade levels: that a gas cannot possibly provide the mass of a grown plant.

The remainder of the video explores student thinking related to this topic in elementary, middle, and high school classes and considers the type of instruction that leads to common misconceptions about plant growth. We encourage you to watch the video if you haven't already done so and consider implications for your own teaching.[1]

Overview

In this chapter, we explore the misconception that carbon from carbon dioxide is the source of a plant's mass. We also look at other common, research-identified misconceptions that make it difficult for students to understand photosynthesis and to connect the photosynthetic processes in a plant cell to the plant and its surroundings. We will discuss photosynthesis in the context of the various levels of biological organization, although we won't address applications to the ecosystem. Of course, we understand the importance of photosynthesis in the food chain and more broadly its relation to topics such as global climate change, but our emphasis is on general cellular processes, actual plants as a contexts for learning, and gas exchange with the surroundings (refer to the left side of Figure 4.1 on p. 122).

We focus on photosynthesis as a mechanism for harnessing energy and generating organic carbon from atmospheric carbon. We also briefly discuss what happens to that carbon in the plant once photosynthesis is complete and we discuss gas exchange in plants during respiration. We will not address food chains or animal respirations. (*Note:* All tables are grouped together at the end of the chapter, beginning on p. 133. They are followed by Recommended Resources and Endnotes.)

We consider photosynthesis the foundation on which students can build their understandings about flow of energy and cycling of matter in the ecosystem, as well as the interdependence of life, further explored in Chapter 7.

Topic: Photosynthesis
Go to: *www.scilinks.org*
Code: HTB004

Topic: Factors affecting photosynthesis
Go to: *www.scilinks.org*
Code: HTB005

Figure 4.1

Carbon Cycling in Environmental Systems[2]

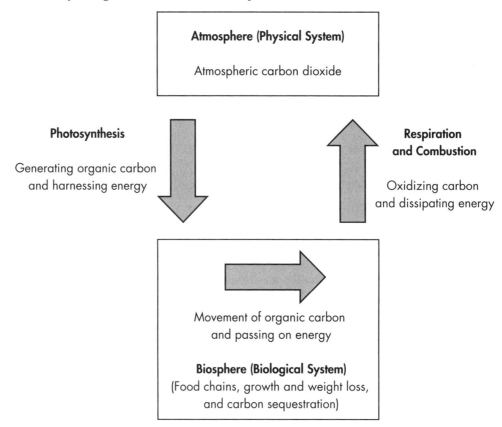

Source: Adapted from Mohan, L., J. Chen, and C. W. Anderson. 2007. Developing a K–12 Learning Progression for Carbon Cycling in Socio-Ecological Systems. *http://edr1.educ.msu. edu/EnvironmentalLit/index.htm*. Retrieved May 26, 2008, and reprinted with permission from the author.

Instructional Planning Framework: *Predictive Phase*

Because the *predictive phase* of the Instructional Planning Framework was thoroughly covered in Chapter 3, we limit our coverage in this chapter to a brief review of this phase and show its application to a lesson on photosynthesis. First, however, we include here expectations for adult science literacy to remind you of our end target, or anchor, for learning about photosynthesis (Figure 4.2, p. 123).

Figure 4.2

Adult Science Literacy Expectations Regarding Photosynthesis

"However complex the workings of living organisms, they share with all other natural systems the same physical principles of the conservation and transformation of matter and energy. Over long spans of time, matter and energy are transformed among living things, and between them and the physical environment. In these grand-scale cycles, the total amount of matter and energy remains constant, even though their form and location undergo continual change.

"Almost all life on earth is ultimately maintained by transformations of energy from the sun. Plants capture the sun's energy and use it to synthesize complex, energy-rich molecules (chiefly sugars) from molecules of carbon dioxide and water. These synthesized molecules then serve, directly or indirectly, as the source of energy for the plants themselves and ultimately for all animals and decomposer organisms (such as bacteria and fungi)." (AAAS 1989, p. 66)

We did our initial planning for the *predictive phase* based on the adult-science-learning expectations in Figure 4.2. We used the process outlined in Chapter 3 to determine the conceptual target, the learning sequence required to help students understand photosynthesis,[3] and the criteria that would be used to demonstrate student understanding. Figure 4.3 shows a summary of this process.

Figure 4.3

Planning in the Predictive Phase

1. Identify the essential understandings for the lesson.
   a. Begin with the descriptions of adult science literacy to determine an anchor goal.
   b. Consider the middle school and high school standards and benchmarks.
   c. Optional: Study existing research on learning progressions. A good resource (*www.project2061.org/publications/2061Connections/2007/2007-04a-resources.htm*) is found in the 2061 Connections online newsletter (AAAS 2007a).
   d. Dig a bit deeper and think about the concepts included in the standards.
   e. Decide what is essential and what can be pruned.
2. Develop a logical sequence of learning targets for the lesson.
   a. Consider first the middle school experiences students should have had.
   b. Outline the key ideas embedded in the high school standards and benchmarks.
   c. Sequence the key ideas in a way to build student understanding.
   d. Consider connections from one lesson to the next.
3. Identify the criteria for demonstrating understanding. (*Note*: Steps b and c are completed later, after a review of research).
   a. Identify one criterion for each Learning Target.
   b. Identify one criterion for your selected standards-based strategy (Inquiry, HOS, or NOS).
   c. Identify one criterion for your selected metacognitive strategy.

The result of our planning was the beginning of a Teacher Work Template for this topic, completing the *predictive phase*. Carefully study the completed work shown in Table 4.1 (p. 133). Following the steps outlined in Figure 4.3, we completed the template with the national standards that would be addressed, previous conceptual learning from middle school, prior instruction in the biology course itself, and the essential understandings, knowledge, and skills that are the targets of this lesson. In addition, we developed our learning sequence targets, each of which is included in the Teacher Work Template on page 134 and in Figure 4.4.

Reflection and Application

This is our second look at the process used (Figure 4.3) to complete the *predictive phase*. The first was is Chapter 3. Take a moment to reflect on the application of the *predictive phase* to the topic of photosynthesis:

1. How have you taught this topic in the past?
2. In what ways does your past instruction align with the work in the *predictive phase* for this topic? In what ways is it different?
3. Are there changes you might make in your instruction based on your answers to questions #1 and #2?

Figure 4.4

Photosynthesis Learning Sequence

Target #1: The vast majority of plants are able to convert inorganic carbon in CO_2 into organic carbon through photosynthesis. Carbon dioxide and water are used in the process to create biomass. The surrounding environment is the source of raw materials for photosynthesis	**Target #2:** Photosynthesis captures the energy of sunlight that is used to create chemical bonds in the creation of carbohydrates. Chloroplasts in the cells of plant leaves contain compounds able to capture light energy. Photosynthesis utilizes CO_2 and the hydrogen from water to form carbohydrates, releasing oxygen.	**Target #3:** Carbohydrates produced during photosynthesis in leaves can be used immediately for energy in the plant, stored for future use, or converted to other macromolecules that help the plant grow and function.	**Target #4:** A variety of gases move into and out of plant leaves. Leaves use CO_2 and release O_2 during photosynthesis. When they respire, leaves use O_2 and release CO_2. Other gases enter the leaf as well, but are excreted.

Essential Understandings: Plants have the ability to capture the energy of sunlight and use it to combine low-energy molecules (carbon dioxide and water) to form higher energy molecules (glucose and starches). This is called *photosynthesis*. They can use the glucose immediately as a source of energy, convert it into other molecules that help their cells function, or store it for later use. Regardless, the total amount of matter and energy in the system stays the same.

Instructional Planning Framework: *Responsive Phase*

You are now ready to consider the *responsive phase* of the Instructional Planning Framework and determine how to help your students reach each target in the learning sequence shown in Table 4.1 on page 134. Remember that the *responsive phase* is not a linear process but rather iterative in nature. Teachers need to use ongoing formative assessment processes to determine what their students do or don't understand and address these gaps with instruction (Hipkins et al. 2002). Though teachers can flesh out an initial instructional plan, conducting formative assessments along the way might require that they modify instruction. Regardless, the work for the *responsive phase* must be completed, and it is to that work that we turn our attention.

Identifying Preconceptions

The primary purpose of this chapter is to model the first portions of the Instructional Planning Framework's *responsive phase*: identifying, eliciting, and confronting preconceptions and becoming aware of research-identified misconceptions (Figure 4.5, p. 126).

Why do teachers need to be concerned about their students' preinstructional ideas or about typical misconceptions that have been identified in the research? The answer is that learning occurs when students make connections and construct patterns, and doing so depends on their prior knowledge (Lowery 1990).[4] This means that teachers must gear their lessons to the developmental level of their students and provide multiple pathways to understanding (Weiss et al. 2003). They must provide opportunities for their students to express and confront their own preconceptions and those of their classmates if the students are to develop conceptual understanding.

Learning About Research-Identified Misconceptions

You can learn a lot by conducting your own review of your students' misconceptions about photosynthesis. It can be time consuming, but if you are, for instance, involved in a study group with other biology teachers and want to improve instruction for a specific standard, research on misconceptions and effective strategies to address those misconceptions might be a rich area of study for your group. Or if there is a content area in which you are not as strong as in others, this type of review can help you dig deeper into the content. If you decide that this is something you want to do for another topic, consider the steps and resources shown in Figure 4.6 on page 126. These steps are sequenced, based on how easy it may be for you to obtain the resources. They are also sequenced by simplicity of use.

Figure 4.5

Instructional Planning Framework: Responsive Phase

Planning is based on the learning targets and the essential understandings established during the predictive phase.

Responsive Phase

Building on the foundation of the predictive phase, the teacher plans for and implements instruction during the responsive phase, one learning target at a time.

Identifying Preconceptions
Teacher identifies preconceptions and uses information in instructional planning and implementation

Eliciting and Confronting Preconceptions
Teacher orchestrates experiences designed to confront students' preconceptions

Sense Making
Teacher provides opportunities for students to make sense of learning and explain understandings* **

**If student explanations fail to demonstrate understanding, teacher provides additional opportunities to confront students' preconceptions.

*If student explanations align with criteria for demonstrating understanding, instruction can proceed to the next learning target in the sequence and repeat this cycle.

We understand that many of you do not have time to conduct this type of research review, so we completed a literature review that resulted in an extensive list of misconceptions about photosynthesis in particular and carbon cycling in general. We then sorted the misconceptions by the Learning Targets established in the *predictive phase.* Finally, we added these misconceptions to the *responsive phase* portion of the Teacher Work Template for photosynthesis (Table 4.2, p. 135).

Figure 4.6

Steps for a Misconception Literature Review

1. Review *Benchmarks for Science Literacy* (AAAS 1993) for misconceptions discussed there. Chapter 15 of the book includes research findings organized by benchmark. If you do not have a copy of the book, you can read it online at *www.project2061.org/publications/ bsl/online/ index.php?txtRef=&txtURlOld=%2Fpublications%2Fbsl%2Fonline%2Findex.*
2. Complete a web search for misconceptions on the selected topic. Simply run a search for your topic and misconceptions (e.g., "photosynthesis + misconceptions"). If you run your search at Google Scholar (*http://scholar.google.com*), you will gain access to numerous resources. In some cases you will only access an abstract, but in others you will find entire documents. This process is more time-consuming than step #1 but yields additional resources.
3. An excellent source for a summary of students' misconceptions is *Making Sense of Secondary Science: Research into Children's Ideas* (Driver et al. 1994). The book is outlined by science topic and provides a rich summary of research on children's ideas about these topics.

Reflection and Application

Take a moment to reflect on misconceptions on photosynthesis that we found in the research (Table 4.2). Consider also the process that we used ("Identifying Student Perceptions" in the table). Then answer the the following questions:

1. The authors of this book identified photosynthesis as a hard-to-teach topic. If you agree, what do you think makes it hard to teach?
2. If you conducted your own review of the research, what aspects of the review were most helpful to you? Why were they helpful?
3. How might the research review conducted by the authors help you in your instruction? What might you do differently in your current lesson on photosynthesis, based on the research we summarized?

Identifying Our Students' Preconceptions

Misconceptions that have been identified by researchers can vary by age, sex, geography, and student motivation or interest (Westcott and Cunningham 2005). There is extensive research on how to elicit students' prior ideas in science and how, by taking students' ideas into account, to develop teaching strategies that move them toward science ideas.[5] (The Instructional Tools in Chapter 2 include many of these strategies for use in planning.)

In the ideal situation, teachers would identify their students' preconceptions just prior to planning a unit or lesson. However, the reality of day-to-day teaching requires that teachers plan well ahead of the actual instructional time. We recommend that teachers start planning for each learning target with the research-identified misconceptions; teachers should also determine their own students' preconceptions. To do this, we used the process outlined in Figure 4.7, and we suggest that you complete the steps yourself.

Study the Instructional Strategy Sequencing Tool (2.1). It provides an extensive list of strategies that teachers can use to uncover their students' preconceptions. We selected annotated drawings, concept cartoons, concept mapping, informational text strategies, and questioning. Study that list. Can you see how we determined the strategies on the list?

Figure 4.7

Strategy Selection: Identifying, Eliciting, and Confronting Student Preconceptions

1. Use the Instructional Strategy Sequencing Tools in Chapter 2 (starting on p. 29) to identify possible strategies that work to identify, elicit, and confront student preconceptions.
2. Review the strategies in the Instructional Tools. See the Metacognitive Strategy Tools (Instructional Tools 2.2–2.4, starting on p. 33), the three Standards-Based Strategy Tools (Instructional Tools 2.5–2.7, starting on p. 43, and the seven Sense-Making Strategy Tools (Instructional Tools 2.8–2.14, starting on p. 55).
3. Carefully review the research and application recommendations for each of the strategies.
4. Determine several strategies that fit well with the particular content you are teaching.
5. Review the resources in each Instructional Tool to more fully understand the strategies and to determine what they might look like in application.
6. Select one metacognitive strategy, one standards-based strategy, and two or three sense-making strategies for use in your lesson. (Recall that these strategies will be used to differentiate instruction and to provide further instruction if formative assessments indicate that some or all students do not demonstrate understanding of the learning targets.)
7. Determine one criterion to demonstrate understanding for each metacognitive and standards-based focus.

As we continue our planning, we reviewed the various Instructional Strategy Tools (Steps #2–4 in Figure 4.7). That helped us to narrow the list of possible strategies; some have been shown to be particularly effective for developing student understandings of abstract topics such as photosynthesis (e.g., annotated drawings, concept cartoons, and concept maps). To narrow our choices further, we covered steps #5 and #6 in Figure 4.7. We then examined the strengths of each sense-making approach (Table 4.3, p. 140).

How did we determine which of the three strategies in Table 4.3 would best suit our needs? First, all three strategies have been shown to be effective for eliciting preconceptions and promoting conceptual change, especially of abstract concepts such as photosynthesis. Second, each strategy engages students in the learning process, motivates them to deal with the concepts, and requires them to grapple with their ideas, thus serving a metacognitive function.

Annotated drawings and concept cartoons might have some advantage over concept mapping, especially in diverse classrooms. *Annotated drawings* tend to involve more students in the learning process because (1) students who might not express themselves in words are given a different option for expression, and (2) students are free to choose what they draw and to draw from their own experiences. *Concept cartoons* have several advantages: (1) they create an environment that promotes participation in class discussion and lessens students' anxiety over the wrong answer, (2) they present cognitive conflict that requires students to consider explanations for the situations in the cartoons, confronting both their own and their peers' preconceptions, and (3) they lead naturally to decisions about possible investigations (and photosynthesis is an ideal topic for student-designed investigations).

The third strategy—concept mapping—is effective in support of conceptual change and requires students to show relationships among concepts. Annotated drawings and concept cartoons, however, are more effective at eliciting student preconceptions. Furthermore, regarding photosynthesis, annotated drawings help contextualize photosynthesis in the plant, which is important if you want students to be able to visualize the process—thus making it more accessible (Russell, Netherwood, and Robinson 2004).

The strategies fit our lesson and should provide a good entry into this content. We then add these strategies to our Teacher Work Template (see Table 4.2, "Identifying Student Preconceptions") as our means of determining our students' general preconceptions about photosynthesis. We began our lesson with one of these activities to specifically elicit and confront misconceptions about Learning Target #1 (Table 4.2).

We next consider the metacognitive and standards-based strategies that best align with this content and the selected sense-making strategies. Remember, we decided to use annotated drawing and concept cartoons to contextualize photosynthesis in the plant. We required that students make a claim, and we prepared them for investigations. We chose to focus on openness to other students' ideas as students gathered evidence to support claims. We also focused on having students contrast their personal claims with those of historical theories, helping them better understand both the history and nature of science. We then developed criteria for each of these areas of focus and added them to the work template (see "Criteria to Demonstrate Understanding," Table 4.1).

Description of Assessment for Preconceptions

What do these three strategies look like in practice? Let's start with students' general understandings about photosynthesis and use some of the strategies we just discussed to determine their preconceptions. Our plan begins with use of annotated drawings and is outlined below.

- Show a time-lapsed video of a seed growing into a plant to provide the context for the preassessment activities. A variety of videos are available online (see Technology Applications and Websites at the end of this chapter, p. 141).

- Ask each student to prepare an annotated drawing in response to the probe, "How did the seed change into a seedling and finally into a ____?" Write an appropriate probe depending on the video you choose. Also ask students to write paragraphs that describe what is happening in their drawings. Circulate around the room, asking open-ended, probing questions of students to further determine their individual understandings. (*Note*: You can conduct this activity at the close of a class period, collect all student responses, and use them to modify your lesson prior to the next day's instruction.)

- Ask students to share their drawings in small groups, discuss their drawings, and make a composite drawing on poster paper that reflects the group's thinking. Again, you should circulate around the room asking probing questions of each group. The resulting posters can be posted, reflected on, and modified during the course of the lesson. You can use this information to inform further lesson development.

- Facilitate a full-class discussion about the posters and generate a list of student questions about the depicted processes. Point out common ideas and areas of disagreement. Let students know that these ideas will be explored during the lesson.

This activity engages students through various learning modes: drawing, writing, small-group and whole-class discussion, and personal and collaborative reflection. It also requires students to stay open to others' ideas as they generate claims.

Reflection and Application

Let's take another moment to reflect. Consider the process used and the tools developed to identify your own students' preconceptions. Ask yourself the following questions:

1. What aspects of this research-review process were most helpful to you in your instruction? Why were they helpful? What was most difficult and why?
2. Does this modify your thinking about beginning a lesson? If so, how?
3. Consider your current lesson on photosynthesis. How might you modify it based on the tools and resources provided?

Eliciting and Confronting Preconceptions

Let's revisit the Learning Target #1 in our learning sequence (Table 4.2) before moving forward with the lesson. The Learning Target reads as follows: "The vast majority of plants are able to convert inorganic carbon in CO_2 into organic carbon through photosynthesis. Carbon dioxide and water are used in the process to create biomass. The surrounding environment is the source of raw materials for photosynthesis."

We continue to determine our students' preconceptions, with the specific purpose of eliciting and confronting preconceptions they have about this Learning Target. Notice that each of the research-identified misconceptions in Table 4.2 revolves around the source of biomass in the plant or what causes the plant to grow. Students attribute mass in the growing plant to almost anything but the carbon in carbon dioxide. We use a concept cartoon because it provides the students with alternative conceptions that include the scientific explanation as well as research-identified misconceptions and sets the stage for student dialogue and determination of possible areas of investigation. The intent is to display the concept cartoon (Figure 4.8) and ask each student which response he or she most agrees with. Students then record their own responses in their journals; the responses should be in the form of explanations that support the stances they have taken.

Figure 4.8

Concept Cartoon: Where Does a Plant's Mass Come From?

Question: This large tree started as a little seed. What provided most of the mass that made the tree grow so large?

Next, groups of students determine the group's "best answer" to the cartoon, confronting their individual conceptions as well as those of their peers. They consider the stance taken in their answer and respond to the probe, "How would you test your claim?" Although there are many resources the teacher can use to help students test their claims, we suggest using one of two options.

Option #1: Students mass out radish seeds in three batches, each batch weighing 1.5g, and apply to the seeds various experimental treatments (choices might include seeds on moist paper towels in the light, seeds on moist paper towels in the dark, and seeds not moistened in the light). They grow them for one week, dry them overnight in an oven, and measure total biomass in grams. Prior to revealing results, students predict the biomass of the plants receiving various treatments (Ebert-May 2003).

Option #2: Students design experiments using Wisconsin Fast Plants to test their claims. Information about use of Fast Plants as well as developed activities can be found at *www.fastplants.org*.

Reflection and Application

Let's take a final moment to reflect now that we have considered a tool—concept cartoons—that elicits and confronts preconceptions.

1. How might the use of concept cartoons help to elicit and confront your own students' preconceptions about photosynthesis?
2. Consider cartoons you might develop to use with each of the other learning targets. How would you need to change your current instruction to further implement this strategy?

Completing the *Responsive Phase*: Sense Making and Demonstrating Understanding

Rather than complete a detailed description of the remainder of the lesson on photosynthesis at this time, we briefly summarize it in the Teacher Work Template for the *responsive phase* (Table 4.2). We include a brief description of how to elicit and confront student conceptions for Learning Targets #2, #3, and #4. We also outline how the lesson addresses sense making and demonstrating understanding. A fully developed lesson would include teacher support materials and student work materials; Table 4.2 provides an outline that you can use as you develop a lesson for use in your own classroom.

Once you study the remaining aspects of the Instructional Planning Framework developed in this book, you can further flesh out this lesson, using the framework as your guide. Further description of "eliciting and confronting preconceptions" is provided in Chapter 5, while "sense making" and "demonstrating understanding" are covered in the remaining chapters.

Table 4.1

Teacher Work Template: **Predictive Phase**

Lesson Topic—Flow of Energy and Matter: Photosynthesis			
Conceptual Target Development	**National Standard(s) Addressed**	*From 9–12 NSES:* • Plant cells contain chloroplasts, the site of photosynthesis. Plants and many microorganisms use solar energy to combine molecules of carbon dioxide and water into complex, energy rich organic compounds and release oxygen to the environment. This process of photosynthesis provides a vital connection between the sun and the energy needs of living systems. (p. 184) • The atoms and molecules on the earth cycle among the living and nonliving components of the biosphere. (p. 186) • Energy flows through ecosystems in one direction, from photosynthetic organisms to herbivores to carnivores and decomposers. (p. 186) • The energy for life primarily derives from the sun. Plants capture energy by absorbing light and using it to form strong (covalent) chemical bonds between the atoms of carbon-containing organic molecules. These molecules can be used to assemble larger molecules with biological activity (including proteins, DNA, sugars, and fats). In addition, the energy stored in bonds between the atoms (chemical energy) can be used as sources of energy for life processes. (p. 186)	*From 9–12 Benchmarks:* • Plants alter the earth's atmosphere by removing carbon dioxide from it, using the carbon to make sugars and releasing oxygen. This process is responsible for the oxygen content of air. (p. 74) • The chemical elements that make up the molecules of living things pass through food webs and are combined and recombined in different ways. At each link in a food web, some energy is stored in newly made structures but much is dissipated into the environment. Continual input of energy from sunlight keeps the process going. (p.121)
	Previous Conceptual Learning	*From middle grade NSES:* • For ecosystems, the major source of energy is sunlight. Energy entering ecosystems as sunlight is transferred by producers into chemical energy through photosynthesis. That energy then passes from organism to organism in food web. (p.158)	*From middle grade Benchmarks:* • Food provides the fuel and the building material for all organisms. Plants use the energy from light to make sugars from carbon dioxide and water. This food can be used immediately or stored for later use…. (p. 120) • Over a long time, matter is transferred from one organism to another repeatedly and between organisms and their physical environment. As in all material systems, the total amount of matter remains constant, even though its form and location change. (p. 120) • Energy can change from one form to another in living things…. Almost all food energy comes originally from sunlight. (p. 120)
		From prior instruction in the biology course: Basic cell structure and function, types of organic molecules, both monomers and polymers that comprise biomolecules, cellular respiration	

Table 4.1 (continued)

Conceptual Target Development (continued)	**Knowledge and Skills**	***Essential knowledge:*** See **Learning Targets #1–#2** and unpack for embedded knowledge. ***Subtopics that may be pruned:*** Details about the steps of photosynthesis, including photosystems, electron transport, ATP formation, dark reactions, and the Calvin cycle. ***Essential vocabulary:*** *photosynthesis, biomass, cellular respiration, glucose versus sugar* ***Vocabulary that may be pruned:*** *electron transport chain, polysaccharide*
Essential Understandings		Plants have the ability to capture the energy of sunlight and use it to combine low-energy molecules (carbon dioxide and water) to form higher energy molecules (glucose and starches). This process is called *photosynthesis.* Plants can use the glucose immediately as a source of energy, convert it into other molecules that help their cells function, or store it for later use. Regardless, the total amount of matter and energy in the system stays the same.
Learning Sequence Targets		
Learning Target #1		The vast majority of plants are able to convert inorganic carbon in CO_2 into organic carbon through photosynthesis. Carbon dioxide and water are used in the process to create biomass. The surrounding environment is the source of raw materials for photosynthesis.
Learning Target #2		Photosynthesis captures the energy of sunlight that is used to create chemical bonds in the creation carbohydrates. Chloroplasts in the cells of plant leaves contain compounds able to capture light energy. Photosynthesis uses CO_2 and the hydrogen from water to form carbohydrates, releasing oxygen.
Learning Target #3		Carbohydrates produced during photosynthesis in leaves can be used immediately for energy in the plant, stored for future use, or converted to other macromolecules that help the plant grow and function.
Learning Target #4		A variety of gases move into and out of plant leaves. Leaves use CO_2 and release O_2 during photosynthesis. When they respire, leaves use O_2 and release CO_2. Other gases enter the leaf as well, but are excreted.
Criteria to Demonstrate Understanding		• Predict the source of biomass in plants and thoroughly justify claims based on experimental results. • Find patterns in data to determine the possible role of light in photosynthesis and design an experiment to test claims that are made based on these data. • Carefully perform analyses to determine the various plant products that make up a plant's biomass. • Propose and support a well-crafted explanation for the variations in levels of oxygen and carbon dioxide during daytime and nighttime.

Table 4.2

Teacher Work Template: **Responsive Phase**

Lesson Topic—Flow of Energy and Matter: Photosynthesis	
Identifying Student Preconceptions	Two major activities are used to determine students' preconceptions in this lesson. The first targets the "big ideas" for the lesson and the second is used with Learning Target #1, which addresses a major misconception related to photosynthesis and plant growth. 1. Use a concept cartoon to probe students' understandings about carbon as the source of plant biomass. 2. Use student-developed, annotated drawings to determine students' ideas about the processes and resources a plant uses to grow from seed to mature plant. The intent is to determine students' current understandings about flow of matter and cycling of energy in a plant system.

Learning Sequence Targets

Learning Target #1	The vast majority of plants are able to convert inorganic carbon in CO_2 into organic carbon through photosynthesis. Carbon dioxide and water are used in the process to create biomass. The surrounding environment is the source of raw materials for photosynthesis.

Research-Identified Misconceptions Addressed

- When asked to describe a plant's needs, some students attribute anthropomorphic characteristics to plants, such as breathing, drinking, and eating (Barman et al. 2006; Ebert-May 2006).
- Some students of all ages are unaware that plants make their food internally, thinking instead that they take it in from the outside. They struggle to comprehend that plants make their food from water and air, and that this is their only source of food (AAAS 1993).
- Students think photosynthesis provides energy for uptake of nutrients through roots and building biomass and that no biomass is built through photosynthesis alone (Ebert-May 2006).
- Some students at all ages think plants get most of their food from the soil, through their roots. This is why some students will say that plants need fertilizer (Barker 1995; Barman et al. 2006; Driver et al. 1994; Köse 2008; Russell, Netherwood, and Robinson 2004).
- Many students know that water is absorbed through a plant's roots, but they assume that water is the primary growth material for the plant. Other studies show that students often think minerals are food for plants or that they directly contribute to photosynthesis (Driver et al. 1994).
- There is disbelief that weight increase in plants is due to a gas (CO_2), even if students know that the gas is absorbed by plants (Driver et al. 1994; Ebert-May 2006).
- Only a third of 15-year-olds understand gas exchange in plants or that green plants take in carbon dioxide. Forty-six percent of 16-year-olds do not understand that increased photosynthesis decreases the level of carbon dioxide in a closed system (Driver et al. 1994).

Table 4.2 (continued)

Initial Instructional Plan

Eliciting Preconceptions: Notice that each of the research-identified misconceptions revolves around the source of biomass in the plant or around what causes the plant to grow. Students attribute mass in the growing plant to almost anything but the carbon in CO_2, and the concept cartoon elicits our own students' preconceptions by choosing each student's individual "best answer" to the cartoon.

Confronting Preconceptions: Groups of students now determine the group's "best answer" to the cartoon, confronting their individual conceptions as well as those of their peers. At the same time, teachers should support the metacognitive focus by using a strategy Claim/Support/Question, found at the Visible Thinking website (*www.pz.harvard.edu/vt*). It requires students to clarify claims of truth by making claims, identifying support for their claims, and further questioning their own claims. Have student groups consider the stance taken in their answers and ask them, "How would you test your claim?" There are many resources we can use to help students test their claims. We suggest these two options:

> *Option #1:* Students mass out three batches of radish seeds, each batch weighing 1.5g. Apply various experimental treatments to the seeds (e.g., seeds on moist paper towels in the light, seeds on moist paper towels in the dark, and seeds not moistened in the light). Grow the seeds for one week. Then dry them overnight in an oven and measure biomass in grams. Prior to revealing results, have students predict the biomass of the various treatments (Ebert-May 2003).

> *Option #2:* Students design experiments using Wisconsin Fast Plants (floating leaf discs) to test their claims. Information about use of Fast Plants as well as developed activities can be found at *www.fastplants.org.*

Sense Making: Students write an explanation about the results once results are revealed. If there is not enough time to conduct the Option #1 experiment, the author's (Ebert-May 2003) results can be used (light no water,1.46g; light, water,1.63g; and no light, water, 1.20g). Conclude with a discussion comparing student results to the Van Helmont experiment and his conclusions. Have students discuss in small groups and then record their explanations in their science notebooks.

Additional discussion can help students explore common research-identified misconceptions, including why no soil is required in hydroponics and why soil does not disappear from pots in which plants are growing.

Formative Assessment Plan (Demonstrating Understanding)

1. Student discussions and explanations in their science notebooks serve as formative assessments.
2. Revisit the concept cartoon and ask students to record their current responses in their science notebooks and justify their explanations.
3. Finally, ask students to propose equations for photosynthesis based on their current understanding, record these equations in their science notebooks, and write explanations of their thinking.

Table 4.2 (continued)

Learning Target #2	Photosynthesis captures the energy of sunlight that is used to create chemical bonds in the creation of carbohydrates. Chloroplasts in the cells of plant leaves contain compounds able to capture light energy. Photosynthesis uses CO_2 and the hydrogen from water to form carbohydrates, releasing oxygen.

Research-Identified Misconceptions Addressed

- Some students of all ages confuse energy with other concepts—including food, force and temperature—making it difficult to understand the importance of energy conversions in photosynthesis (AAAS 1993).
- There is confusion about what chlorophyll is and what its role is in plants. Few students understand its role in converting light to chemical energy (Driver et al. 1994).
- Many students believe that plants are green because they absorb green light (Russell, Netherwood, and Robinson 2004).
- Chlorophyll alone is insufficient for plant photosynthesis. Many other enzymes and organic compounds are required. "Chloroplasts" is a better requirement (Hershey 2004).

Initial Instructional Plan

Eliciting and Confronting Preconceptions: Students continue experiments begun in Learning Target #1 and compare the results with other activities that address this target. Provide students with secondary sources that show oxygen concentration around leaves over a 24-hour period. Ask them to find patterns in the data and make a claim, using the data as evidence.

Sense Making: Establish that the evidence supports photosynthesis occurring in the presence of daylight, and ask students to propose investigations that would further test their claims. Students then devise a way to measure photosynthesis under varying conditions, stressing light intensity. Have them make predictions, time the collection of fixed amount of oxygen or use an oxygen probe, graph results, and identify/explain anomalous results. One approach is to use floating leaf discs, an example of which is "Exploring Photosynthesis with Fast Plants," an activity in which students measure rates of photosynthesis by measuring oxygen produced (*www.fastplants.org/pdf/activities/exploring_photosynthesis.pdf*). An optional activity is to read and discuss historical experiments with radioactively tagged water to identify water as the source of oxygen. *Note*: There are difficulties with approaches using the freshwater plant Elodea that tend to produce erroneous data. Photosynthesis does not always cause the bubbles formed on submerged leaves. If you use cold water, bubbles form as the water warms and gases become less soluble. The gas is not always pure oxygen since, as photosynthetic oxygen dissolves, some nitrogen comes out of solution (Hershey 2004).

Close with an activity that requires students to compare their results with those of Joseph Priestley.

Formative Assessment Plan (Demonstrating Understanding)

Students expand or modify their equations for photosynthesis. Require that they explain their reasoning for changes they make to their equations

Table 4.2 (continued)

Learning Target #3	Carbohydrates produced during photosynthesis in leaves can be used immediately for energy in the plant, stored for future use, or converted to other macromolecules that help the plant grow and function.

Research-Identified Misconceptions Addressed

- Students have little understanding of energy transfers in plant metabolism, thinking that food accumulates in a plant as it grows and having little understanding that food provides energy for a plant's life processes (Driver et al. 1994).
- Glucose is not the major photosynthetic product. There is virtually no free glucose produced in photosynthesis. The most common product is starch or sucrose, and students often test leaves for starch (Hershey 2004).

Initial Instructional Plan

Eliciting Preconceptions: Have student groups brainstorm what they know about plant parts and their use as food sources, using one of the brainstorming webs (Instructional Tool 2.10, on page 72. Encourage them to think of all plant parts that might eventually lead them to plant products that include molecules other than glucose.

Confronting Preconceptions: Show students some variegated plants. Ask them to consider why only some parts of the leaves are green and what that might mean about photosynthesis. You can use traditional activities—with green leaves that have parts covered or with variegated leaves— to demonstrate that only green parts of plants make glucose and store it as starch. Have student groups conduct experiments and make sketches of their results. Summarize the results of all groups and discuss consistencies and inconsistencies. Revisit the idea that chlorophyll is necessary to absorb light.

Present students with a wide range of plant products (e.g., cellulose, fats, proteins, starches, sugars) and have them test some for a variety of moles (e.g., fats, proteins, starches, sugars).

Sense Making: Have students research the composition and role of the various plant products in the plant. Establish that these determine the plant's biomass, together with the glucose. A possible extension is to have students find out about the molecular structures of glucose, sucrose, and starch and the relationship among them. At this point, they have not been exposed to respiration in the plant, but this sense-making activity serves as a transition to Learning Target #4.

Formative Assessment Plan (Demonstrating Understanding)

Again have student revisit their equations for photosynthesis, having them modify their equations and write explanations for any modifications.

Table 4.2 (continued)

Learning Target #4	A variety of gases move into and out of plant leaves. Leaves use CO_2 and release O_2 during photosynthesis. When they respire, leaves use O_2 and release CO_2. Other gases enter the leaf as well, but are excreted.

Research-Identified Misconceptions Addressed

- Photosynthesis is often seen as something that plants do for the benefit of animals and people (especially with gas exchange) and that it is not as important to the plant itself (Driver et al. 2004).
- Some students at various ages think that the main job of leaves is to give off carbon dioxide or give off oxygen (Köse 2008).
- Students often think that air is used in opposite ways in plants and animals or they think that plants don't use air (Driver et al. 1994).
- Plants carry on photosynthesis; animals respire (Cottrell 2004; Köse 2008).
- Photosynthesis and respiration function in an opposite and contrasting manner (Köse 2008).
- Plants carry on photosynthesis during the day and respiration during the night (Hershey 2008; Russell, Netherwood, and Robinson 2004). While photosynthesis in plants takes in CO_2 and gives off O_2 during the day, it takes in O_2 and gives off CO_2 at night (Köse 2008).
- Many students think plants require light to grow, including for the germination of seeds (Driver et al. 2004).

Initial Instructional Plan

Eliciting Preconceptions: Raise the question, "If plants produce oxygen, why don't oxygen levels continually rise in the atmosphere?" Students' likely response will be that respiration occurs in animals (since that topic has already been studied).

Confronting Preconceptions:

- Provide students with secondary data sources that indicate O_2 and CO_2 levels around leaves during daytime and nighttime. Ask students what happens at night and how this might be tested. You can again use floating leaf discs (Wisconsin Fast Plants) to have students design and conduct experiments that test their thinking. A wonderful resource explaining use of leaf discs is found *at www.elbiology.com/labtools/ Leafdisk.html* (Williamson, n.d.). It will be helpful with Learning Targets #1 and #4 because it not only explains use of the leaf discs to test oxygen generation in the light, but also includes an extension with discs in the dark.
- You can also consider germinating pea seedlings in the dark over a period of about four weeks. Indeed, you might initiate germination at the beginning of this lesson/unit. O'Connell (2008) provides the steps of the process: (1) obtain uniform lots of peas and begin germination; (2) remove some seedlings from each lot on days 8, 15, and 22, leaving them to air dry; and (3) on days 25 and 26, when the seedlings should be completely dry (the author provides details on how to ensure this), mass out all peas and examine and explain data. Refer to O'Connell (2008) for more detailed information.

Sense Making: Student groups share experimental results. Consistencies and inconsistencies are discussed. Individual students record findings and explanations in their science notebooks.

Formative Assessment Plan (Demonstrating Understanding)

Students finalize their photosynthesis equations, once again justifying any changes.

Table 4.3

Strategies for Teaching Photosynthesis

Strategy	Strengths of the Strategies
Drawings and Annotated Drawings	• They may be best used when teaching nonobservable science concepts (i.e., photosynthesis). • Student-created descriptive drawings are more effective at promoting conceptual change than just writing (without drawing). • They are even more effective when coupled with verbal information (questioning/interviews). • Some students who might find it difficult to express themselves in words may be able to express themselves through drawing. • Annotated illustrations require the student to select, organize, and integrate ideas. These are cognitive processes necessary for meaningful learning. • Annotated drawings make students' knowledge-construction visible and let them grapple with their own ideas and adjust their thinking. Thus, annotated drawings serve a metacognitive function. • Drawings provide information about specific misconceptions, which is helpful to both students and teachers. • They provide information to the teacher that helps determine what strategies to use. • They are less biased than some strategies or assessments because students choose what they draw and draw from their own experiences. This also allows the teacher to respond to the interests, background knowledge, and skills of individual students.
Concept Cartoons	• They have been shown effective in eliciting and addressing student misconceptions about photosynthesis. • They present cognitive conflict, which both provides motivation and challenges a student's misconceptions. • They engage students in the learning process because students are required to focus on construction of explanations for the situations in the cartoons. • They make the flow of learning more continuous because elicitation of student ideas and restructuring of their thinking occur simultaneously. • Students choose between alternative explanations, making the need for investigation evident. They are then responsible for choosing the appropriate investigation, which gives the teacher time to respond to students' individual needs. • They create an environment that promotes participation of all students in class discussion, activates students to support their ideas, and remedies misconceptions. • They may lessen student anxiety over offering a wrong answer.
Concept Maps	• They are effective when working with concept-rich units such as photosynthesis. • They motivate and engage students in the content. • They show relationships among concepts. • They challenge students to analyze their thinking, thereby enhancing metacognition. • Group concept mapping is especially powerful. • Effective use of concept maps requires training for the teacher so that he or she can then train the student. It takes students about eight weeks of school to become proficient at concept mapping.

Recommended Resources

Technology Applications and Websites

Each of the following websites provide video of germination of seeds and continuing plant growth that can be used to elicit student preconceptions:

- Minds of Our Own video (*www.learner.org/resources/series26.html*)

- From Seed to Flower at the Teacher's Domain website (*www.teachersdomain.org/resources/tdc02/sci/life/colt/plantsgrow/index.html*)

- The Giant Sequoia seed germination at the ARKive Images of Life on Earth website (*www.arkive.org/species/GES/plants_and_algae/Sequoiadendron_giganteum/Sequoiadendron_gigant_09c.html*)

- Several time-lapse seed germination videos at the Teacher Tube website, including Wisconsin Fast Plants Life Cycle Time Lapse and Time Lapse Radish (*www.teachertube.com/search_result.php?search_id=seed*)

Two helpful sites for use during investigations include the following:

- Wisconsin Fast Plants website (*www.fastplants.org*)

- "The Floating Leaf Disk Assay for Investigating Photosynthesis" is found at the Exploring Life Community website (*www.elbiology.com/labtools/Leafdisk.html*)

Finally, a summary of misconceptions related to photosynthesis is found at the AIBS website (*www.actionbioscience.org/education/hershey.html*).

Additional resources to support the framework process are found in endnote #3.

Build Your Library

Check out Probes 15 and 16 in *Uncovering Student Ideas in Science, Volume 2: 25 More Formative Assessment Probes* (Keeley, Eberle, and Tugel. 2007). These probes deal with photosynthesis.

Endnotes

1. Annenberg has made video segments available online at *www.learner.org/resources/series26.html*.

2. This diagram is modified from the work of Mohan, Chen, and Anderson (2007). Theirs is a loop diagram for carbon cycling in socio-ecological systems and includes human and economic systems as well as environmental systems. Their diagram was designed to model how humans impact carbon cycling in an ecosystem.

3. Several sources were used to determine the best learning sequence for this lesson. They are rich resources for your further study of carbon cycling broadly and photosynthesis in particular. These sources are

- Environmental Literacy Learning Progressions from the Project 2061 website: *www.project2061.org/publications/2061Connections/2007/media/KSIdocs/anderson_paper.pdf* (5/26/08)

- MIT Hierarchical Framework: *http://web.mit.edu/bioedgroup/HBCF/HBCF_full.htm* (5/22/08)

- The Standards Site, Science KS3: *www.standards.dcsf.gov.uk/schemes2/secondary_science/?view=get* (4/17/08)

- Multiple papers at the Environmental Literacy website at Michigan State University (*http://edr1.educ.msu.edu/EnvironmentalLit/index.htm*) (5/15/08)

4. Students build new knowledge based on what they already know. Although their ideas seem reasonable and appropriate to them, the ideas may not be consistent with scientific explanations or the ideas may be limited in application (Driver et al. 1994). If they are going to change their perceptions, students must become dissatisfied with their existing views by being presented with a new conception that seems reasonable and more attractive than their previous ideas. The new conception must help them explain scientific phenomena and make predictions as they make sense of their world (Strike and Posner 1985).

Conceptual change research is grounded in the idea that students' ideas must be *restructured* rather than replaced (Duit and Treagust 1998). This means that teachers must value their students' ideas and teach them to reflect on the ideas. Then, teachers can help students reach the conceptual targets that the teachers have set (Hipkins et al. 2002). Weiss et al. (2003) summarize four areas in which teachers have the most impact on students' scientific learning. Teachers must (1) engage students in grappling with important science content, (2) motivate students to engage in the content, (3) portray science as a dynamic body of knowledge, and (4) take students where they are and move them forward. "Instruction must begin with close attention to students' ideas, knowledge, skills, and attitudes, which provide the foundation on which new learning builds" (NRC 2005, p. 14).

5. A review of related research (Scott, Asoko, and Driver 1992) categorized two main types of conceptual change teaching strategies. The first is sometimes called the cognitive conflict model and uses strategies that elicit student ideas at the beginning of a lesson and immediately has students contrast the ideas with scientists' ideas. The second is called the conceptual development model and begins with students' ideas, leading them gradually toward scientific ideas. The strategies in Chapter 2 use both of these models.

Instructional Planning Framework

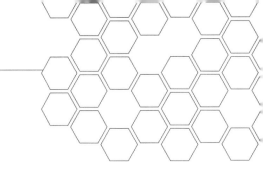

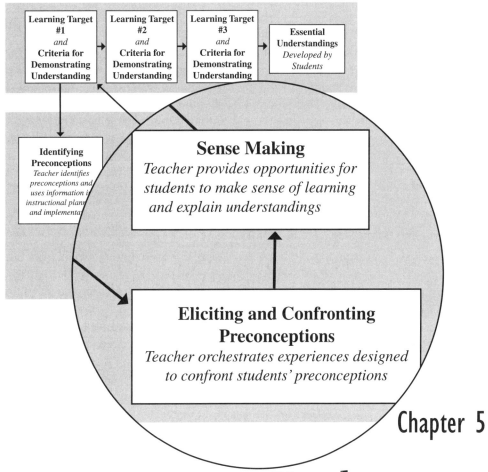

Predictive Phase
The teacher determines the lesson's essential understandings, the sequence of learning targets that lead toward those understandings, and the criteria by which understanding is determined.

Responsive Phase
Building on the foundation of the predictive phase, the teacher plans for and implements instruction during the responsive phase, one learning target at a time.

Learning Target #1 *and* **Criteria for Demonstrating Understanding**	Learning Target #2 *and* **Criteria for Demonstrating Understanding**	Learning Target #3 *and* **Criteria for Demonstrating Understanding**	**Essential Understandings** *Developed by Students*

Identifying Preconceptions
Teacher identifies preconceptions and uses information i[n] instructional plann[ing] and implementa[tion]

Sense Making
Teacher provides opportunities for students to make sense of learning and explain understandings

Eliciting and Confronting Preconceptions
Teacher orchestrates experiences designed to confront students' preconceptions

Chapter 5

Evolution: Natural Selection

"Natural selection is probably the single most misunderstood idea in all of evolution, and thus is a Big Idea or critical concept that binds all of biology together."

—Fisher and Williams 2007, p. 3

Let's begin with a scenario common in many classrooms across the country. A biology teacher of 10 years tells her students that the class will begin a unit on evolution next week. That announcement immediately evokes a variety of heated responses: "Evolution is only a theory and we should be able to study all the theories out there, including creationism." "I don't believe in evolution." "My mother says I can't study evolution because it conflicts with our religion." These objections give the teacher pause. She knows how essential the concept of evolution is to biology but wonders how she can teach about evolution without further antagonizing her students (or their parents). Clearly there are ongoing misunderstandings about what is meant by a theory, how science works, and the differences between science and religion.

Why This Topic?

Evolution is the central organizing principle that biologists use to make sense of the world. It is essential to teach evolution as the core of biology so that students can bring greater order and coherence to their understandings about life (National Academy of Science 1998). Understanding evolution is also essential to students' scientific literacy (NSTA 2003). And, for students to understand evolution, they must understand natural variation and its role in natural selection, a primary mechanism for biological evolution (Ardia 2005). Yet, in "the twentieth century, no scientific theory has been more difficult for people to accept than biological evolution by natural selection" (AAAS 1993, p. 122).

Four factors seem to impede a widespread understanding of evolution: (1) it seems to go against the beliefs some people strongly hold; (2) many students get little or no instruction about it (NAS 1998); (3) secondary textbooks do not often reflect current research about evolution (Gerking 2004); and (4) natural selection is one of the most "misinterpreted and misunderstood concepts" in the field of science (Wuerth 2004). Natural selection is especially difficult to teach because students see it as an abstract process, highly statistical, and takes place over long periods of time (Hilbish and Goodwin 1994).

Overview

Evolutionary biology reconstructs how life on Earth has changed and proposes mechanisms that account for how those changes might occur (Passmore and Stewart 2000). Our focus in this chapter is on the latter area, and we look specifically at natural selec-

Topic: Natural selection
Go to: *www.scilinks.org*
Code: HTB006

tion as an explanatory model of evolution. We do not examine other mechanisms of evolution, such as recombination, random mating, or mutation as sources of variation (which are prerequisites to this lesson). Neither do we discuss genetic drift, evidence for evolution, relatedness/classification of organisms based on evolutionary relationships, natural selection patterns, or speciation (which can be taught after this lesson).

In this chapter, we focus on the responsive phase of the Instructional Planning Framework (Figure 5.1), particularly "eliciting and confronting preconceptions" and "sense making." But first, beginning on page 146, we briefly review the *predictive phase* and its application to this lesson on natural selection. (*Note:* All tables are grouped together at the end of the chapter, beginning on p. 159. They are followed by Recommended Resources and Endnotes.)

Figure 5.1

Instructional Plannning Framework: Responsive Phase

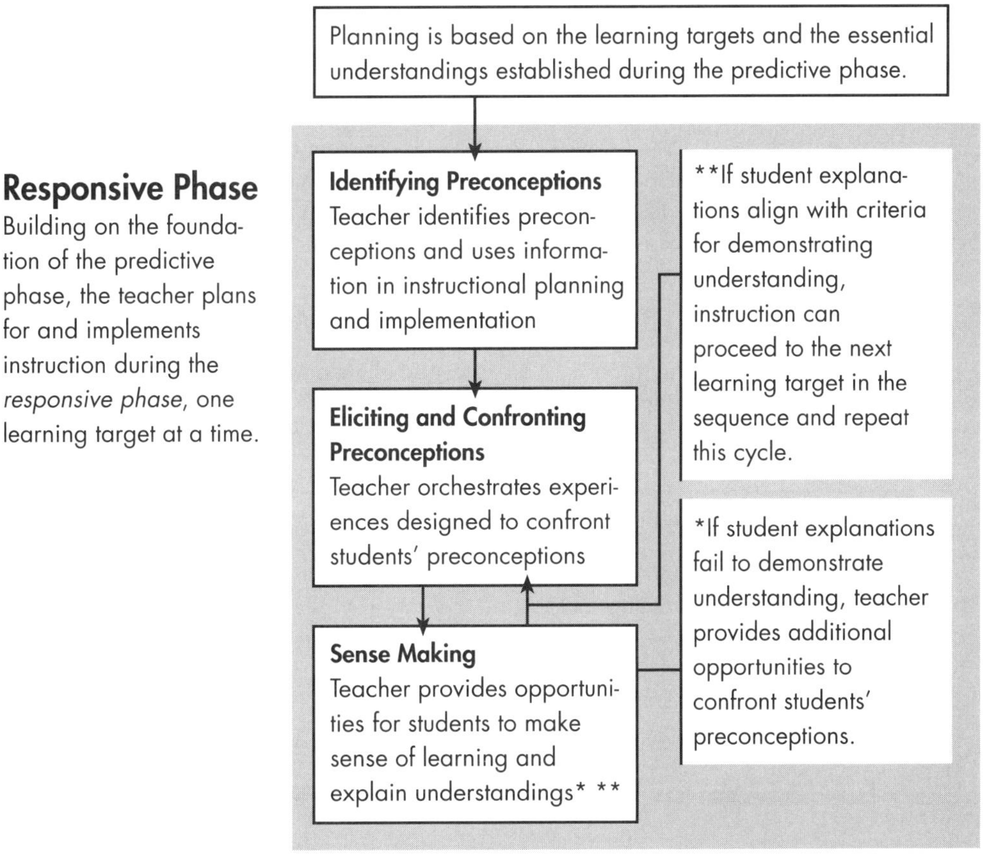

Planning is based on the learning targets and the essential understandings established during the predictive phase.

Responsive Phase
Building on the foundation of the predictive phase, the teacher plans for and implements instruction during the *responsive phase*, one learning target at a time.

Identifying Preconceptions
Teacher identifies preconceptions and uses information in instructional planning and implementation

Eliciting and Confronting Preconceptions
Teacher orchestrates experiences designed to confront students' preconceptions

Sense Making
Teacher provides opportunities for students to make sense of learning and explain understandings* **

**If student explanations align with criteria for demonstrating understanding, instruction can proceed to the next learning target in the sequence and repeat this cycle.

*If student explanations fail to demonstrate understanding, teacher provides additional opportunities to confront students' preconceptions.

Instructional Planning Framework: *Predictive Phase*

Let's look again at *Science for All Americans* to remember what our end target is: the expectations for adult science literacy (Figure 5.2).

Figure 5.2

Natural Selection and Adult Science Literacy

Science for All Americans states that a science-literate adult should know that:

"A central concept of the theory of evolution is natural selection, which arises from three well-established observations: (1) There is some variation in heritable characteristics within every species of organism, (2) some of these characteristics will give individuals an advantage over others in surviving to maturity and reproducing, and (3) those individuals will be likely to have more offspring, which will themselves be more likely than others to survive and reproduce. The likely result is that over successive generations, the proportion of individuals that have inherited advantage-giving characteristics will tend to increase.

"Selectable characteristics can include details of biochemistry, such as the molecular structure of hormones or digestive enzymes, and anatomical features that are ultimately produced in the development of the organism, such as bone size or fur length. They can also include more subtle features determined by anatomy, such as acuity of vision or pumping efficiency of the heart. By biochemical or anatomical means, selectable characteristics may also influence behavior, such as weaving a certain shape of web, preferring certain characteristics in a mate, or being disposed to care for offspring....

"By its very nature, natural selection is likely to lead to organisms with characteristics that are well adapted to survival in particular environments.... Moreover, when an environment changes (in this sense, other organisms are also part of the environment), the advantage or disadvantage of characteristics can change. So natural selection does not necessarily result in long-term progress in a set direction. Evolution builds on what already exists, so the more variety that already exists, the more there can be." (AAAS 1989, 68–69)

We next use the procedures outlined in Chapter 3 to determine the conceptual targets, a logical learning progression, and criteria to demonstrate understanding. A brief summary of these procedures appears again to remind you of the process (Figure 5.3).[1]

Figure 5.3

Planning in the **Predictive Phase**

1. Identify the essential understandings for the lesson.
   a. Begin with the descriptions of adult science literacy to determine an anchor goal.
   b. Consider the middle school and high school standards and benchmarks.
   c. Optional: Study existing research on learning progressions. A good resource (*www.project2061.org/publications/2061Connections/2007/2007-04a-resources.htm*) is found in the 2061 Connections online newsletter (AAAS 2007a).
   d. Dig a bit deeper and think about the concepts included in the standards.
   e. Decide what is essential and what can be pruned.
2. Develop a logical sequence of Learning Targets for the lesson.
   a. Consider first the middle school experiences that students should have had.
   b. Outline the key ideas embedded in the high school standards and benchmarks.
   c. Sequence the key ideas in a way to build student understanding.
   d. Consider connections from one lesson to the next.
3. Identify the criteria for demonstrating understanding. (*Note:* Steps b and c are completed later, after a review of research.)
   a. Identify one criterion for each Learning Target.
   b. Identify one criterion for your selected standards-based strategy (Inquiry, HOS, or NOS).
   c. Identify one criterion for your selected metacognitive strategy.

Also review the natural selection learning sequence and how it leads to the essential understandings for this topic (Figure 5.4, p. 148).

The result of our planning is the Teacher Work Template for the *prescriptive phase* that you see in Table 5.1 (p. 159). Carefully study the criteria to demonstrate understanding at the end of the table so that you can interpret the decisions we made about best approaches to elicit and confront common misconceptions during the *responsive phase*, described in the next portion of this chapter.

Reflection and Application

This is our third experience (see also Chapter 3 and Chapter 4) with the process used to complete the *predictive phase*. Take a moment to reflect on the process as completed for "natural selection."

1. How have you taught this topic in the past?
2. In what ways does your past instruction of this topic align with the steps we have taken so far in the *predictive phase*? In what ways has it been different?
3. Are there changes you might make in your instruction based on the information gained during this process and found in Table 5.1?

Figure 5.4

Natural Selection Learning Sequence

Target #1: Populations produce more offspring than can survive. Individuals in the population are not identical, in part because their genetic material varies. Since it varies, their physical characteristics (including chemical, physical and behavioral traits) also vary. As a result, individual survival is not random since some of them are better at competing due to these randomly produced variations.	**Target #2:** Some traits provide an advantage, and individuals with these traits are more likely to survive and reproduce. If their offspring survive, these individuals pass on their traits/alleles. Natural selection affects only heritable traits, and only individuals are selected.	**Target #3:** Individuals are selected, but only populations evolve. Populations change over time as the percentage of advantageous traits (alleles) increases (changes to the gene pool).	**Target #4:** Natural selection adapts a population to an environment. If an environment changes or mutations occur, the gene pool of the population changes.

Essential Understandings: Natural selection is the most important mechanism for evolutionary change in populations and in development of species. It occurs because 1) not all offspring in a population survive due to competition for limited resources, 2) there is heritable variation among the members of the population, and 3) some of these variations give a survival advantage to the individuals that have those traits. As a result, survivors tend to produce more offspring who inherit the advantage, passing it on and increasing the percentage of individuals in the population with that advantage. Since the initial three conditions exist in nature at all times, populations almost always undergo adaptive change to the environment. Changing environments can put pressures on populations resulting in changes in competitive advantage and, eventually, in an evolving gene pool.

Instructional Planning Framework: *Responsive Phase*

Identifying Preconceptions

In Chapter 4 we began to focus on the *responsive phase* of the framework, specifically on identifying preconceptions. We use the same process in this chapter to (1) determine misconceptions about natural selection uncovered by research (Figure 5.5, steps #1–#3) and (2) identify our own students' preconceptions (Figure 5.5, steps #4 and #6–8).

We applied the process in Figure 5.5 (steps #1–#3) to our lesson on natural selection. The results of our work appear in the Teacher Work Template for the responsive phase (Table 5.2, pp. 161–163). Carefully study the template and use it to complete the reflection on page 150.

Figure 5.5

Planning in the Responsive Phase

Learn About Research-Identified Misconceptions

1. Review *Benchmarks for Science Literacy* (1993) for the misconceptions discussed there. Chapter 15 of that book includes research findings organized by benchmark. If you do not have a copy of the book, you can read it online at *www.project2061.org/ publications/bsl/online/index.php?txtRef=&txtURIOld=%2Fpublications%2Fbsl%2Fonline %2Findex.*

2. Complete a web search for misconceptions on the selected topic. Simply run a search for your topic and misconceptions (e.g., "photosynthesis + misconceptions"). If you run your search at Google Scholar (*http://scholar.google.com*), you will gain access to numerous resources. In some cases you will only access the abstract, but in others you will find the entire document. This process is more time-consuming than step #1 but yields additional resources.

3. This step is the most direct way to access a summary of misconceptions, but it requires that you have a copy of *Making Sense of Secondary Science: Research Into Children's Ideas* (Driver et al. 1994). The book is outlined by topic and provides a rich summary of research on children's ideas about these topics.

Strategy Selection for Identifying, Eliciting, and Confronting Preconceptions and for Sense Making

4. Use Instructional Strategy Sequencing Tool 2.1 (p. 29) to identify strategies that work to identify and elicit/confront student preconceptions as well as strategies that work for sense making. Finally, identify metacognitive and standards-based strategies to review.

5. Find the strategies in the three Metacognitive Strategy Tools (Instructional Tools 2.2–2.4), starting on p. 33), the three Standards-Based Strategy Tools (Instructional Tools 2.5–2.7, starting on p. 43), and the seven Sense-Making Strategy Tools (Instructional Tools 2.8–2.14, starting on p. 55).

6. Carefully review the research and application recommendations for each of the identified strategies.

7. Determine several strategies that fit well with the particular content you are teaching.

8. Review the resources in each Instructional Tool to more fully understand the strategies and to determine what they might look like in application.

9. Select one metacognitive strategy, one standards-based strategy, and two or three sense-making strategies for use in your lesson (recall that these will be used to differentiate instruction and to provide further instruction if formative assessments indicate that students do not demonstrate understanding of the Learning Targets).

10. Determine one criterion to demonstrate understanding for each of your metacognitive and standards-based focuses.

Reflection and Application

This is our second experience (see also Chapter 4) with identifying preconceptions in the *responsive phase*. Take a moment to reflect on the process as completed for natural selection.

1. We identified natural selection as a hard-to-teach topic. If you agree, what, in your opinion, makes it a hard-to-teach topic?
2. How do the results of the research review we conducted and presented in Table 5.2 (p. 161) inform your instruction? What might you do differently in your current lesson on natural selection, based on the research we summarized?
3. How well would the strategies employed to identify students' preconceptions about natural selection (see Table 5.2, top of p. 161) work in your classroom? Would you need to modify them? If so, what might you do?

Before addressing our three Learning Targets (which will be found in Table 5.2), we want to share what the research says about effective teaching of evolution and natural selection. This summary was drawn from research found during our search for common misconceptions. We used it as we identified strategies to elicit and confront preconceptions. These findings apply to each of the Learning Targets in this lesson.

- Effective instruction about evolution works to build understandings about the questions that evolutionary biologists ask and the methods they employ (Cooper 2004). We think this approach has potential for addressing the confusion about evolution that results from misunderstanding the nature of science (as demonstrated in the opening of this chapter) (Scotchmoor and Janulaw 2005).
- Standard approaches to teaching natural selection rely on artificial examples or computer simulations. These approaches show what *could* happen rather than what *does* happen, so students tend to see natural selection as an intangible theory rather than a process that actually occurs. It is better to include real-life demonstrations using living organisms and selection pressures familiar to students (Hilbish and Goodwin 1994).
- "History should not be overlooked. Learning about Darwin and what led him to the concept of evolution illustrates the interacting roles of evidence and theory in scientific inquiry" (AAAS 1993, p. 124). Again, recall the issues addressed at the beginning of this chapter.
- Teachers must be careful in their use of terms because students' misconceptions are exacerbated by terms—such as *fitness* and *theory*—that mean different things in daily life and to scientists (Bishop and Anderson 1990; Wescott and Cunningham 2005). Teachers should be explicit about how scientists, as opposed to the general public, use certain terms.

Eliciting and Confronting Preconceptions and Sense Making

What are appropriate strategies to elicit and confront preconceptions related to our Learning Targets for this lesson? First, consider the results from the Conceptual Inventory for Natural Selection (CINS), the assessment we selected as best able to identify common preconceptions in your classroom. Student responses to these questions help identify particular areas of difficulty. The CINS is found at *www.biologylessons. sdsu.edu/*, and the answer key is available at *http://bioliteracy.net/Readings/Natural%20 Selection%20CI.pdf* (Anderson, Fisher, and Norman 2002).

Next, use the methods first outlined in Chapter 4 and shown again in Figure 5.5 (steps #4–#10) to select strategies that are appropriate both to elicit and confront preconceptions on this topic and to help students in sense making.

Using these methods, what are the best strategies to use when teaching natural selection? It seems that several would be especially productive for eliciting and confronting student preconceptions: concept cartoons, dynamic models, concept maps, the various "writing to learn" strategies, and discourse. Effective sense-making strategies include some of the same strategies, in addition to some of the standards-based strategies, especially those summarized in the Instructional Tool 2.5, "Standards-Based Approaches for Inquiry," p. 43). The standards-based and sense-making strategies that seem most effective for the study of natural selection are summarized in Table 5.3, p. 164. For further information on sense-making strategies, refer to Instructional Tools 2.8–2.14 (beginning on p. 55).

As you will see in Table 5.3, there is a strong overlap among many of the strategies for eliciting preconceptions and for sense making. Let's look at that overlap.

1. As we learned in Chapter 4, concept cartoons effectively elicit and confront preconceptions and serve as an entry into student discourse and writing. The cartoons require students to make a claim and provide reasoning for that claim; doing so ties nicely to the use of discourse, writing, and formulating explanations.

2. Dynamic models (including computer simulations) are effective when learning complex ideas and making sense of concepts that are difficult or impossible to observe (as is true of natural selection). Simulations can probe students' thinking and modify preconceptions, especially when combined with hands-on laboratory experiences. Earlier we discussed the importance of real-life demonstrations using living organisms and selection pressures familiar to students (Hilbish and Goodwin 1994), not just computer simulations. These experiences require students to build explanations based on evidence.

3. Formulating explanations from evidence and connecting explanations to scientific knowledge are dependent on literacy strategies, including discourse and writing. These aspects of inquiry also address our earlier concern about evolution and the nature of science. Using the methods of evolutionary biologists,

teachers can address the confusion about evolution that results from misunderstanding the nature of science (Scotchmoor and Janulaw 2005).

4. Writing and discourse are essential to develop and communicate explanations. However, these are complex strategies for teachers to learn and for students to master. The Science Writing Heuristic (SWH) process (for information go to *http://avogadro.chem.iastate.edu/SWH/homepage.htm*) beautifully ties together various literacy strategies and requires students to make claims based on evidence and to use reasoning that connects claims to evidence. But full implementation requires adequate understanding on the teacher's part. Teachers who are familiar with the SWH process will find it ideal for use in this lesson. Teachers unfamiliar with SWH should either learn more about it before implementation or investigate subsets of the strategies used in this chapter (e.g., aspects of discourse and science notebooks).

Now we use all the information presented in this section, especially the contents of Table 5.3, to determine the best ways, for each Learning Target, to elicit and confront preconceptions and to help students in sense making.

At this point, recall our metacognitive focus and our standards-based focus for this lesson. With the metacognitive focus, we seek to improve students' abilities to distinguish between experimental observations and inferences about natural selection (NOS focus). The standards-based focus is employed to help students make personal claims based on evidence and generate alternative claims based on that evidence. These focuses tie nicely with the strategies outlined in Table 5.3 and in the four-item list that begins on page 151.

The focus of the chapter, as we have said, is not on demonstrating understanding. We don't show how we reached decisions to use particular formative assessments for the Learning Targets or how the results might be used. Instead, we summarize the formative assessments, including them in our Teacher Work Template for the *responsive phase* (Table 5.2).

We look at each Learning Target in turn.

Learning Target #1: *Populations produce more offspring than can survive. Individuals in the population are not identical, in part because their genetic material varies. Because it varies, their physical characteristics (including chemical, physical, and behavioral traits) also vary. As a result, individual survival is not random, because some individuals are better at competing due to these randomly produced variations.*

Based on middle school experiences, students should understand the first sentence in Learning Target #1 because they should have studied population growth and the impact of biotic and abiotic factors on this growth (see Table 5.1, p. 159). However, depending on your student results from the CINS, you may have to review the concepts with them. If you find that is necessary, here are four experiences you might use.

1. Population Growth: Eliciting and Confronting Preconceptions

We suggest the use of concept cartoon #9 at the San Diego State University website (*www.biologylessons.sdsu.edu/cartoons/concepts.html*) to *elicit* your students' preconceptions If student responses and CINS data indicate the need, the following activities are options to further elicit and confront student preconceptions about population growth.

- We suggest Population Explorer (see Recommended Resources, p. 166) as a quality simulation.
  - Begin with a student engagement activity, targeting specific aspects of Population Explorer's "Budgie Population." (Carefully review the materials listed in this chapter's Recommended Resources before using the simulation.) Your students can learn about budgies, and you can limit the aspects of Population Explorer that students visit, focusing at this point only on growth of the population and observation of the population curve. You can choose to do this as a demonstration or a small-group activity. In either case, have students use their science notebooks to record observations and generate questions. Caution them to list only observations, making no inferences at this time. Students share observations and questions either in whole-group discussion or in small groups followed by whole-group discussion.
  - Follow with a general population study to address some of the questions asked and observations made during the simulation. Yeast population studies are easily found on the web and in textbooks. These traditional experiments can be completed by student groups, with each group conducting a standard experiment or with each pursuing a question that was generated during the simulation activity. Students should make claims prior to completing the study, basing their claims on what they learned in the simulation. The focus of the study is again on observations but also on gathering data (population counts) that are graphed. (We chose yeast, as it is easy to grow. More interesting options include duckweed or flour beetles, but they are slower growing. Make your choice based on the time available.)

2. Population Growth: Sense Making

At the end of the experiment, students write individual explanations (using reasoning to connect the evidence to their claims about population growth), discuss them with group members, and generate an explanation for the group. Small-group members share and compare their explanations, based on the data they collect (graphs from population counts). Students then use textbooks or other print materials to compare their claims to those of experts.

3. Variation and Differential Mortality: Eliciting and Confronting Preconceptions

We again suggest using concept cartoons available at the SDSU website to *elicit* preconceptions. Cartoon #38 is effective for variation; #7, #27, and #34 address competition; #29 is about randomness; and #15 ties Learning Target #1 to Learning Target #2 (on p. 156). Use them in conjunction with the following activities designed to *confront* student preconceptions.

- Various activities can help students understand intraspecific variation, an important concept since genetic variation in a population (gene pool) is the raw material for natural selection. Remember that a combination of simulations and experimental activities have been shown to be effective. Select from the following:
  - Return to the budgie population in Population Explorer and have students study the variations in the population. Have them first add the default 100 organisms. Then have them double-click on the various colors to find out more about individual genotypes that lead to various colors. Note that students can find out about budgies at the Budgerigar Homepage *www.geocities.com/RainForest/3298,* especially at the links for "histories of varieties" and "genetics."
  - Examine an array of variations in particular populations, both physical and biochemical, using graphs or tables showing distribution of traits in populations.
  - Study variations using concrete examples. We suggest beginning research that will last throughout the Learning Targets for this lesson, selecting one of the following two options:
    1. An online study of plumage color and beak morphology in birds. This lesson originally appeared in the American Biology Teacher (Ardia 2005). The full lesson can also be seen and downloaded at *http://csip.cornell.edu/curriculum_resources/csip/ardia.* Ardia describes procedures to elicit understandings about variations in bird coloration and builds on this understanding, having students study variations in plumage and bill morphology. Students use specimens or online images. For this activity, complete the exercise to the point that students generate frequency histograms for one color variable and one bill size measure.
    2. A study of variation in populations known to students. We suggest using dandelions, as this ties with an activity that can be used throughout the Learning Targets for this lesson. Students can measure natural variations of shoot length and root length in dandelions. A full description of how this is done will be found in the American Biology Teacher (Hilbish and Goodwin 1994). At the same time students study these variations. Then, dandelion seeds should be collected from two areas (one that has not been mowed for many years and one where mowing regularly occurs), planted,

and grown for two to three months. Students observe the plants' growth. These observations will later be used in Learning Target #4. At this point, students should be asked to predict which plants will have a greater shoot-to-root ratio—those from the mowed area or those from the area that has not been mowed for many years. As students proceed through the lesson, they can refer to these populations for their explanations.

In each case, probe your students' thinking about the sources of variation, connecting to past learning about recombination, random mating, and mutation. (*Note*: Various other studies—including development of resistance to insecticides (flour beetles and Malathion) and antibiotic resistance in bacteria—are options to consider.)

Now you are ready to have students consider the advantage of variation in a population. To do this, you can extend any of the activities selected to tie variation to competition. First, regardless of the chosen experiment or simulation, probe your students' thinking about why variation might be important. Have them make a claim about the importance of a trait to an organism's survival in competing for scare resources (e.g., for budgies, their beak morphology). Proceed with the activity.

- Return to Population Explorer and click on "edit rules" to introduce a survival advantage. Follow the directions for editing rules found in the Concord Consortium newsletter article (see Recommended Resources, p. 166). Have students run the simulation and provide an explanation for the results.
- Return to the bird specimen experiment and have students, using their frequency histograms, predict the relationship between one selected trait (plumage or beak) and survival. Share the graphs that show the relationship between body and bill size and survival in birds, and discuss as a whole class the implications of these data.
- Return to the dandelion experiment and have students predict the relationship between one selected trait (shoot length or root length) and survival.

4. Variation and Differential Mortality: Sense Making

Students revisit their claims, discuss them with group members, and revise their explanations. Students use textbooks or other print materials to compare their explanations with those of experts. Then, students individually expand their explanations to include what they learned through the simulations and the evidence they have gathered. Finally, students reflect on how their thinking has changed.

Learning Target #2: Some traits provide an advantage, and individuals with these traits are more likely to survive and reproduce. If their offspring survive, these individuals pass on their traits/alleles. Natural selection affects only heritable traits, and only individuals are selected.

Students now need to understand that fitness is important not only for survival but also for reproductive success. Again, there are activities that help elicit and confront student preconceptions about fitness, building on the learning so far in this lesson. Some of these activities continue ongoing work with simulations and experimentation.

Eliciting and Confronting Preconceptions

Once again use concept cartoons from the SDSU website (*www.biologylessons.sdsu.edu/cartoons/concepts.html*) to elicit student preconceptions. Appropriate cartoons for this Learning Target are #11 (ties Learning Target #1 to #2), #5 (deals directly with fitness), #12 (deals with use and disuse), and #13 (addresses acquired traits versus inheritability). Select a cartoon and have student groups choose the response with which they most agree and explain why.

An excellent option for an appropriate simulation is EvoTutor (*www.evotutor.org*). When you visit the site, select "online simulations," then "selection," and then "requirements." Students can explore the interactions of variation, heritability, and differential mortality. This links what students learned in Learning Target #1 to Learning Target #2.

We understand that some of you have limited computer access in the classroom. Other options include (1) blocking computer lab time; (2) small-group explorations of the site, cycling students through a computer station while other students have alternate assignments; or (3) using the simulation as a reference during a whole-class interactive lecture.

Sense Making

Students now apply what they learned in the simulations to their ongoing inquiry on bird plumage or beak morphology (or other chosen inquiry). For the ongoing bird study, give students the various graphs related to fitness (plumage coloration and reproduction, plumage color and number of feeding visits per hour, and bill length and reproductive success). Small groups hold discussions and update their explanations.

For homework, assign the reading of "Survival of the Sneakiest," a cartoon about fitness found at *http://evolution.berkeley.edu/evosite/evohome.html*. (To find this resource, go to the site, select "teaching evolution," then "search for lessons," and simply search for "fitness.") Students read the cartoon and respond to the questions. They also write explanations of how cricket fitness and selection are similar to and different from fitness and selection in their experimental populations.

Learning Target #3: *Individuals are selected, but only populations evolve. Populations change over time as the percentage of advantageous traits (alleles) increases (changes to the gene pool).*

Eliciting and Confronting Preconceptions

Show students SDSU Concept Cartoon #24, and ask individual students to choose an answer and record it in their science notebooks (eliciting preconceptions). Ask students to explain the thinking that prompted them to select their responses. Small groups then discuss their responses, come to group consensus, and share their responses with the whole class. (Student preconceptions are confronted in the last step as students hear alternative explanations from other group members.) Lead a class discussion to determine how students used their understandings from the first two Learning Targets to reach this point and to identify any lingering misconceptions about the fact that populations, not individuals, evolve.

Then use EvoTutor and/or Population Explorer to further students' understandings. Ask students to pay special attention to what happens to individual organisms versus what happens to the population of organisms.

Sense Making

Students apply their understandings to their ongoing experiments (e.g., dandelions, insecticide resistance), using science notebooks and classroom discourse. Have them make and support predictions about what might happen to changing percentages of alleles in the gene pool.

Learning Target #4: Natural selection adapts a population to an environment. If an environment changes or mutations occur, the gene pool of the population changes.

Eliciting and Confronting Preconceptions

For Learning Target #4, use SDSU concept cartoon #23 or #30 to elicit students' preconceptions. Small groups discuss the cartoon, make a choice, and share those choices with the class.

Once again, students visit Population Explorer, where they create multiple terrains, set up different rules for each, and observe the impact on the population. They then explore the Peppered Moth Simulation (*www.biologycorner.com/worksheets/peppepredmoth.html*) and make connections to their observations at Population Explorer. A possible extension to this activity is to return to Population Explorer, introduce mutations, and determine impact.

Sense Making

By this time, all dandelions should be harvested. Students have measured the various shoot and root lengths and/or weights for the mowed area and the area that was not mowed. Students develop frequency diagrams of shoot-to-root ratios and compare actual data to their predictions. They then develop full explanations for the results, tying their original claims to the evidence. They also provide an alternative explanation, if at all possible. A full description of this procedure is found in an article in *The American Biology Teacher* (Hilbish and Goodwin 1994).

Similarly, if you chose another experiment for students to study (insecticide resistance or antibiotic resistance), you should now be able to bring closure to the experi-

Hard-to-Teach Biology Concepts

ment. Regardless of the experiment completed, at this point all student explanations should incorporate the key components of natural selection. All findings and interpretations should be recorded in the students' science notebooks, as well as thoroughly discussed in small groups and shared with the whole class. It is important that teachers determine the degree of understanding demonstrated in the notebooks and ask probing questions to further guide learning. Finally, students compare their findings to those of Darwin. To do this use the textbooks and other text resources listed in Recommended Resources, page 166.

A brief outline of this planned instruction completes the Teacher Work Template for natural selection (Table 5.1). Also see the initial instructional plan for each Learning Target in Table 5.2 (pp. 161–163).

Reflection and Application

You have just completed the second use of the process for identifying strategies for eliciting and confronting preconceptions (introduced in Chapter 4 but examined more carefully in this chapter) For the first time you have considered strategies for sense making (more on sense making in Chapter 6). Take a moment now to reflect on the process as completed for the topic of natural selection.

1. What about this process challenges you? What about the process makes it difficult, and why?
2. If challenges exist, how would you overcome them?
3. How well would the selected strategies work in your classroom? Would you need to modify them? If so, what might you do?

Table 5.1

Teacher Work Template–**Predictive Phase**

Lesson Topic—Evolution: Natural Selection			
Conceptual Target Development	National Standard(s) Addressed	*From 9–12 NSES:* Species evolve over time. Evolution is the consequence of the interactions of (1) the potential for a species to increase its numbers, (2) the genetic variability of offspring due to mutation and recombination of genes, (3) a finite supply of the resources required for life, and (4) the ensuing selection by the environment of those offspring better able to survive and leave offspring. (p. 185)	*From 9–12 Benchmarks:* • Natural selection provides the following mechanism for evolution: Some variation in heritable characteristics exists within every species; some of these characteristics give individuals an advantage over others in surviving and reproducing; and the advantaged offspring, in turn, are more likely than others to survive and reproduce. As a result, the proportion of individuals that have advantageous characteristics will increase. (p. 125) • Heritable characteristics can be observed at molecular and whole-organism levels—in structure, chemistry, or behavior. These characteristics strongly influence what capabilities an organism will have and how it will react, and therefore influence how likely it is to survive and reproduce. (p. 125) • Natural selection leads to organisms that are well suited for survival in particular environments.... When an environment changes, the survival value of some inherited characteristics may change. (p. 125)
	Previous Conceptual Learning	*From middle grade NSES:* • The number of organisms an ecosystem can support depends on the resources available and abiotic factors, such as quantity of light and water, range of temperatures, and soil composition. Given adequate biotic and abiotic resources and no disease or predators, populations (including humans) increase at rapid rates. Lack of resources and other factors, such as predation and climate, limit the growth of populations in specific niches in the ecosystem. (p. 158) • Biological evolution accounts for the diversity of species developed through gradual processes over many generations. Species acquire many of their unique characteristics through biological adaptation, which involves the selection of naturally occurring variations in populations. Biological adaptations include changes in structures, behaviors, or physiology that enhance survival and reproductive success in a particular environment. (p. 158)	*From middle grade Benchmarks:* • In all environments...organisms with similar needs may compete with one another for resources, including food, space, water, air, and shelter. In any particular environment, the growth and survival of organisms depend on physical conditions. (p. 117) • Individual organisms with certain traits are more likely than others to survive and have offspring. Changes in environmental conditions can affect the survival of individual organisms and entire species. (p. 124) (*Note:* The focus at the 9–12 level shifts from selection of individuals to changing proportions of a trait in populations.)

Hard-to-Teach Biology Concepts

Table 5.1 (continued)

<table>
<tr>
<td rowspan="5">Conceptual Target Development (cont.)</td>
<td>Previous Conceptual Learning (cont.)</td>
<td>From prior instruction in the biology course: DNA as a source of continuity of traits between generations and variation that can arise; meiosis, sexual reproduction, and mutations as sources of variation; artificial selection and pedigrees; diversity and relatedness of species; evolution as the historical change in life forms; and evidence of evolution including an understanding of how fossils form</td>
</tr>
<tr>
<td>Knowledge and Skills</td>
<td>Essential knowledge: See Learning Targets #1–#4 and unpack for embedded knowledge.
Subtopics that may be pruned: reproductive isolation, gradualism, adaptive radiation
Essential vocabulary: variation, heritability, fitness, gene pool
Vocabulary that may be pruned: N/A</td>
</tr>
<tr>
<td>Essential Understandings</td>
<td>Natural selection is the most important mechanism for evolutionary change in populations and in the development of species. It occurs because (1) not all offspring in a population survive due to competition for limited resources, (2) there is heritable variation among the members of the population, and (3) some of these variations give a survival advantage to the individuals that have those traits. As a result, survivors tend to produce more viable offspring who inherit the advantage, passing it on and increasing the frequency of individuals in the population with that advantage. Because the initial three conditions exist in nature at all times, populations almost always undergo adaptive change to the environment.</td>
</tr>
<tr>
<td colspan="2" align="center">Learning Sequence Targets</td>
</tr>
<tr>
<td>Learning Target #1</td>
<td>Populations produce more offspring than can survive. Individuals in the population are not identical, in part because their genetic material varies. Because it varies, their physical characteristics (including chemical, physical, and behavioral traits) also vary. As a result, individual survival is not random, because some individuals are better at competing due to these random variations.</td>
</tr>
<tr>
<td colspan="2"></td>
<td></td>
</tr>
</table>

<table>
<tr>
<td>Learning Target #2</td>
<td>Some traits provide an advantage, and individuals with these traits are more likely to survive and reproduce. If their offspring survive, these individuals pass on their traits/alleles. Natural selection affects only heritable traits, and only individuals are selected.</td>
</tr>
<tr>
<td>Learning Target #3</td>
<td>While individuals are selected, populations evolve. They change over time as the percentage of advantageous traits (alleles) increases (changes to the gene pool).</td>
</tr>
<tr>
<td>Learning Target #4</td>
<td>Natural selection adapts a population to an environment. If an environment changes or mutations occur, the gene pool of the population changes.</td>
</tr>
<tr>
<td>Criteria to Demonstrate Understanding</td>
<td>
<ul>
<li>Accurately describe the relationship among population growth, resource availability, genetic variations in a population, and individual survival.</li>
<li>Evaluate the importance of certain traits to individual survival and heritability in particular environments.</li>
<li>Make sense of changes to a gene pool over time.</li>
<li>Predict the impact of a changing environment or a mutation on a population and provide reasoning for this prediction, using the basic concepts of natural selection.</li>
<li>Carefully distinguish between experimental observations and inferences made about natural selection (NOS focus)</li>
<li>Objectively consider a personal claim based on evidence and generate alternative claims based on the same evidence (metacognitive focus)</li>
</ul>
</td>
</tr>
</table>

Table 5.2

Teacher Work Template—Responsive Phase

Lesson Topic—Evolution: Natural Selection	
Identifying Student Preconceptions	A wonderful instrument to determine student preconceptions about natural selection is CINS, Concept Inventory of Natural Selection (Anderson, Fisher, and Norman. 2002). It is found at San Diego State University's Biology Lessons for Prospective and Practicing Teachers site: *www.biologylessons.sdsu.edu*. An answer key for CINS is found at *http://bioliteracy.net/Readings/Natural%20Selection%20CI.pdf*. Use of this instrument clearly defines preconceptions and measures student understandings during and after the course of instruction. Concept cartoons are also available at this site and can be used throughout the lesson to identify student preconceptions, particularly those aligned with individual Learning Targets.

Learning Sequence Targets

Learning Target #1	Populations produce more offspring than can survive. Individuals in the population are not identical, in part because their genetic material varies. Because it varies, their physical characteristics (including chemical, physical, and behavioral traits) also vary. As a result, individual survival is not random because some individuals are better at competing due to these random variations.

Research-Identified Misconceptions Addressed

- Many people think evolution means that life changes "by chance." Although some aspects of evolution are random (random mutation as a source of variation), natural selection is not random. Individuals that survive better in an environment and successfully reproduce have more offspring and that is certainly not random (University of California Berkeley n.d.).
- Students have little understanding that chance alone produces new heritable characteristics by forming new combinations of existing genes or by mutations of genes (Clough and Wood-Robinson 1985).
- Students often fail to recognize that natural selection depends on variation among individuals in a population (Haury 1996; Wescott and Cunningham 2005).

Initial Instructional Plan

Population Growth

Eliciting Preconceptions: Use concept cartoon #9 from San Diego State University's website (*www.biologylessons.sdsu.edu*).

Confronting Preconceptions: Use computer simulation (Population Explorer: *www.concord.org/resources/browse/172*) and yeast population study.

Sense Making: Write claims and explanations based on data. Compare to explanations of experts.

Variation and Differential Mortality

Eliciting Preconceptions: Select various concept cartoons from the SDSU website.

Confronting Preconceptions: Study variations in populations and the advantages of those variations during competition, using both Population Explorer (simulation) and concrete examples as students begin an investigation that continues throughout the lesson.

Sense Making: Revisit claims and revise explanations based on growing understandings.

Table 5.2 (continued)

Formative Assessment Plan (Demonstrating Understanding)

Analyze student discourse and review science notebooks, making sure that students can accurately describe the relationships among population growth, resource availability, genetic variations in a population, and individual survival.

Learning Target #2	Some traits provide an advantage, and individuals with these traits are more likely to survive and reproduce. If their offspring survive, these individuals pass on their traits/alleles. Natural selection affects only heritable traits, and only individuals are selected.

Research-Identified Misconceptions Addressed

- Students believe that transmitted characteristics are acquired during the lifetime of the organism, that individuals can adapt to a changing environment, and that these adaptations are heritable (Berthelsen 1999).
- Students often attribute new variations to an organism's need, environmental conditions, or use (NRC 1996).
- Many students believe that environmental conditions are responsible for changes in traits, that organisms develop new traits because they need them to survive, or that organisms over use or under use certain bodily organs or abilities (Bishop and Anderson 1990).
- Students struggle with the word *adaptation*. They tend to think that it is a conscious process or happens with purpose to an individual, rather than being an inadvertent change in populations over generations (AAAS 1993; Driver et al. 1994).
- Students often have Lamarckian views (individuals can adapt to environmental changes and pass adaptations on to their offspring) or teleological views (individual change out of need or desire to fulfill a future requirement) (Driver et al. 1994; Wilson et al. 2006).
- Students also have difficulties understanding that changing a population results from the survival of a few individuals that preferentially reproduce, not from the gradual change of all individuals in the population (Brumby 1979; Haury 1996).

Initial Instructional Plan

Eliciting Preconceptions: Select appropriate concept cartoons, have individual students choose their best answers, and then have groups agree on the best answer, providing rationales for their choices.

Confronting Preconceptions: Use EvoTutor (*www.evotutor.org/TutorA.html*) to have students explore the interactions of variation, heritability, and differential mortality.

Sense Making: Revise explanations related to ongoing experimentation, based on new learning. As homework, have students read "Survival of the Sneakiest" (*http://evolution.berkeley.edu/evosite/evohome.html*) and have them compare cricket "fitness" to fitness of organisms in their ongoing experimentations.

Formative Assessment Plan (Demonstrating Understanding)

Revisit concept cartoons. Have students evaluate the importance of certain traits to individual survival and heritability in particular environments.

Learning Target #3	While individuals are selected, populations evolve. They change over time as the percentage of advantageous traits (alleles) increases (changes to the gene pool).

Research-Identified Misconceptions Addressed

- Students are often unable to integrate two processes: the occurrence of new traits in a population and their effects on long-term survival. They merge them into a process in which species change over time because of environmental pressures, assuming there is gradual change over time of the traits themselves (Bishop and Anderson 1990; Haury 1996; Wescott and Cunningham 2005).

Table 5.2 (continued)

- Students often fail to consider the diversity in populations and its role in evolutionary change (Wilson, Zesaguli, and Anderson 2006). They fail to connect new variations in a population to the impact of those variations on the long-term survival of a species (NRC 1996).
- Students often struggle to understand that differential reproduction (some individuals produce more offspring than others) leads to population change. Instead they believe that individuals in a population change (NRC 1996).
- Students have difficulty relating an individual's adaptation to environment, with changes in species phenotypes occurring over a long period of time due to selection (Berthelsen 1999).

Initial Instructional Plan

Eliciting Preconceptions: Use concept cartoon #24 (*www.biologylessons.sdsu.edu*) to begin small-group discussion and share "best answers" with the class.

Confronting Preconceptions: Use EvoTutor and/or Population Explorer to focus on changes in a population versus changes in individuals.

Sense Making: Apply understanding to ongoing experimentation, revising and expanding explanations.

Formative Assessment Plan (Demonstrating Understanding)

Student explanations should include understandings of a changing gene pool over time.

Learning Target #4	Natural selection adapts a population to an environment. If an environment changes or mutations occur, the gene pool of the population changes.

Research-Identified Misconceptions Addressed

- Students often fail to consider the diversity in populations and its role in evolutionary change (Wilson, Zesaguli, and Anderson. 2006). They fail to connect new variations in a population to the impact of those variations on the long-term survival of a species (NRC 1996).
- Many people think that evolution leads to "progress" and that organisms are always getting better. Instead, some organisms have changed little over time and even those that have aren't necessarily better. What is missing here is that what was "better" once may not be in the future because fitness is tied to the environment and environments change (University of California Museum of Paleontology n.d.).

Initial Instructional Plan

Eliciting Preconceptions: Use concept cartoon #23 or #30 (*www.biologylessons.sdsu.edu*). Once again facilitate small-group and whole-class discourse.

Confronting Preconceptions: Once again use Population Explorer, but change terrains and/or introduce mutations. Students can also explore the Peppered Moth simulation.

Sense Making: Complete ongoing investigations and apply understandings of natural selection to explanations. Require students to include alternative explanations. Compare to textbooks or other text materials. Include, in these comparisons, the work of Darwin.

Formative Assessment Plan (Demonstrating Understanding)

Given a new scenario, have students predict the impact of a changing environment or a mutation on a population and provide reasoning for this prediction, using the basic concepts of natural selection. Also, administer again the CINS and determine changes in student understandings.

Table 5.3

Strategies to Teach Natural Selection

Sense-Making Strategy	Strengths of the Strategies
Concept Cartoons	• They present cognitive conflict, which motivates and challenges preconceptions. • They engage students since they require students to focus on constructing explanations for the cartoon situations. • They allow for a continuous flow of learning, with simultaneous idea-elicitation and restructuring of thinking. • They create an environment that promotes participation of all students in class discussion, activates them to support their ideas, and remedies misconceptions. • They may lessen student anxiety over offering a wrong answer. • Students are required to choose between alternative explanations, making the need for investigation evident. They can then choose an appropriate investigation, giving the teacher time to respond to students' individual needs.
Dynamic Models	• Computer simulations can enhance students' conceptual understandings, as well as improve achievement on complex concepts, more quickly than traditional instruction. Simulations help when instruction involves scientific models that are difficult or impossible to observe. They can also simplify complex systems. • They probe preconceptions and can be used individually or in small groups. • Combining computer modeling and hands-on laboratories is effective. It is also helpful to support use of dynamic models with scaffolding, including specific instructions and guiding questions. • Use of simulations can promote misconceptions unless teachers explicitly identify the limitations of the simulated model.
Concept Maps	• Mapping tools are helpful in elucidation of the difference between scientific conceptions and alternative conceptions, both for the teacher and the student. • Concept maps show relationships among concepts and are effective when working with concept-rich units. • They engage students in the content and challenge students to analyze their thinking (enhancing metacogntion). They also decrease anxiety, improve self-confidence, and promote positive attitudes. • Effective use of concept maps requires training for the teacher. It takes students about eight weeks of school to become proficient at concept mapping.
Writing Scientific Explanations	• Support for students to construct explanations results in improved understandings about inquiry, science content, and science literacy. Learning to construct explanations while learning content is hard, so teacher support is essential. • One framework for writing scientific explanations includes three components: (1) make a claim, (2) provide evidence for the claim, and (3) provide reasoning that links the claim to the evidence. • Five effective steps for the teacher to take are to (1) make the framework explicit, (2) model the construction of explanations, (3) provide a rationale for constructing explanations, (4) connect scientific explanations to everyday explanations, and (5) assess and provide feedback to students.

Table 5.3 (continued)

Sense-Making Strategy	Strengths of the Strategies
Science Notebooks	• The first goal of writing in science is to understand because writing is a tool with which to think. If students use their science notebooks during discussions, it helps them construct meaning from the science phenomena they observe. • Science notebooks focus on making sense of phenomena and give priority to evidence in responding to questions. They require students to be responsible for their learning, promoting metacognition. • One model of a guide to using science notebooks includes seven parts (focus question, prediction/hypothesis, planning, data, claims and evidence, making meaning conference, conclusion/reflection). • Active science learning that includes science notebooks is useful for assessment when (1) most of the work in the notebook is narrative and centered around authentic science tasks, (2) the notebook work is purposeful, with students investigating their own questions, (3) "right" answers or conclusions are uncommon, and (4) the notebook provides information not only to the teacher, but also to the student and possibly a parent.
Science Writing Heuristic	• The SWH positively impacts student understanding and metacognition. • It has been used in a variety of classrooms across grade levels and science disciplines, impacting learning gains. • Students identify preinstructional ideas, think about concepts during prelaboratory activities, complete a laboratory activity, share and compare data among small groups, compare ideas to those of textbooks/print resources, reflect and write, and explore postinstruction understanding. Each component is essential and requires attention by the teacher. • Instructor preparation is essential for successful integration of SWH.
Discourse	• Large- and small-group discourse can promote learning about concepts, metacognition, and understanding the NOS. Such discussions also promote positive attitudes, rapport, and equity and expectations. • Discussion improves if students discern several plausible viewpoints, promoting self-motivation and self-sustaining conversation, and resulting in students determining their own theories. Alternative viewpoints are effectively presented via concept cartoons because they create cognitive conflict. Accountable talk deepens conversation and understanding. It requires students to ask for clarification, justification, and evidence for claims and arguments. • Students build on each other's ideas as they form explanations in small groups. Whole-class discussion works best in the context of an activity in which the focus of the discussion is on shared experiences. Whole-class discourse increases demands for explanatory power of students' products and challenges students' ideas. Balancing whole-class and small-group discussions is important and reflects two types of scientific discourse (within and among laboratories). • Student-generated questions, open-ended questions, student choice of inquiry topics, and time for student research and exploration all encourage deeper discussion and investigation. Effective discussion requires students to produce an outcome as the result of discussion. Carefully selected materials for students focus discussion and decision-making.

Table 5.3 (continued)

Standards-Based Strategy	Strengths of the Strategies
Formulate Explanations From Evidence	• Learning increases if students think about how evidence supports or does not support their personal theories. But we cannot assume students know how to write explanations. They need explicit instruction, especially with evidence and reasoning (less with writing a claim). Teachers should provide specific definitions and examples of what is meant by claim and evidence. Student discussion of what students think evidence means is a productive strategy. • It is important to (1) make the framework (claim, evidence, and reasoning) explicit, (2) model and critique explanations, (3) provide a rationale for creating explanations, (4) connect scientific to everyday explanations, and (5) assess and provide feedback to students. • Students can improve in this area of inquiry if they are given raw data and primary sources from which to develop explanations. Reading, discussion, and research are also beneficial. It is important to model and critique explanations, in written or verbal form. • Producing new science knowledge requires a balance of interpretation and argumentation that includes the following strategies: (1) conjectures are made (or presented as in concept cartoons), (2) relevance of facts and information is judged, (3) evidence and counterevidence is found for each conjecture, and (4) the sufficiency and coherence of evidence is assessed. • Concept cartoons can focus argumentation and discussion, provide a safe environment, and sharpen the conceptual and metacognitive focuses during argumentation.
Connect Explanations to Scientific Knowledge	• "Alternative explanations may be reviewed as students engage in dialogues, compare results, or check their results with those proposed by the teacher or instructional materials" (NRC 2000, p. 27). It is important to make sure students connect their results with currently accepted scientific knowledge appropriate to their developmental level. Well-structured materials that make evidence for scientific theories apparent are necessary. • We must provide specific definitions and examples of what is meant by "reasoning." Specific discussions are required so students understand the need to write the underlying scientific principle used to select their evidence.

Recommended Resources
Technology Applications and Websites

• Population Explorer (*www.concord.org/resources/browse/172*) is a powerful simulation. In addition, you can download the Concord Consortium newsletter article software at *www.concord.org/publications/newsletter/2005-fall/thursday.html*, which outlines how to use Population Explorer.

• EvoTutor includes a set of simulations about evolution (*www.evotutor.org*).

• On evolution, see this rich site developed by PBS (*www.pbs.org/wgbh/evolution*), with an evolution library, as well as links for teachers and students that include case studies, lessons, and videos. It also includes information on Darwin.

- The Virtual Fossil Museum (*www.fossilmuseum.net/Evolution/Darwin.htm*) is a good site for information on Darwin.

- Understanding Evolution for Teachers (*http://evolution.berkeley.edu*) is a rich site that includes misconceptions, lessons, Evolution 101, and a link to information on Darwin.

- Harvard University's Evolution links (*http://golgi.harvard.edu/biopages/evolution.html*) include, among other things, general resources and software.

- Don't miss the AIBS article on natural selection (*www.actionbioscience.org/evolution/futuyma.html*), which includes a wonderful interview with Douglas Futuyma on natural selection and an amazing set of links to other resources.

Build Your Library

These three resources can support your teaching of evolution.

- Biological Sciences Curriculum Study (BSCS). 2005. *The nature of science and the study of biological evolution.* Arlington VA: NSTA Press.

- Bybee, R. W., ed. 2004. *Evolution in perspective: The science teacher's compendium.* Arlington, VA: NSTA Press.

- National Academy of Sciences. 1998. *Teaching about evolution and the nature of science.* Washington, DC: National Academy Press.

Endnote

1. The same resources used in previous chapters were used to determine appropriate standards; prior understandings; knowledge, skills, and vocabulary to include or exclude; and the Learning Targets.

Instructional Planning Framework

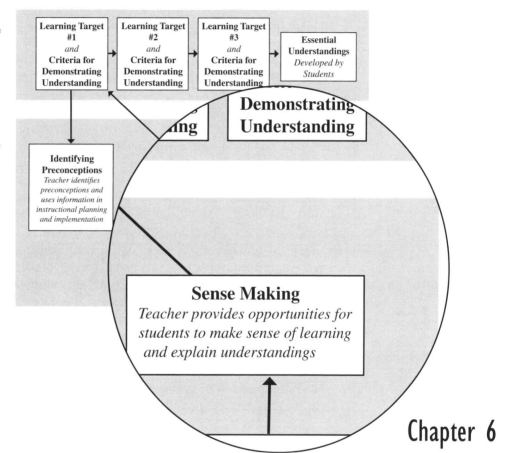

Predictive Phase
The teacher determines the lesson's essential understandings, the sequence of learning targets that lead toward those understandings, and the criteria by which understanding is determined.

Responsive Phase
Building on the foundation of the predictive phase, the teacher plans for and implements instruction during the responsive phase, one learning target at a time.

Learning Target #1
and
Criteria for Demonstrating Understanding

Learning Target #2
and
Criteria for Demonstrating Understanding

Learning Target #3
and
Criteria for Demonstrating Understanding

Essential Understandings
Developed by Students

Demonstrating Understanding

Identifying Preconceptions
Teacher identifies preconceptions and uses information in instructional planning and implementation

Sense Making
Teacher provides opportunities for students to make sense of learning and explain understandings

Chapter 6

Molecular Genetics: Proteins and Genes

"Because molecular biology will continue into the twenty-first century as a major frontier of science, students should understand the chemical basis of life not only for its own sake, but because of the need to take informed positions on some of the practical and ethical implications of humankind's capacity to manipulate living organisms."

—*National Research Council 1996, p. 181*

Why This Topic?

At the same time that the media are filled with commentary about stem-cell research, gene therapy, and genetic modification of foods, few people understand the relationship between gene function, the production of proteins, and phenotype—a relationship essential to understanding each of those issues. Molecular genetics is a topic likely to have an immediate effect on and direct relevance to students' lives in the 21st century, yet traditional teaching methods are not adequate to motivate and educate students about that topic (Eklund et al. 2007; Sinan, Aydin, and Gezer 2007).

Genetics is a difficult topic to understand (Bahar, Johnstone, and Hansell 1999; Mertens and Walker 1992) for a variety of reasons, including that students must integrate information from multiple levels of biological organization (Bahar, Johnstone, and Hansell 1999; Duncan and Reiser 2003; Kindfield 1994; Lewis and Wood-Robinson 2000). This is also the problem when it comes to the molecular basis of heredity because students must connect what happens at the molecular level during transcription and translation to the resulting cellular proteins and they must understand how that impacts the appearance and function of cells, tissues, and organisms.

These difficulties are compounded by the common approach to teaching genetics—that is, Mendelian inheritance is taught before DNA, and DNA is unconnected to the actions of proteins (Roseman et al. 2006). Also, passive instruction using lecture and textbooks, typical for this topic, relies on abstract, complex figures and chemical formulas, posing difficulties for typical high school students (Rotbain, Marbach-Ad, and Stavy 2005). Finally, "this area of science is moving so quickly that the majority of us lack appropriate content training" (Texley and Wild 2004, p. 89).

Overview

In this chapter, we focus conceptually on the connection between genotype and phenotype, specifically the role of genes and proteins in that connection. We also consider the importance of proteins to the work of cells and the impact of proteins on the structures

Topic: Factors affecting population growth
Go to: *www.scilinks.org*
Code: HTB007

Topic: Genotypes
Go to: *www.scilinks.org*
Code: HTB008

Topic: Phenotypes
Go to: *www.scilinks.org*
Code: HTB009

and functions of organisms. We do not cover the details of transcription and translation but, instead, stress the importance of the process in the production of proteins essential to life. Nor will we discuss regulation of gene expression. In terms of the Instructional Planning Framework, our focus is on *sense making* and *demonstrating understanding*. (*Note:* All tables are grouped together at the end of the chapter, beginning on p. 183. They are followed by Recommended Resources and Endnotes.)

At this point, meet Mr. Adams, a teacher who has tried in many ways to improve his instruction yet is met with less than adequate student understanding (Figure 6.1). We'll use Mr. Adams's context as we delve into the biological content of this chapter and sense making and demonstrating understanding.

Figure 6.1

Case Study About Protein Synthesis Instruction

Mr. Adams worked for years to improve his students' understandings about protein synthesis. He took a course on technologies appropriate to molecular genetics, attended a workshop on multiple intelligences, and learned through district professional development about cooperative learning and reading in the content area. He even completed a graduate degree with a focus on molecular biology. In his classroom, he used a good combination of interactive lectures and hands-on experiences. His students completed activities that included laboratory-based activities and simulations. He thought he understood what his students knew and the things that were most difficult for them. But regardless of his attempts, they still struggled to understand the central importance of protein synthesis. What might be the problem?

Instructional Planning Framework: *Predictive Phase*

We limit coverage of the *predictive phase* in this chapter to its application in a lesson about molecular genetics. First though, we revisit *Science for All Americans* to remember our end target, the expectations for adult science literacy (Figure 6.2).

Figure 6.2

Adult Science Literacy Expectations for Molecular Genetics

"The work of the cell is carried out by the many different types of molecules it assembles, mostly proteins. Protein molecules are long, usually folded chains made from 20 different kinds of amino acid molecules. The function of each protein depends on its specific sequence of amino acids and the shape the chain takes as a consequence of attractions between the chain's parts. Some of the assembled molecules assist in replicating genetic information, repairing cell structures, helping other molecules to get in or out of the cell, and generally in catalyzing and regulating molecular interactions. In specialized cells, other protein molecules may carry oxygen, effect contraction, respond to outside stimuli, or provide material for hair, nails, and other body structures. In still other cells, assembled molecules may be exported to serve as hormones, antibodies, or digestive enzymes.

"The genetic information encoded in DNA molecules provides instructions for assembling protein molecules. This code is virtually the same for all life forms. Thus, for example, if a gene from a human cell is placed in a bacterium, the chemical machinery of the bacterium will follow the gene's instructions and produce the same protein that would be produced in human cells. A change in even a single atom in the DNA molecule, which may be induced by chemicals or radiation, can therefore change the protein that is produced. Such a mutation of a DNA segment may not make much difference, may fatally disrupt the operation of the cell, or may change the successful operation of the cell in a significant way (for example, it may foster uncontrolled replication, as in cancer)." (AAAS 1989, pp. 63–64)

Using these expectations of adult science literacy as our ultimate goal, we use the procedures outlined in Chapter 3 to determine the conceptual targets, a logical learning progression, and the criteria to demonstrate understanding (Figure 6.3).[1]

Figure 6.3

Planning in the Predictive Phase

1. Identify the essential understandings for the lesson.
    a. Begin with the descriptions of adult literacy to determine an anchor goal.
    b. Consider the middle school and high school standards and benchmarks.
    c. Optional: Study existing research on learning progressions. A good resource (*www. project2061.org/publications/2061Connections/2007/2007-04a-resources.htm*) is found in the 2061 Connections online newsletter (AAAS 2007a).
    d. Dig a bit deeper and think about the concepts included in the standards.
    e. Decide what is essential and what can be pruned.
2. Develop a logical sequence of learning targets for the lesson.
    a. Consider the middle school science experiences students should have had.
    b. Outline the key ideas embedded in the high school standards and benchmarks.
    c. Sequence the key ideas in a way to build student understanding.
    d. Consider connections from one lesson to the next.
3. Identify the criteria for demonstrating understanding. (*Note:* Steps b and c are completed later, after a review of research.)
    a. Identify one criterion for each Learning Target.
    b. Identify one criterion for your selected standards-based strategy (Inquiry, HOS, or NOS).
    c. Identify one criterion for your selected metacognitive strategy

The work completed during the process in Figure 6.3 was added to the Teacher Work Template (Table 6.1, p. 183) for the topic "proteins and genes." This template lays the foundation for this lesson. Also review the learning sequence and how it leads to the essential understandings for this topic during the *responsive phase* (see Figure 6.4).

Figure 6.4

Proteins and Genes Learning Sequence

| **Target #1:** Proteins carry out the major work of cells and are responsible for both the structures and functions of organisms. An organism's traits (phenotype) are a reflection of the work of proteins. | **Target #2:** Genetic information (genes) coded in DNA provides the information necessary to assemble proteins. The sequence of subunits (nucleotides) in DNA determines the sequence of amino acids in proteins. | **Target #3:** The sequence of amino acids determines not only the kind, but also the shape of the protein, and thus its function. | **Target #4:** Mutations, changes in the DNA, impact protein production. Errors in the DNA (mutation) can result in missing proteins or ones that function inadequately. This results in a change in phenotype/trait. |

Essential Understandings: Proteins carry out the major work of cells but, if they are not made properly, cell function can be affected. Changes (mutations) in the gene/DNA can impact not only the code but also the protein, cells, and tissues. Though some mutations can be helpful, they might also stop or limit the protein's ability to function and potentially lead to physiological disorder in the organism.

Reflection and Application

We have implemented the *predictive phase* process (Figure 6.3) in Chapters 4, 5, and this one. Reflect, once again, about this process as related to "proteins and genes."

1. How have you taught this topic in the past?
2. In what ways does your past instruction align with the work in the *predictive phase* for this topic? In what ways is it different?
3. Are there changes you might make in your instruction based on this information?

Instructional Planning Framework: *Responsive Phase*

Identifying, Eliciting, and Confronting Preconceptions

Recall that in Chapter 4 we focused on how to learn about research-identified student misconceptions (also see Figure 6.5). The Instructional Tools on pages 33–87 show how to select appropriate strategies to determine our own students' preconceptions. In Chapter 5, we built on the Chapter 4 example of identifying strategies to elicit and confront student preconceptions (steps #4–#10 in Figure 6.5). We completed all of the steps outlined in Figure 6.4, and added them to the Teacher Workshop Template (Table 6.1 on p. 183) for the topic "proteins and genes.

Figure 6.5

Planning in the Responsive Phase

Learn About Research-Identified Misconceptions

1. Review *Benchmarks for Science Literacy* (AAAS 1993) for misconceptions discussed there. Chapter 15 of the book includes research findings organized by benchmark. If you do not have a copy of the book, you can read the book online at *www.project2061.org/ publications/bsl/online/ index.php?txtRef=&txtURIOld=%2Fpublications%2Fbsl%2Fonline %2Findex.*

2. Complete a web search for misconceptions on the selected topic. Simply run a search for your topic and misconceptions (e.g., "photosynthesis + misconceptions"). If you run your search at Google Scholar (*http://scholar.google.com*), you will gain access to numerous resources. In some cases you will only access the abstract, but in others you will find the entire document. This process is more time-consuming than step #1 but yields additional resources.

3. This step is the most direct way to access a summary of misconceptions, but it requires that you have a copy of *Making Sense of Secondary Science: Research into Children's Ideas* (Driver et al. 1994). The book is outlined by topic and provides a rich summary of research on children's ideas about these topics.

Strategy Selection: Identify, Elicit, and Confront Preconceptions

4. Use the Instructional Strategy Sequencing Tool in Chapter 2, page 29, to identify possible strategies to identify student preconceptions, as well as strategies to elicit and confront those preconceptions. Finally, identify metacognitive and standards-based strategies to review.

5. In Chapter 2 find the strategies in the three Metacognitive Strategy Tools (Instructional Tools 2.2–2.4), the three Standards-Based Strategy Tools (Instructional Tools 2.5–2.7), and the seven Sense-Making Strategy Tools (Instructional Tools 2.8–2.14).

6. Carefully review the research and application recommendations for each of the identified strategies.

7. Determine several strategies that fit well with the particular content you are teaching.

8. Select one metacognitive strategy, one standards-based strategy, and two or three sense-making strategies for use in your lesson (recall that these will be used to differentiate instruction and to provide further instruction if formative assessments indicate that students do not understand the learning targets.

9. Determine one criterion to demonstrate understanding for each of your metacognitive and standards-based focuses. Add these to the existing criteria in the Teacher Work Template.

10. Review the resources listed in the Instructional Tools to more fully understand the strategies and to determine what they might look like in application.

It is important that you study the completed Teacher Work Template (Table 6.1, p. 183). It shows the foundation for our upcoming work, for the selection of strategies that will help students make sense of their experiences, and for helping us understand what our students have really learned from the experiences.

Before proceeding to our discussions of sense making and demonstrating understanding, we share some information related to proteins and genes that we found during our review of the research. Here are the keys ideas:

- Student understanding of proteins, genes, the connection between them, and genomes all increased when teachers did the following: integrated proteins into the same context as genes; introduced the importance of proteins before introducing genes; and scaffolded students' written explanations of a trait at the levels of gene, protein, cell, tissue, and organisms (Eklund et al. 2007).
- Students' limited understanding of the specific contexts at the cellular, tissue, and whole organism levels may be a reason students struggle to make a connection between protein and trait. The examples teachers use should be simple and familiar to students. In addition, activities should be spread throughout the lesson not just used at the end of the lesson (Eklund et al. 2007).
- Lewis and Kattmann (2004) recommend using sickle-cell anemia as an example that links the gene, the structure/function of the gene product, and the resulting phenotype. Other research recommends that the teacher cover a number of different disease traits as well as nondisease traits to provide context (Eklund et al. 2007).
- Attention should be paid to confusing terms (*proteins* and *amino acids*, *gene*, *mutation*) but not to unnecessary words (*transcription* and *translation*) (Eklund et al. 2007).

Reflection and Application

Take a moment to reflect on the process of identifying, eliciting, and confronting preconceptions for "proteins and genes."

1. We identified "proteins and genes" as a hard-to-teach topic. What, in your opinion, makes it hard-to teach?
2. Based on the research we summarized in the bullet list above and in Table 6.1, what might you do differently in your current lesson on proteins and genes?
3. How well would the strategies work in your classroom? Would you need to modify them to work in your context? If so, what might you do?

Sense Making: Strategies to Address Preconceptions

We looked briefly at sense making in Chapter 5, but we are now ready to more clearly define how to select and implement sense-making strategies. This is the primary focus of this chapter. We also look at how students demonstrate understanding through formative assessments and how we can use those assessments to inform instruction. It is here that we also consider the iterative nature of the *responsive phase* of the Instructional Planning Framework.

First, what do we mean by *sense making*? Eliciting and confronting students' preconceptions will not, by itself, promote conceptual understanding. Effective instruction requires that students make sense of the ideas with which they grapple, connecting what they already understand with the learning intent of the lesson, linking the ideas to the larger scientific body of knowledge, organizing that knowledge, and applying the ideas to new contexts. It is not likely that students will make all these connections by themselves, so it is important that teachers facilitate this process (Banilower et al. 2008). Sense making should occur throughout the lesson, even as teachers elicit and confront student preconceptions. The lesson in this chapter uses teacher questioning, group discussions, student reflection, and more.

However, our lesson on proteins and genes (as we have developed it so far in this chapter) does not yet require interactive activities followed by sense making. Recall our case study of Mr. Adams's biology class. His instruction, similar to our lesson so far, does not include adequate opportunities for student sense making. We need to consider strategies that will help Mr. Adams and other teachers like him to introduce sense making effectively.

We use the same process to identify effective sense-making and formative assessment strategies that we did to identify strategies to elicit and confront preconceptions (see Figure 6.5, steps #4–#7). Step #4 asks you to look at the Instructional Strategy Sequencing Tool (Instructional Tool 2.1, p. 29). Take a moment to review this tool once again. In that tool, under "Sense Making," you will find the following four categories:

1. Perceiving, interpreting, and organizing information
2. Connecting information
3. Retrieving, extending, and applying information
4. Using knowledge in relevant ways

These categories support sense making. It is from these categories that teachers should select strategies. And, we suggest, the further teachers move through the instructional learning sequence, the more they should move to the right among those four categories

Demonstrating Understanding

In this sample approach to the topic and the application of the Instructional Planning Framework, we need to determine the best formative assessments. We must also consider the iterative nature of the *responsive phase*. Up to this point in the book we have modeled the process of *planning* for instruction. Now we need to think about how formative assessments might inform our *actual implementation of the plan*. What if our formative assessments during Learning Target #1 in Table 6.1, page 186, indicate that students just didn't "get it" or understood part of the concept but not all? Instead of a linear path through the lesson—charging ahead because we constructed the lesson in

Figure 6.6

Planned Learning Sequence

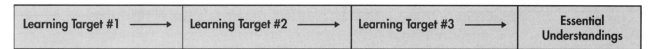

Implemented Learning Sequence

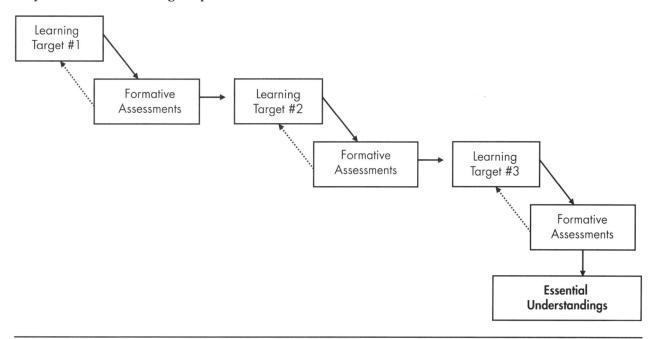

that way—we need to give students other experiences with the same content so that they have additional opportunities to learn.

What does it look like when we "double back" in our lesson? Take a look at Figure 6.6. Notice the "planned learning sequence," similar to the one in our Instructional Planning Framework (Figure 1.1, p. 6). It is linear in nature and appears quite predictable. However, as teachers know, things are not always so clear-cut during implementation. Now, refer to the "implemented learning sequence." The formative assessments might indicate a need to provide additional instruction for some or all of the concepts for the Learning Target. On the other hand, it is possible that we could proceed directly from the formative assessments to Learning Target #2 if students demonstrate clear understanding of Learning Target #1. This is true for each of the learning targets and demonstrates the iterative nature of the responsive phase of our framework.

Sense Making and Demonstrating Understanding for the Learning Targets

Now we are ready to determine the best sense-making strategies for each learning target. Review the sense-making strategies in Instructional Strategy Sequencing Tool 2.1 (p. 29), both linguistic and nonlinguistic representations, and consider which best suit this lesson. It is important to keep in mind that the strategies and activities chosen for Learning Target #1 (student research using text and web resources) are likely to be quite different from those used in Learning Targets #2–#4 (using and interpreting dynamic models).

Learning Target #1 (Table 6.1, p. 185)

It is appropriate to focus on linguistic representations for this learning target because we chose to elicit and confront student preconceptions in ways that require students to read for information (as well as comprehension) as they research a particular disorder. Linguistic representations should help support students' reading, the organization of their thinking as they read and gather information, and the representation of their understanding when they present, in some way, what they have learned. Our chosen sense-making activities employ individual learning logs with four components:

1. Two-column notes (an informational text strategy for active reading that students use as they research their topics. See *http://printables.familyeducation.com/ skill-builder/graphic-organizers/51680.html.*
2. Tree maps (a thinking-process map) to help students sort their information into various organizational levels and consider how each level is impacted
3. Individual reflections on the reading and writing processes, students' emerging content understandings, and any questions they have
4. Individual written explanations to summarize students' understanding of how their disorder impacts the various levels of organization in the human system

Small groups then share and critique their individual summaries from their learning logs, discuss their findings, and summarize their thinking as a group. They then prepare a poster to share with the class, describing what they learned. Posters are hung around the room and used in a round-robin session during which student groups visit other posters to critique, look for similarities and differences among the posters, and pose questions. Finally, the teacher facilitates a class discussion that summarizes the thinking and generates questions, making a record of thinking on poster paper or a SmartBoard. Summarizations and questions are retained for ongoing thinking throughout the lesson.

The selected sense-making strategies also serve nicely as formative assessments. Two-column notes, learning logs, and tree maps are reviewed to determine students' understandings. The teacher provides comments in student journals that are designed to provoke further thinking, work, and learning. Questions and probes during student group work also further student understanding and inform the teacher about student conceptions. Student posters and presentations are assessed for clarity and accuracy, and poster presentations allow teachers and peers to probe student thinking and assess understanding.

Remember that though we outline the assessments separately to bring them to your attention, they occur as close to the sense-making experience as possible, and in the case of questioning and probes, they occur concurrently. These "in the moment" assessments continually probe student understandings and provide information to modify instruction, as needed. In addition, as students become more self-aware during the sense-making process, self-reflection and peer assessments deepen understanding. The close interactions of sense making, reflection, and formative assessment are essential to the learner-centered, knowledge-centered, and assessment-centered classroom that establishes a community of science learners (Bransford, Brown, and Cocking 1999).

But what happens if students are unable to demonstrate understanding? What if students have a pretty good understanding about the diverse and robust roles of proteins in cells but struggle a bit to clearly link the role of proteins at the various levels of organization, resulting in the phenotype? What might now be done to provide additional instructional support?

We recommend that if the majority of students are still struggling with the concepts that you explicitly walk through the research process as a whole-class activity, using a disorder not previously studied by a student group. First, demonstrate to the class, using a think-aloud approach, how you would extract information from selected text and organize that information in an appropriate graphic organizer. Then give each small group text (or links to websites) that addresses the impact of the disorder at a different level of organization. After students read the text individually, they discuss the text in their small groups. The teacher then facilitates whole-class mapping using small-group input. This round of sense making models for students the use of informational text to perceive and organize information. It also demonstrates how to use concept mapping to organize and connect information. Students then can revisit their work on the original assigned trait, modifying their explanations. Thus, they extend and apply what they have just learned.

What happens if most of the students understand the basic ideas but a portion of students are still struggling to understand them? For those students who have mastered the basic ideas, we suggest that they work with the Concord Consortium materials (*www.concord.org/resources/browse/172*). This resource is rich with interactive experiences, and students should be able to explore further on their own without intensive teacher support. The teacher is then free to work with the small group of students who do not yet understand the basic ideas. The teacher probes their thinking, perhaps using more-structured graphic organizers and reading extracts or simply has a small-group discussion to clarify ideas.

Reflection and Application

Before proceeding to the next learning targets, let's consider the process we just used and reflect on its application in your context. See Figure 6.7 and review Learning Target #1 in Table 6.1, page 185.

1. What about this iterative process makes sense to you? What works easily in your context?
2. What about this process makes your instruction difficult and why?
3. If challenges exist, how would you overcome those challenges?

Figure 6.7

Finalizing the Process to Promote Understanding

Use these steps to select and implement sense making and formative assessment strategies.

Strategy Selection
1. As before, review the Instructional Strategy Sequencing Tool (Instructional Tool 2.1, p. 29) to identify strategies for sense making, including
   a. perceiving, interpreting, and organizing information,
   b. connecting information,
   c. retrieving, extending, and applying information, and
   d. using knowledge in relevant ways.
2. Also review Instructional Tool 2.1 for potential formative assessment strategies.

Strategy Implementation
3. Implement the selected strategies for sense making in Instructional Tool 2.1 and gather data using the formative assessment strategies for a learning target.
4. If formative assessments indicate that all students understand the concepts, move forward with the next learning target.
5. If they do not understanding the ideas, then
   a. use a different strategy to provide additional learning experiences for the students or
   b. extend the learning for students who demonstrate understanding and provide additional small-group and/or individualized instruction for those who still struggle to understand.

Learning Targets #2–#4 (Table 6.1, pp. 186–188)

Learning Targets #2–#4 have several things in common. They all benefit from the use of dynamic modeling, primarily because dynamic models are effective for teaching abstract concepts and complex systems and connecting what happens at the submicroscopic and macroscopic levels (Calwetti 1999; Trunfio et al. 2003). Clearly, dynamic models will be helpful when you are teaching "genes and proteins." Also, remember that we use expressed models to help our students develop mental models that align with scientific models.

What sense-making activities support the use of models? And what are some key, research-based ideas to keep in mind as we select strategies? Here are some important research findings to remember (see Instructional Tool 2.9 on p. 66 for a complete list of ideas):

- Conceptual development is enhanced if students are able to construct and critique their own models (Hipkins et al. 2002).
- Students who receive instructions and guiding questions along with a model better understand molecular genetics (Rotbain, Marbach-Ad, and Stavy 2005).
- An interactive dynamic model combined with scaffolding improves students' abilities to explain human inheritance and evolutionary phenomena, connecting their ideas about phenotypes, chromosomes, and gametes (Schwendimann 2008).
- Simulations can promote misconceptions unless teachers work explicitly with students to identify limitations of the models (Calwetti 1999).
- Teachers should model scientific modeling to their students, encourage the use of multiple models in science lessons, and encourage negotiation of model meanings. Systematic presentation of in-class models using the Focus, Action, and Reflection (FAR) Guide to socially negotiate model meanings is effective (Harrison and Treagust 2000).

We recommend the following sense-making strategies to address these ideas:

- Written explanations that interpret dynamic models and text
- Group concept mapping that translates student experiences with the dynamic model into students' own mental and written models
- Large- and small-group discourse to interpret and apply interactions with the models
- Comparison of interactive models and student concept maps with text (scientific explanations)
- Creating and critiquing analogies to extend and apply mental models, using the FAR Guide.[2]

In addition, Learning Target #4 requires students to make predictions (claims) about mutations, gather evidence using a protein folding interactive developed by the Concord Consortium, and use this evidence to further explain the impact of their chosen disorders. The development, critique, and support of these explanations address both "retrieving, extending and applying information" and "using knowledge in relevant ways" (as cited in Instructional Strategy Sequencing Tool 2.1).

As we consider ways for students to demonstrate understanding, we recall that the sense-making activities for Learning Targets #2–#4 include embedded formative assessments. In addition, student explanations in Learning Target #4 can be reviewed and critiqued by you, other students, and the students themselves. Critique of explanations is most effective when clear targets and rubrics that include the criteria for success are made available before instruction. Sutherland, McNeill, and Krajcik (2006) propose that the components of the rubric include a critique of the claim (that it responds to the question asked or problem posed), the evidence (that scientific data are used to provide support for the claim), and the reasoning (that students use scientific principles to explain why the data provide evidence to support the claim). Keeley (2008) describes a formative assessment strategy, "Explanation Analysis," that builds on this thinking. It is an appropriate strategy because we expect students to develop quality scientific explanations.

Study Table 6.1, pages 186–188, to see how we apply the information in the table to sense making and demonstrating understanding for Learning Targets #2–4.

***

Chapter 6 has used "proteins and genes" as the context for focusing on aspects of the *responsive phase*, primarily on sense making. We considered how to select and implement formative assessments and demonstrated how these assessment data inform ongoing instruction. For the first time, we modeled the iterative nature of the *responsive phase*. Our chapter-by-chapter approach to modeling the implementation of our Instructional Planning Framework is now complete. In Chapter 7 we walk through the entire process, letting you see its application in full.

Table 6.1

Teacher Work Template for "Molecular Genetics: Proteins and Genes"

Lesson Topic—Molecular Genetics: Proteins and Genes			
Predictive Phase			
Conceptual Target Development	**National Standard(s) Addressed**	*From 9–12 NSES:* • Cells store and use information to guide their functions. The genetic information stored in DNA is used to direct the synthesis of the thousands of proteins that each cell requires. (p. 184) • In all organisms, the instructions for specifying the characteristics of the organism are carried in DNA, a large polymer formed from subunits of four kinds (A, G, C, and T). The chemical and structural properties of DNA explain how the genetic information that underlies heredity is both encoded in genes (as a string of molecular "letters") and replicated (by a templating mechanism). Each DNA molecule in a cell forms a single chromosome. (p. 185)	*From 9–12 Benchmarks:* • The work of the cell is carried out by the many different types of molecules it assembles, mostly proteins. Protein molecules are long, usually folded chains made from 20 different kinds of amino-acid molecules. The function of each protein molecule depends on its specific sequence of amino acids and its shape. The shape of the chain is a consequence of attractions between its parts. (p.114) • The genetic information encoded in DNA molecules provides instructions for assembling protein molecules. (p. 114)
	Previous Conceptual Learning	*From middle grade NSES:* Cells carry on the many functions needed to sustain life. They grow and divide, thereby producing more cells. This requires that they take in nutrients, which they use to provide energy for the work that cells do and to make the materials that a cell or an organism needs. (p. 156)	*From middle grade Benchmarks:* Within cells, many of the basic functions of organisms...are carried out. The way in which cells function is similar in all living organisms. (p. 112)
		From prior instruction in the biology course: *NSES:* In all organisms, the instructions for specifying the characteristics of the organism are carried in DNA, a large polymer formed from subunits of four kinds (A, G, C, and T). The chemical and structural properties of DNA explain how the genetic information that underlies heredity is both encoded in genes (as a string of molecular "letters") and replicated (by a templating mechanism). Each DNA molecule in a cell forms a single chromosome. *Benchmarks:* Within the cells are specialized parts for the transport of materials, energy capture and release, protein building, waste disposal, passing information, and even movement.	

Table 6.1 (continued)

Conceptual Target Development (cont.)	**Knowledge and Skills**	**Essential knowledge:** *See Learning Targets #1–#4 and unpack for embedded knowledge.* **Subtopics that may be pruned:** • Specific descriptions of how proteins function (e.g., enzyme catalysis, muscle contraction) • Details about transcription and translation • Names and structures of nucleotides • RNA and its structure • Primary, secondary, and tertiary structure of proteins • Differentiation between hydrophobic and hydrophilic amino acids. • Peptides and peptide bonds • Nucleic acids and nucleotides • Transcription and translation **Essential vocabulary:** *protein, amino acid, gene, code, phenotype/trait. Nucleotide, if used, should be followed by "a subunit of DNA."* **Vocabulary that may be pruned:** *peptide bond, polymer, ribosome, adenine, guanine, thymine, cytosine, purines, pyramidines, ribonucleic acid, phosphate group, ribose, messenger RNA, transfer RNA, ribosomal RNA, codon*
Essential Understandings		Proteins carry out the major work of cells but, if proteins are not made properly, cell function can be affected. Changes (mutations) in the gene/DNA can impact not only the code but also the protein, cells, and tissues. Though some mutations can be helpful, they might also stop or limit the proteins' ability to function and potentially lead to physiological disorder in the organism.
Criteria to Demonstrate Understanding		• Describe the central role of proteins and link the action of a particular protein across levels of organization (cell, tissue, organ, organism), explaining how an organism's phenotype reflects the work of the protein. • Model how DNA coding determines the sequence of amino acids in a protein. • Illustrate how amino acid sequence determines the shape of a protein and correlate protein shape and function. • Determine the impact of a mutation on a phenotype/trait, including a discussion of the protein's role in the process. • Make connections between personal explanations based on a protein synthesis simulation and scientific explanations of the process (standards-based focus). • Be open to others' ideas to establish thinking about proteins and genes (metacognitive focus—creativity using brainstorming).

Responsive Phase

Identifying Student Preconceptions	• Use an anticipation/reaction guide and include common misconceptions about the relationship of proteins, genotype, and phenotype. Examples of anticipation guides can be found at *www.gystc.org/6thGrdCur/documents/s6e2/c/es_1.pdf* or *www.ncrel.org/sdrs/areas/issues/students/learning/lr1anti.htm*. • Use the response to the guide as a preparation for a preliminary discussion on one or more of the ideas. This discussion could be via a Socratic seminar, a jigsaw discussion, or small-group dialogue.

Table 6.1 (continued)

Learning Sequence Targets	
Learning Target #1	Proteins carry out the major work of cells and are responsible for both the structures and functions of organisms. An organism's traits (phenotype) are a reflection of the work of proteins.

Research-Identified Misconceptions Addressed

- It may be easier for students to understand the cell as the unit of structure than the cell as the unit of function (AAAS 1993).
- Students demonstrate confusion over levels of organization, particularly with cells and molecules. They tend to think of molecules as related to the physical sciences and cells to life science. Some students even think that proteins are made of cells and that molecules of protein are bigger than cells (Driver et al. 1994).
- Because students are not aware that proteins play a role that is central to living things (most/all genetic phenomena are mediated by proteins) and robust (many functions), it hampers their ability to provide mechanistic explanations of genetic phenomena (Duncan and Reiser 2005).
- The majority of upper-division biology students and future science teachers recognize the physical constitution of an organism as its phenotype, yet do not understand the role of genes and proteins in producing the phenotype (Elrod n.d.).

Initial Instructional Plan

Eliciting Preconceptions: Facilitate a brainstorming session using the probe, "What are proteins and why are they important?" This can be as a whole-class or in small groups (but share as a whole class after small-group work). You can use one of the brainstorming webs (Instructional Tool 2.10, p. 72) or use the understanding routine, Think/Puzzle/Explore, found at the Visible Thinking website (see Instructional Tool 2.5, p. 44, Engage in Scientifically Oriented Questions). During the class discussion, elicit ideas about various proteins and introduce the concept that missing or ill-functioning proteins can significantly impact functions and, in many cases, cause disease. The goal is to ensure that students understand the robust and important functions of proteins. End the discussion by generating student questions.

Confronting Preconceptions: Show the YouTube video "Protein Functions in the Body" (see Recommended Resources at the end of this chapter). Provide student groups with a list of various proteins and the associated disorders than can arise if the protein is missing or malfunctioning. Have each group choose a disorder. Their task is to research the protein and disorder and determine the impact of the missing or malfunctioning protein on the various levels of organization (cells, tissues, organs, organisms). Model what this would look like, using sickle-cell anemia as an example (students revisit sickle cell in Learning Target #3). Do not focus on the actual mutation, but on the impact of sickle cell at the various levels of organization. Two resources that students can use as a starting point is a summary of disorders (*www.usoe.k12.ut.us/CURR/SCIENCE/core/bio/genetics/home%20page.htm*) and a resource at the Your Genes, Your Health website (*www.ygyh.org*).

Sense Making: Review with students the use of two-column notes and tree maps before they begin research. Facilitate their use during small-group work, probing for student understanding of both concepts and use of the tools. Require students to prepare both individual summaries in their learning logs, share and critique their summaries (as a group), and prepare a poster presentation to share with the entire class. Support students during individual learning log summary development and during poster preparation. Use a round-robin approach to poster sharing, during which students rotate from poster to poster, critiquing the work, looking for similarities and differences among posters, and generating questions. Facilitate a whole-class discussion, summarizing key ideas, and generating questions (poster paper or SmartBoard).

Table 6.1 (continued)

Formative Assessment Plan (Demonstrating Understanding)

- Teacher review of learning logs, including two-column notes
- Analysis of tree maps for inclusion of key ideas
- Questions and probes during small-group work and class discussion
- Final posters and poster critiques using pre-established rubrics

Learning Target #2	Genetic information (genes) coded in DNA provides the information necessary to assemble proteins. The sequence of subunits (nucleotides) in DNA determines the sequence of amino acids in proteins.

Research-Identified Misconceptions Addressed

- Some students think a gene is a trait or that the DNA makes proteins (Elrod n.d.).
- Because some students do not connect genes to proteins to phenotypes (Lewis and Wood-Robinson 2000), they assume that genes directly express traits in organisms (Lewis and Kattmann 2004).
- Less than half of upper-division biology students and future science teachers understand the nature of the genetic code (Elrod 2007). Only 22% of undergraduate students with some biological science course work defined the gene in terms of nucleotide sequences involved in protein synthesis (Chattopadhyay and Mahajan 2006).
- Though students usually equate genes with traits, they do not understand that genes code for specific proteins and that the production of these proteins results in the traits (Friedrichsen and Stone 2004).
- Students often think that genes code for more than proteins. They also often think that the genes code for information at multiple levels of organization (e.g., the gene "tells" a tissue or organ to malfunction), which bypasses the need for students to provide a mechanistic explanation of molecular genetics phenomena (Duncan and Reiser 2005).
- 30–52% of upper-division biology students and future science teachers do not recognize RNA as the product of transcription. 50–75% of introductory biology and genetics students in college and future science teachers do not identify proteins as the product of translation (Elrod 2007; Fisher 1985).

Initial Instructional Plan

Eliciting Preconceptions: Begin with the idea that all the work students just completed was about genetic disorders. Ask them how genes are related to the proteins just studied. Provide students with a list of the essential vocabulary terms and ask them to use all the terms in the list to write their best explanations of the relationship. Share in small groups and then discuss selected explanations as a whole class. Now share an animation that provides an overview of protein synthesis (see Resources, below). Have small groups discuss and map connections to previous understandings, interpretations of the overview, and any questions they have. Facilitate discussions in small groups and then as whole class, focusing on the ideas in the learning target.

Confronting Preconceptions: Have students read about protein synthesis from their text or other print resource and modify their maps and explanations based on what they learn. Next, have them complete a shockwave activity available at the DNA Workshop site, choosing the protein synthesis option (see Resources, below) or one of the activities at the Concord Consortium's Molecular Logic Project (see Resources, below). Note that students are not responsible for all vocabulary used in either resource, unless this is expected in your school district. The idea is to provide visual images of the connection between genes and proteins.

Sense Making: Have students revisit concept maps, explanations, and questions, revising based on new experiences. Assign to students sections of text (print/electronic sources) on protein synthesis. Once again, have them modify concept maps and explanations. Facilitate the work of each group with probes and questions. Then use student questions as guides for class discussion.

Table 6.1 (continued)

Formative Assessment Plan (Demonstrating Understanding)

- Questions and probes during small-group work and class discussion
- Analyze student explanations using a rubric
- Analyze student concept maps (peer critique of maps can also be included)
- Use student questions to indicate ongoing areas of misunderstanding and elicit ideas using questions as a guide for class discussion

Learning Target #3	The sequence of amino acids determines not only the kind, but also the shape, of the protein, and thus its function.

Research-Identified Misconceptions Addressed

- It may be easier for students to understand the cell as the unit of structure than the cell as the unit of function (AAAS 1993).
- Many students think that a gene is a trait or that the DNA makes proteins (Elrod 2007).
- Though students usually equate genes with traits, they do not understand that genes code for specific proteins and that the production of these proteins results in the traits (Friedrichsen and Stone 2004).
- Though 80% of undergraduates knew that a disease could be linked to a gene, only 35% correctly represented a flow diagram between the genes and disease. Even if they could explain the concept of the central dogma, they could not extrapolate their understanding to a real-life situation (Chattopadhyay and Majahan 2006).

Initial Instructional Plan

Eliciting Preconceptions: Go to *http://molo.concord.org/database/activities/76.html* and show "How a Protein Gets Its Shape: The Role of Charge." Run the "original chain" as a demonstration, also showing how the simulation works. Share your mental model of the process, thinking out loud. Have students run the additional demonstrations (individual or with a partner). Then have them discuss, in small groups or as partnered problem solving (see Table 2.4, p. 39, Classroom Implications for Talk About Thinking), why they think protein shape is important. Share ideas with the whole class and facilitate a discussion.

Confronting Preconceptions: Go to *http://molo.concord.org/database/activities/225.html* and have students complete "Protein Folding: Stepping Stones Full Interactive," screens #1–#4. As they complete the activities, they generate a report that is submitted at the end of the activity. However, this will not be complete until after Learning Target #4.

Sense Making: Model for students how to develop an analogy for protein synthesis. Make sure to identify the concept and the analog, discuss how the two are similar and how they are different, and reflect on the effectiveness of the analogy. What about it was effective and what was confusing? "Building a house" is one analog for protein synthesis, recommended by Harrison and Coll (2008). They outline an application of the FAR Guide in their book (see Resources, below). Once you model this, have students identify and develop an analogy.

Formative Assessment Plan (Demonstrating Understanding)

- Questions and probes during small-group work and class discussion
- Even though the student reports for the protein-folding interaction are not complete until the completion of Learning Target #4, you can review student work online during the interactions and use this information to gauge level of understanding
- Critiques of student analogies by self, peers, and teacher, using the FAR Guide if available

Table 6.1 (continued)

Learning Target #4	Mutations, changes in the DNA, impact protein production. Errors in the DNA (mutation) can result in missing proteins or ones that function inadequately. This results in a change in phenotype/trait.

Research-Identified Misconceptions Addressed

- It may be easier for students to understand the cell as the unit of structure than the cell as the unit of function (AAAS 1993).
- Most students are unable to explain a situation where a change to the DNA sequence does not change the protein sequence (Eklund et al. 2007).

Initial Instructional Plan

Eliciting Preconceptions: Have students continue the protein-folding activity started in Learning Target #3. It now introduces mutation, focusing on sickle-cell anemia. Students are asked to predict the impact of a change to the DNA sequence before completing the simulation. Have them make this prediction (claim) and share their explanations as a class. Recall that scientific explanations require students to make claims, provide evidence for their claims, and link the claims to the evidence.

Confronting Preconceptions: Have students complete screens #5–#8. They can now complete and generate their report. They can also complete the activity, Modeling Mutations, further described at *www.concord.org/publications/newsletter/2004-spring/mondayslesson.html.*

Sense Making: Then have students refer to their textbooks or other print resources to research other types of mutations and their potential impact. They should connect this information back to their original research on their selected disorder. They should also revise their explanations and expand their analogies developed during Learning Target #3 to include what they learned in this part of the lesson.

Formative Assessment Plan (Demonstrating Understanding)

- Questions and probes during small-group work and class discussion
- Student reports generated by the protein-folding interaction
- Critique of scientific explanations by students and teacher (see description in text) or using the "Explanation Analysis" strategy (Keeley 2008)
- Critiques of student analogies by self, peers, and teacher, using the FAR Guide if available

Recommended Resources

Technology Applications and Websites

- The YouTube video "Protein Functions in the Body" (*www.youtube.com/watch?v=T500B5yTy58*) presents the wide array of proteins that make up living organisms.

- Two resources that students can use as a starting point as they research different disorders are *www.usoe.k12.ut.us/CURR/SCIENCE/core/bio/genetics/home%20page.htm* and Your Genes, Your Health website (*www.ygyh.org*).

- Teachers Domain (*www.teachersdomain.org*) offers a flash interactive—Cell Transcription and Translation—that includes an overview of protein synthesis as well as more detailed interactions with transcription and translation (*www.teachersdomain.org/ resource/lsps07.sci.life.stru.celltrans*); at this point, we recommend sharing only the overview, not the details. If you do not have a Teachers Domain account, you can register at no cost.

- The DNA Workshop site (*www.pbs.org/wgbh/aso/tryit/dna/#*) has a protein synthesis shockwave. Also, more extensive explorations are available at the Concord Consortium's Molecular Logic Project (*http://molo.concord.org*). Many of the explorations are linked to specific biology textbooks, perhaps including one your district uses.

- For your personal content learning, the NSTA SciPack "Cell Structure and Function" is a good option. In particular, the last Science Object called "The Most Important Molecule" relates directly to this chapter. Visit the NSTA Science Store (*www.nsta.org/ store/?lid=tnavhp*) and search for "protein."

Build Your Library
- A great resource for formative assessments, which we used to construct the Instructional Planning Framework, is *Science Formative Assessment: 75 Practical Strategies for Linking Assessment, Instruction, and Learning* (Keeley 2008). You might also consider any or all of the three *Uncovering Student Ideas in Science* volumes (Keeley, Eberle, and Farrin 2005; Keeley, Eberle, and Tugel 2007; Keeley, Eberle, and Dorsey 2008).
- An excellent resource to learn more about the use of analogies in secondary science classrooms is *Using Analogies in Middle and Secondary Science Classrooms: The FAR Guide—An Interesting Way to Teach With Analogies* (Harrison and Coll 2008).
- Chapter 11, "How Nature Builds Itself: Self-Assembly," in *Nanoscale Science: Activities for Grades 6–12* (Jones et al. 2007), ties in nicely with some of the Concord Consortium dynamic models used in this lesson.
- Black and Harrison (2004) provide examples and suggestions for descriptive feedback for students in *Science Inside the Black Box: Assessment for Learning in the Science Classroom*.

Endnotes

1. The same resources used in previous chapters were used to determine appropriate standards; prior understandings; knowledge, skills, and vocabulary to include or exclude; and the learning targets. The identified learning sequence was based on three different resources: Roseman et al. (2006); Duncan, Rogat, and Yarden (2007); and Eklund et al. (2007).

2. The FAR Guide has three main aspects:

   1. Consider the focus. Look at the concept itself (difficult? unfamiliar? abstract?), the ideas the students bring to the table, and whether the analog is familiar to students.

2. What is the action? Discuss how the concept is like the analog (similarities) and unlike the analog (differences).

3. Take time to reflect. After using the analog, determine if it was clear or confusing and if it achieved the desired outcomes. Also consider any changes you would make in future use.

We urge you to learn more about the entire FAR Guide process prior to implementation. This summary, in itself, is not adequate for implementation.

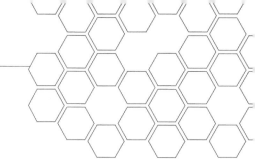

Instructional Planning Framework

Predictive Phase

The teacher determines the lesson's essential understandings, the sequence of learning targets that lead toward those understandings, and the criteria by which understanding is determined.

Responsive Phase

Building on the foundation of the predictive phase, the teacher plans for and implements instruction during the responsive phase, one learning target at a time.

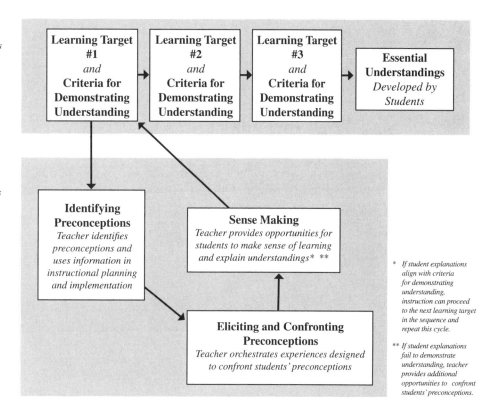

Learning Target #1 *and* **Criteria for Demonstrating Understanding**

Learning Target #2 *and* **Criteria for Demonstrating Understanding**

Learning Target #3 *and* **Criteria for Demonstrating Understanding**

Essential Understandings *Developed by Students*

Identifying Preconceptions *Teacher identifies preconceptions and uses information in instructional planning and implementation*

Sense Making *Teacher provides opportunities for students to make sense of learning and explain understandings* ***

Eliciting and Confronting Preconceptions *Teacher orchestrates experiences designed to confront students' preconceptions*

* *If student explanations align with criteria for demonstrating understanding, instruction can proceed to the next learning target in the sequence and repeat this cycle.*

** *If student explanations fail to demonstrate understanding, teacher provides additional opportunities to confront students' preconceptions.*

Chapter 7

Interdependence: Environmental Systems and Human Impact

"[S]tudying science in the context of the environment is doubly productive. It shows how scientific knowledge and ways of thinking, coupled with the process of making decisions about our collective interaction with nature, can illuminate each other to the advantage of both."
—*Environmental Literacy Council and National Science Teachers Association 2007, p. xiii*

Why This Topic?

The quote above emphasizes the importance of environmental literacy as well as the key role of scientific literacy in reaching that end. Both components drove our decision to include "environmental systems and human impact" as a chapter topic in this book. We know that it is common for students to graduate from high school without having had experiences that help them understand the nature of science. In addition, these graduates rarely understand the impact of humans on the environment because they did not develop environmental literacy during their years in school.

But environmental literacy is difficult to develop because it requires understanding complex systems that span space and time. The task is made more difficult since high school students have had many experiences with the environment and bring misconceptions based on these experiences to the classroom (Carnegie Mellon University 2003). Another difficulty is that reasoning about living systems involves relating different levels of organization—from molecule to biosphere—and understanding how living systems are structured at each level.

However, the functions of living systems at these levels, as well as the interactions among living systems and how they depend on one another to carry out their functions, are important concepts for students to understand. Student understandings about species interaction in an ecosystem, the dynamics of population growth and decline, the use of resources by multiple species, the impact of multiple species on their environments, and the complex interactions among all these factors have enormous consequences to the survival of all species, including humans (WestEd and CCSSO 2007). Furthermore, when students understand about the environmental systems that more directly reflect scientific understanding of these systems, our country will have a more educated public that can make informed decisions.

Topic: Ecosystem interactions
Go to: *www.scilinks.org*
Code: HTB010

Overview

This chapter covers the entire Instructional Planning Framework process, including both the *predictive* and *responsive phases*. Each aspect of the framework you learned about in a stepwise manner in Chapters 3–6 is reviewed again and seen as an entire process. Our content focus is on a local ecosystem. We will be studying the interactions of system components, fluctuations in populations, inputs and outputs, and so forth. We do not trace the flow of energy or matter through the ecosystem, though connections are made to these concepts, as we assume both concepts were studied prior to this lesson. The key ideas of the lesson are (1) the possible long-term stability of ecosystems, (2) the interactions of populations in those ecosystems, and (2) the impact of humans in the same systems. We draw connections to broader systems, pointing to global impact, but these ideas are better explored more thoroughly in a following lesson.

We selected a particular ecosystem for the lesson context, but you should select one typical of your area. Although students should learn about many different ecosystems, it is best for them to learn first about those close to home (AAAS 1993). (*Note:* All tables are grouped together at the end of the chapter, beginning on p. 217. They are followed by Recommended Resources and Endnotes.)

Instructional Planning Framework: *Predictive Phase*

Let's briefly review the planning steps in the *predictive phase* (Figure 7.1). They are identifying the conceptual targets, establishing the learning target sequence, and determining the criteria for understanding.

Figure 7.1

Planning in the Predictive Phase

1. Identify the essential understandings for the lesson (conceptual target).
   a. Begin with the descriptions of adult science literacy to determine an anchor goal.
   b. Consider the middle school and high school standards and benchmarks.
   c. Optional: Study existing research on learning progressions. A good resource (*www.project2061.org/publications/2061Connections/2007/2007-04a-resources.htm*) is found in the 2061 Connections online newsletter (AAAS 2007a).
   d. Dig a bit deeper and think about the concepts included in the standards.
   e. Decide what is essential and what can be pruned.
2. Develop a logical sequence of learning targets for the lesson.
   a. Consider first the middle school experiences students should have had.
   b. Outline the key ideas embedded in the high school standards and benchmarks.
   c. Sequence the key ideas in a way to build student understanding.
   d. Consider connections from one lesson to the next.
3. Identify the criteria for demonstrating understanding. (*Note:* Steps b and c are completed later, after a review of research).
   a. Identify one criterion for each Learning Target.
   b. Identify one criterion for your selected standards-based strategy (Inquiry, HOS, or NOS).
   c. Identify one criterion for your selected metacognitive strategy.

What Are the Conceptual Targets? What Are the Essential Understandings?

Clarification of the conceptual targets begins with adult science learning expectations and then drills down to determine what is appropriate at the grade level as well as what is most essential and what we can let go of.

Adult Science Literacy

We start with adult science literacy expectations as aligned with our topic (Figure 7.2) that are drawn from *Science for All Americans* (AAAS 1989).

Figure 7.2

Adult Science Literacy Expectations for Interdependence of Organisms

"The interdependence of organisms in an ecosystem often results in approximate stability over hundreds or thousands of years. As one species proliferates, it is held in check by one or more environmental factors: depletion of food or nesting sites, increased loss to predators, or invasion by parasites. If a natural disaster such as flood or fire occurs, the damaged ecosystem is likely to recover in a succession of stages that eventually results in a system similar to the original one.

"Like many complex systems, ecosystems tend to show cyclic fluctuations around a state of approximate equilibrium. In the long run, however, ecosystems inevitably change when climate changes or when very different new species appear as a result of migration or evolution (or are introduced deliberately or inadvertently by humans)." (AAAS 1989, 65–66)

Middle and High School Standards

As we discussed in Chapter 3, we consider adult science literacy to be a result of what is taught not only in our high school science courses, but also during the middle grades. It is in the middle grades where the conceptual foundations are built for the students in our biology classes. According to the National Science Education Standards (NSES) (NRC 1996), middle schools students should come to high school with the foundational understandings of life science, leaving more abstract knowledge (e.g., scale including molecules and biosphere) to be taught during the high school years (NRC 1996).

According to *Benchmarks for Science Literacy* (referred to as "Benchmarks" in this chapter) (AAAS 1993), middle schoolers "should be guided from specific examples of the interdependency of organisms to a more systematic view of the kinds of interactions that take place among organisms" (AAAS 1993, p. 117). However, a full development of the concept of ecosystem should wait until high school, when a better understanding of systems in general allows for understandings about ecosystems. These understandings include "interdependence of parts, feedback, oscillation, inputs, and outputs. Stability and change in ecosystems can be considered in terms of variables such as population size, number and kinds of species, and productivity" (AAAS 1993, p.117).

Our review of the NSES and Benchmarks led us to the standards specific to the topic of this chapter. They are found in the Teacher Work Template for environmental systems and human impact (Table 7.1, p. 217). We suggest that you study the selected high school standards that align with our topic and the middle school standards that prepare students to tackle these high school ideas.

Digging Further Into the Standards

We now have a sense of how middle and high school standards lead to our adult science learning target, but we need to dig a bit deeper into the standards. In our work, we used the Benchmarks and the NSES, studied the *Atlas of Science Literacy, Volume 2* (AAAS 2007b), and reviewed *Pathways to the Science Standards*—both the high school edition (Texley and Wild 2004) and the middle school edition (Rakow 2000).[1] Let's first take a look at a portion of the map for "Interdependence of Life" found in the second atlas volume (Figure 7.3, p. 196).

The map has four strands: (1) interactions among organisms, (2) dynamic nature of ecosystems, (3) dependence of organisms on their environment, and (4) human impact. As you can see, the focus in the middle grades is on understanding how organisms, including humans, interact with each other and the environment. By high school, the focus is on the interdependence of organisms in ecosystems and includes the more abstract ideas of stability and change in systems (AAAS 2007b).

The full map in the *Atlas of Science Literacy, Volume 2* (AAAS 2007b) stresses links with the Earth sciences. If your district infuses some of these standards into the biology curriculum (as is occasionally done), be sure that the appropriate standards are included. These might include standards related to Earth's resources and weather and climate. There are clear links from this map to "Science in Personal and Social Perspectives" in the NSES and "Science and Society" in the Benchmarks. Including some of these standards introduces ethical choices and decision making that can personalize the lesson for students.

The *Pathways to the Science Standards* series, especially the High School Edition, provides some additional information. High school biology students should be able to predict the effects of one variable on a population, graphing those data. And given appropriate support, they should be able to predict changes over time and understand the effect of several variables on ecosystems. However, it is difficult for most introductory biology students to understand the potential of a single variable as the limiting factor in a complex ecosystem (Texley and Wild 2004).

Figure 7.3

Concept Map for *The Living Environment:* "*Interdependence of Life*"

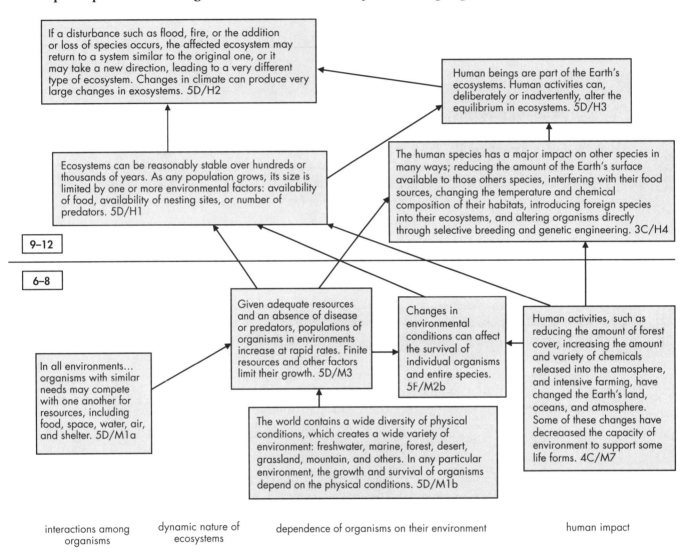

interactions among organisms   dynamic nature of ecosystems   dependence of organisms on their environment   human impact

Source: American Association for the Advancement of Science (AAAS). 2004. *Atlas of Science Literacy, Volume 2.* Washington, DC: AAAS, p. 33. Extract printed with permission.

Abbreviations: 3C/H4, 4C/M7, 5D/H1, 5D/H2, 5D/H3, 5D/M1a, 5D/M1b, 5D/M3, and 5F/M2b refer to the chapter, section, and number of the corresponding statement in *Benchmarks for Science Literacy.* American Association for the Advancement of Science (AAAS). New York: Oxford University Press, 1993.

Research on Learning Progressions

You may not have time to do research on learning progressions, so we provide the information for you. (We remind you, however, that research about learning progressions can extend your own understandings of the content you teach.) The most informative learning progression research connected to our topic appears in Figure 7.4. We look particularly at the research on developing environmental literacy

Anderson (2007), from whose work we adapted Figure 7.4, suggests that the figure presents three key implications for science curriculums:

1. When we teach about something in this system (i.e., environmental systems) we need to think about the entire loop.
2. The current science curriculum is largely inside the "environmental systems" box.
3. When we teach what is in the "environmental systems" box, we need to connect it to the arrows.

Figure 7.4

Structures and Processes of Socio-Ecological Systems (Loop Diagram)

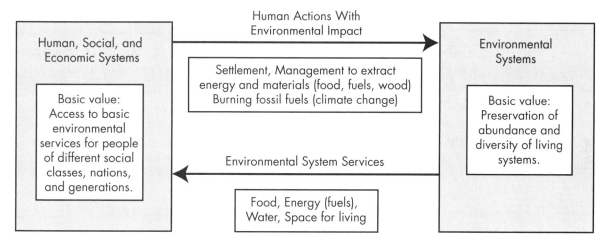

Adapted from Anderson, C. W., Environmental literacy learning progressions, *http://edr1.educ.msu.edu/EnvironmentalLit/publicsite/files/2007KSI/plenary/707KSIPlenaryEnvLit.pdf* (retrieved September 5, 2008) with permission from the author.

We apply this information in three major ways.

1. If you refer back to Figure 7.3 and study the portion of the atlas map for grades 9–12, you see that the focus is primarily *in* the "environmental systems" box. However, the focus on humans as part of that system requires us to consider the

remainder of the map. As we said earlier, our focus in this chapter is on a local ecosystem to study the interactions of system components. However, once we extend our thinking to include human impact in that local ecosystem and then possibly to include regional and global levels, we move *outside* the "environmental systems" box. Our focus is on natural and agricultural populations and communities; the relationship among populations with different niches, habitats, and survival strategies; the impact of natural disturbances on the ecosystem; and human impact on populations and communities (reduction of niches and habitats, as well as invasive species).

2. We do not address tracing matter or energy through the system, but leave that for different lessons. However, we do include "tracing information" through the system. As Anderson (2007, p. 7) says, "A key characteristic of living systems is that they maintain continuity in structure and function even as their subsystems disappear and are replaced…. For example…populations maintain continuity as individuals live and die, and ecosystems maintain continuity as populations change size or are replaced." If students understand this concept, their abilities to understand ecosystems are enhanced.

3. Finally, we believe that students need to understand the complexity of changing environmental systems because the systems involve multiple causes and possibly involve feedback loops. To address this requisite understanding, we contrasted processes of succession during the preindustrial era (which approximately balanced species diversity with reductions in population sizes or local extinctions) with postindustrial "agricultural and settlements practices…[that] vastly increase the rate of selection processes that reduce genetic variability and species diversity" (Anderson 2007, p. 8).

Pruning the Content

We used *Designs for Science Literacy* (AAAS 2001b) to decide where to "unburden" the curriculum. We reviewed the listing of possible subtopics to prune and listed them in the Teacher Work Template (see Table 7.1, p. 217).

What about vocabulary? In general, if students can understand the concepts without the technical vocabulary, then we should consider not using that vocabulary. An exception should be made if these potentially "unnecessary" terms are required by your school district. When you are using these required terms, we encourage you to first teach the concepts and then address the vocabulary. Other exceptions for using technical vocabulary are when the technical vocabulary is also a concept and when the term is so common that it is used over and over during various lessons (e.g., *ecosystem*) (AAAS 2001b).

What Is a Logical Learning Sequence?

The next step in the predictive phase requires that we identify learning targets and determine the logical sequence for these targets. Refer back to Figure 7.1 (step #2). According to that step, teachers must consider students' middle school experiences in order to build on the understandings that arose from those experiences, outline the key ideas embedded in the high school standards and benchmarks, sequence the key ideas in a way to build student understanding, and consider connections from one lesson to the next. Let's see how we used these steps for our lesson on interdependence.

Build on Middle School Experiences

In middle school, students should have experiences with field and laboratory work that focus on specific examples of interdependency of organisms, and they should begin to understand the types of interactions that occur among organisms (AAAS 1993; Rakow 2000). High school teachers need to build on that foundational learning. Students should also have general understandings about population growth and the role of resources in limiting that growth. High school teachers will build on those understandings to help students learn about the rough equilibrium that can be established in ecosystems and how this tentative equilibrium can be disrupted by natural and human events.

In other words, teachers need to help students move from specific examples from contexts they understand to more complex interactions with multiple variables that more clearly reflect how systems work (AAAS 1993). The first learning target should build on these middle school experiences before the more complex aspects of system dynamics are introduced.

Tease Apart the Components of the High School Standards

Let's look at the following group of standards, which we selected for this lesson's focus. Key ideas are in italics.

- *Organisms both cooperate and compete in ecosystems.* The *interrelationships and interdependencies* of these organisms *may generate ecosystems that are stable for hundreds or thousands of years* (NRC 1996, p. 186).
- Living organisms have the *capacity to produce populations of infinite size*, but *environments and resources are finite*. This fundamental *tension has profound effects on the interactions between organisms* (NRC 1996, p. 186).
- Ecosystems *can be reasonably stable over hundreds or thousands of years*. As any *population* of organisms grows, it is *held in check by one or more environmental factors*: depletion of food or nesting sites, increased loss to increased numbers of predators, or parasites. *If a disaster* such as flood or fire *occurs*, the damaged *ecosystem is likely to recover in stages that eventually result in a system similar to the original one* (AAAS 1993, p. 17).

- Like many complex systems, *ecosystems tend to have cyclic fluctuations around a state of rough equilibrium*. In the long run, *however*, ecosystems *always change when climate changes or when one or more new species appear as a result of migration or local evolution* (AAAS 1993, p. 117).

We reviewed these key ideas and they became Learning Targets #1, #2, and #3. Learning Target #4 was derived from the following standards

- *Human beings live within the world's ecosystems. Increasingly, humans modify ecosystems* as a result of population growth, technology, and consumption. Human destruction of habitats through direct harvesting, pollution, atmospheric changes, and other factors are threatening current global stability, *and if not addressed, ecosystems will be irreversibly affected* (NRC 1996, p. 186).
- *Human beings are part of the earth's ecosystems. Human activities can*, deliberately or inadvertently, *alter the equilibrium in ecosystems* (AAAS 1993, p. 117).

The last learning target in any learning sequence should build connections to the next lesson. We focused primarily on local ecosystems in this lesson. Even as we transition to talk about human impact, we stress the local ecosystem under study. Students, however, can begin to think about how their learning connects to broader, global issues.

Having completed the process to determine a logical learning sequence, we now look at our four Learning Targets and decide how they lead to the essential understandings (see Figure 7.5). Also, refer to Table 7.1, which includes the four Learning Targets.

What Criteria Should We Use to Determine Understanding?

Our final planning step in the predictive phase is to establish criteria to determine understanding (Figure 7.1, step #3). As we have in past chapters, we will complete only the first aspect of this work now—that is, the development of one criterion per learning target. At this point we focus on three facets of understanding: explanation, interpretation, and application (McTighe and Wiggins 2004). We also work more toward application as the lesson progresses, reflective of typical learning cycles. The perspective, empathy, and self-knowledge facets apply more clearly to the metacognitive criterion that we will write once we select our metacognitive focus for the lesson (during the responsive phase). Once again, we provide only the criteria so that you have flexibility to apply these criteria and develop a summative assessment that best fits your context. Refer to Table 7.1 and review the criteria we included for each Learning Target.

Reflection and Application

We have completed, for the last time in this book, the predictive phase (Figure 7.1). Take a moment to reflect on this phase as completed for "environmental systems and human impact."

1. How have you taught this topic in the past?
2. In what ways does your past instruction align with the work in the *predictive phase* for this topic? In what ways is it different?
3. Are there changes you might make in your instruction based on this information?

Figure 7.5

Environmental Systems and Human Impact

Target #1: Populations have the capacity to grow but are held in check by environmental factors/resources. This effects the interactions among organisms.	**Target #2:** Ecosystems can be relatively stable over very long periods of time, even though the roles (e.g., competition and cooperation) and populations of organisms within the ecosystem can vary. Ecosystems fluctuate but in a cyclic way around a state of rough equilibrium.	**Target #3:** Various natural factors (including natural disasters, climate change, and the appearance of new species) can disrupt this equilibrium and the balance within the ecosystem can change. Depending on the severity of the disruption, the ecosystem can gradually recover to a system similar to the original system.	**Target #4:** Humans are part of the ecosystem, and our modifications to ecosystems can disrupt the established equilibrium. Ecosystems have the potential to recover from these disruptions, as they do when disrupted by natural factors. But sometimes the disruptive influences can overload the systems ability to maintain balance so ecosystems are irreversibly altered.

Essential Understandings: Ecosystems can remain relatively stable over long periods of time, fluctuating around a state of rough equilibrium. The roles and interactions of individual organisms and populations may change but ecosystems retain continuity. This can be disrupted by various natural factors or human interference. The ecosystem may gradually recover if the natural event is not too severe or the disruptive human influence is removed.

Instructional Planning Framework: *Responsive Phase*

We now translate what we learned during the predictive phase into a lesson. We will determine effective strategies to identify, elicit, and confront preconceptions, to support students' sense making, and to decide how students will demonstrate understanding. We will model the entire *responsive phase*, demonstrating its planning aspects as well as its iterative nature. This coverage of the entire phase reinforces the step-by-step coverage of the phase in Chapters 4–6.

Identifying Preconceptions

Students' preconceptions are important for teachers to be aware of because students make connections and construct patterns when they learn, based on their prior knowledge (Lowery 1990). We begin by identifying the student misconceptions that have been identified in the research literature. We also determine ways to identify our own students' preconceptions. That process is shown in Figure 7.6.

Figure 7.6

Identifying Preconceptions

Learn About Research-Identified Misconceptions

1. Review *Benchmarks for Science Literacy* (1993) for misconceptions discussed there. Chapter 15 of this book includes research findings organized by benchmark. If you do not have a copy of the book, you can read it online at *www.project2061.org/publications/ bsl/online/ index.php?txtRef=&txtURIOld=%2Fpublications%2Fbsl%2Fonline%2Findex.*
2. Complete a web search for misconceptions on the selected topic. Simply run a search for your topic and misconceptions (e.g., "photosynthesis + misconceptions"). If you run your search at Google Scholar (*http://scholar.google.com*), you will gain access to numerous resources. In some cases you will only access the abstract, but in others you will find the entire document. This process is more time-consuming than step #1 but yields additional resources.
3. The most direct way to access a summary of misconceptions is the book *Making Sense of Secondary Science: Research into Children's Ideas* (Driver et al. 1994). The book is outlined by topic and provides a rich summary of research on children's ideas about these topics.

Select Strategies to Identify Student Preconceptions

4. Use the Instructional Strategy Sequencing Tool in Chapter 2 to identify possible strategies that work to identify student preconceptions.
5. Find the strategies in the Sense-Making Instructional Tools (Chapter 2, Instructional Tools 2.8–2.14).
6. Carefully review the research and application recommendations for each of the identified strategies.
7. Determine several strategies that fit well with the particular content you are teaching.
8. Review the listed resources available to you to more fully understand the strategies and to determine what they might look like in application.
9. Select one or two for use in your lesson.

Research-Identified Misconceptions

We used our framework process to complete a search for research-identified misconceptions. (We encourage teachers to conduct this type of search themselves, since it is a rich learning experience.) We followed steps #1–#3 in Figure 7.6 and began with a review of *Benchmarks for Science Literacy* (AAAS 1993). We then completed a web search and reviewed the work of Driver et al. (1994), identifying additional misconceptions. The misconceptions we found are in Table 7.1, sorted by Learning Target.

As we conducted this search, we also found additional information about the development and implementation of this lesson. This information is as follows:

- By high school, students can predict the impact of one variable on a population and graph population data. It is easier for them to understand the effect of multiple variables on a population than to understand the impact of a single variable on a complex ecosystem. To understand the interdependence of organisms, teachers must give students opportunities to move from concrete to formal reasoning. Coupling classroom or computer modeling with field studies is an ideal approach to formalize their understandings. Field-work can be of multiple types: (1) model classroom environments such as terrariums and aquaria let students test hypotheses, (2) simple but extended studies of small, simple communities (e.g. quadrats, creeks) contrast with classroom models and extends student thinking, and (3) since today's environmental science relies on large quantities of data and worldwide communications, students can partner with scientists as researchers of natural phenomena in studies such as river watches and large scale migrations (Texley and Wild 2004). Field studies can gather data from year to year, modeling the work of scientists and engaging students in authentic research.

- It is important to address the nature of systems, stressing the interaction of biotic and abiotic factors in change and in reaching equilibrium. It is also essential to confront egocentric and anthropocentric conceptions of the human place in the ecosystem. The use of conceptual change approaches should be of help to teachers (Tanner and Allen 2005), in particular (1) concept mapping and system dynamics models and animations, and (2) confronting learners with evidence, historical experiments, or data-based problems consistent with scientific explanations and in opposition to common misconceptions.

- Recommendations to promote environmental literacy suggest that we address contexts (situated learning), connections (of concepts and phenomena to one another), competence (application of knowledge and skills), and conscience (understanding the value systems of society today) (Carnegie Mellon University 2003).

- Education on population and environmental issues will be improved if (1) linkages among population size, consumption, and environmental quality are taught; (2) the effects of individual actions on environmental quality are emphasized; and (3) environmental education is tailored to local issues (Holl et al. 2002).

- Appropriate phenomena for observation include human disturbances to ecosystems and environments, both local and global, as well as responses of ecosystems to changes, both natural and human-induced. Appropriate expectations of students include an ability to provide qualitative descriptions of biodiversity of various ecosystems and of fluctuations in populations due to human-induced change, as well as an analysis of quantitative data on biodiversity (WestEd and CCSSO 2007).

- Understandings of human impact on the environment should be connected to understandings about solutions. Making this connection explicit should promote an awareness that people can make decisions about what life on Earth survives and a sense of responsibility about using that power. Students also should learn that people can not shape every aspect of life to their own liking (AAAS 1993).

Identifying Students' Preconceptions

Teachers need to consider their own students' preconceptions, since the misconceptions identified in the research can vary by age, sex, geography, student motivation, and interest (Westcott and Cunningham 2006). (It is helpful—though not always possible—to collect this information ahead of instruction so that you can build your lesson around your own students' preconceptions.) Refer back to steps #4–#9 in Figure 7.6 to review the process for selecting strategies that identify student preconceptions.

In Table 7.2, we listed some basic ideas about strategies that we thought would be useful in identifying our students' understandings prior to instruction. Each of these strategies also can be used throughout the lesson to reflect on ongoing student understanding. Here are two additional strategies:

- We particularly like Keeley's (2008) FACT (formative assessment classroom technique) called "Learning Goals Inventory." You will need her book *Science Formative Assessment* to carry out these strategies.
- We also like the use of drawing to determine students' understandings prior to instruction. A simple probe for the drawing might be, "Make a drawing of an ecosystem that exists in our schoolyard and include annotations that describe your drawing." (For more on the use of drawing, see Chapter 4.)

We use another strategy—circle maps—in this lesson. Students (or teachers) may not have used circle maps before. Here are instructions for creating a circle map: (1) Draw a large circle with a smaller circle in the center. (2) Place the word *ecosystems* in the center circle. (3) Write down phrases or words or draw pictures in the outside circle that you associate with ecosystems. (These indicate students' current thinking about ecosystems.) (4) Write down words or phrases outside the outer circle that describe your prior knowledge or experiences that may have influenced what you wrote down in step #3. In step #4, also include aspects of your personal life and culture that may have influenced your perspective about, and understanding of, ecosystems.

Have students complete this process individually at the end of the class period. Gather the maps from all students and review them for use in your lesson planning. Once you begin the lesson, you can have students work in groups to complete a group circle map on chart paper. This process lets students understand each other's perspectives. These maps can be revisited throughout the lesson. An introduction to thinking maps, samples of circle maps, and a podcast about circle maps are available at the ThinkingMaps website: *www.opencourtresources.com/thinking_maps*.

Reflection and Application

Let's pause once more for reflection. Take a moment to reflect on the process outlined in Figure 7.6 and respond to the following questions.

1. Why do you think environmental systems and human impart are hard to teach?
2. What did you learn from the research-identified misconceptions that challenges the way in which you have taught about ecosystems? How would this new learning change your instruction?
3. Which of the strategies to identify your own students' preconceptions works best for you? Why?

During our search of the literature for common misconceptions, we found new information that can be applied to the strategy selection process. Effective strategies include

- coupling classroom or computer modeling and field studies;
- concept mapping and system dynamics models and animation;
- confronting learners with evidence, historical experiments, or data-based problems that are consistent with scientific explanations and in opposition to common misconceptions;
- situated learning (in this case, a familiar ecosystem);
- teaching the effects of individual actions on environmental quality;
- developing qualitative descriptions of biodiversity and of fluctuations in populations due to human-induced change; and
- connecting understandings about human impact to solutions.

This list, coupled with our instructional experiences, lead us to highly recommend field experiences that let students compare in-class modeling with field work. In the field, they can gather data and build explanations that they can contrast to scientific explanations. Field work also allows them to study an area, provide qualitative descriptions, and connect potential issues to solutions.

Eliciting and Confronting Preconceptions, Sense Making, and Demonstrating Understanding

As teachers know, students come to school with ideas previously gathered from personal experiences, books, television, and many other sources. These ideas both help and hurt their learning. So, teachers must elicit their ideas and help students to test these conceptions in the context of new learning experiences.

However, confronting student preconceptions, by itself, will not ensure understanding. Students need to make sense of these ideas, reflecting on their current thinking, comparing their conceptions to those of their peers and of scientists, and building mental models that best explain their thinking about phenomena. Students are not likely to do this type of thinking on their own. Teachers need to provide opportunities for their students to make sense of the ideas by helping them connect these ideas to their previous knowledge and organize these understandings into a larger science framework (Banilower et al. 2008). Sense making should occur throughout the lesson.

Teachers also must use formative assessments to both demonstrate student understanding and inform instruction. Though teachers can plan a lesson, these assessments may require that teachers provide additional learning opportunities for students who do not understand the concepts and extended-learning opportunities for those ready to move on to new ideas. In the remainder of the chapter, we model both the initial planning process and the iterative nature of the *responsive phase* of our Instructional Planning Framework.

Strategy Selection

First, we need to select strategies for our initial plan. But we also need alternative strategies, in case we need to provide additional learning experiences for some students in our class. Once again, we use the process shown in Figure 7.7 (steps #1–#7) to identify strategies for eliciting and confronting preconceptions and for sense making.

Figure 7.7

Finalizing the Process to Promote Understanding

Strategy Selection

1. Use the Instructional Strategy Sequencing Tool in Chapter 2 to identify possible strategies that work to *elicit and confront* student preconceptions, as well as strategies that work for *sense making* and *demonstrating understanding*. Finally, identify metacognitive and standards-based strategies to review.
2. Find the strategies in the three Metacognitive Strategy Tools (2.2–2.4), the three Standards-Based Strategy Tools (2.5–2.7), and the seven Sense-Making Strategy Tools (2.8–2.14).
3. Carefully review the research and application recommendations for each of the identified strategies.
4. Determine several strategies that fit well with the particular content you are teaching.
5. Review the listed resources available to you to more fully understand the strategies and to determine what they might look like in application.
6. Select one metacognitive strategy, one standards-based strategy, and two or three sense-making strategies for use in your lesson (recall that these will be used to differentiate instruction and to provide further instruction is formative assessments indicate that students have not demonstrated understanding of the learning targets.
7. Determine one criterion to demonstrate understanding for each metacognitive and standards-based focus. Add these to the existing criteria in the work template.

Strategy Implementation

8. Implement, for each learning target, the selected strategies to *elicit and confront preconceptions, sense making,* and *demonstrating understanding*. Gather data *using the formative assessment strategies* for a learning target.
9. If formative assessments indicate that all students understand the concepts, move forward with the next learning target.
10. If they do not understanding the ideas, then use a different strategy to provide additional learning experiences for the students.
11. Extend the learning for students who demonstrate understanding and provide additional small-group and/or individualized instruction for those who still struggle to understand.

Refer to Instructional Tool 2.1 and review the strategies listed under eliciting and confronting preconceptions, as well as strategies for sense making and demonstrating understanding. A review of the strategy tools, coupled with the ideas gleaned from the research-base and listed on page 205, lead us to consider the following options:

- Metacognitive Approach: Self-regulated thinking strategies to enhance effectiveness of planning for and implementing fieldwork (Instructional Tool 2.4, p. 38)
- Standards-Based Approach: Inquiry strategies employed during fieldwork (Instructional Tool 2.5, p. 43)

- Sense-Making Approach: Writing and speaking to learn to develop explanations and solutions (Instructional Tool 2.9, p. 66)
- Models to contrast with fieldwork (Instructional Tool 2.9, p. 66)
- Nonlinguistic representations—thinking-process maps (Instructional Tool 2.12, p. 79)

Now let's review the various strategy tools, selecting possible strategies for our lesson. We separately consider options for each approach. Recall that we select one metacognitive strategy and one standards-based strategy.

Metacognitive Approach Strategies

Let's focus our review on self-regulated thinking and consider each of the strategies listed in Instructional Tool 2.4. Obviously they are all important. But we need to focus on a particular strategy to help students learn this aspect of metacognition. The strategy that aligns most with our thinking about this lesson is "plan and self-regulation." The description says, "Planning and self-regulating include estimating time requirements, organizing materials, scheduling procedures required to complete an activity, and developing criteria for evaluation." These are important skills both in preparation for work in the field and for completion of fieldwork. We can use the "Peel the Fruit" thinking routine or prepare our own format for students to plan and manage their investigations. Individual students and groups can assess their progress in plan implementation.

Standards-Based Approach Strategies

Now let's look at Instructional Tool 2.5, p. 43, and review our strategy options for inquiry, first by a quick review of the strategy descriptions. Remember that these groups of strategies align with the essential feature of inquiry. Any one of these strategies applies, since we are planning for students to conduct fieldwork and to assess the impact of humans on a selected ecosystem. However, our lesson occurs later in the school year. We would already have exposed our students to asking questions, gathering evidence in response to questions, and formulating explanations. As the year progresses, we would spend more time on evaluating and communicating explanations. So we focus on "connect explanations to scientific knowledge."

As we review the information in Instructional Tool 2.5 more closely, we see it is important that students review alternative explanations by engaging in dialogues, comparing results, and checking their results with those proposed by the teacher or instructional materials. It is especially important to make sure students connect their results with currently accepted scientific knowledge appropriate to their developmental level. We also must provide students with specific definitions and examples of what is meant by *reasoning*. It is important to hold specific discussions that help them understand that they need to write down the underlying scientific principle they used to select their evidence. We should model and critique explanations, either in written or verbal form (McNeill and Krajcik 2008).

Notice how well these first two selected strategies reinforce each other. For instance, the metacognitive skills (which include developing criteria for evaluation) help students with their inquiry skills (which include comparing and evaluating explanations). We now add criteria to demonstrate understanding of the selected metacognitive skill and of the inquiry focus (refer to Table 7.1).

Sense-Making Approach Strategies

We used Instructional Tools 2.9, 2.10, and 2.13 to review strategies that might work for eliciting and confronting preconceptions, sense making, and demonstrating understanding. We began with a quick review of the strategy descriptions and then looked more closely at the research base and the classroom implications. Based on this information, we chose as possibilities those strategies included in Table 7.3, p. 223.

The overlap of strategies and their potential to work together is clear. Teachers can use any of these strategies to elicit and confront preconceptions, provide sense-making opportunities for their students, and identify formative assessments to use to have students demonstrate understanding. Indeed, there are plentiful options in Table 7.3 to use as formative assessments if teachers need to revisit ideas with additional instruction. We draw on these strategies as we describe our lesson design.

Planning Instruction for the Learning Targets

We now outline our plans for each Learning Target. Refer to Table 7.3, the Teacher Work Template (Table 7.1), and Figure 7.5 before proceeding. These documents lay the foundation for our thinking and planning. As we determine the best sequence of activities for each Learning Target, we add them to our Teacher Work Template. We also make suggestions, for each Learning Target, to provide additional instruction if formative assessment indicates it is needed (see Figure 7.7, steps #8–#11).

Learning Target #1

Revisit Table 7.1 and review Learning Target #1. We assume that students understand, from previous instruction in the course, general population growth and the role of intraspecific competition as it drives natural selection. However, students have not yet studied the role of environmental factors, including interspecific competition, on population growth. This is the focus of Learning Target #1.

How does a teacher best elicit and confront students' preconceptions for this target? The teacher wants to (1) ensure that students are able to apply their previous understandings about population growth to this new content, (2) determine their preconceptions about the role of environmental factors in population growth, and (3) provide students the opportunity to begin model development and write explanations for the ideas in this lesson.

So, you can use graphic models and students' interpretations of them as a starting place with models and to *elicit* student preconceptions. Show the class two typical population growth curves (a logistic or sigmoid growth curve, and a curve representing a stabilized and oscillating curve resulting from intraspecific competition). Do not expect students to learn these terms, but they should be able to explain the curves. Ask students to write an explanation for the shapes of the curves in their science notebooks. You can extend the activity in order to *confront* student preconceptions, using these steps:

1. Small groups share explanations, write a group explanation on chart paper, post charts around the room, and use a quick round-robin exercise to review and critique explanations. Students then share their ideas and write a class explanation.
2. Connect this thinking to new ideas in this learning target. Distribute various graphs to different groups, each representing the interactions of a different environmental factor on population growth (e.g., seasons, food supply, interspecific competition, predation, or parasitism). Many of these graphs are available in standard biology texts. If these are not available to you, retrieve "Ecosystems & Human Impact" from the Biology Mad website (see Recommended Resources, p. 225). The site provides sample, reproducible graphs. Groups discuss their assigned graphs and prepare group explanations of the graphs.

Though sense making occurs throughout the process already described, we now focus on it. We continue the previous activity to extend sense making. Groups share their explanations and other groups critique these explanations. Remind the groups about the following points about a model (in this case, the graphs and the students' mental models of what they portray).

1. A model can *explain all observations*.
2. A model can be used to *predict* the system's behavior if manipulated specific ways.
3. A model is *consistent with other models* in science and *with ideas people have about how the world works* (National Center for Mathematics and Science 2002).

When students interpret graphs in front of their peers, it helps them understand what is represented by the graphical representation. A teacher might ask such questions as (1) Can the data be extrapolated? (2) Does the graph represent actual data or summaries of data? (3) What about this graph supports/does not support your mental model?

Then hold a class discussion to pull together ideas shared in the various explanations. Use a teacher "think-aloud" to model for students how they might think through the differences and similarities of two of these graphs. Then small groups use modeling software (e.g., Model It) or prepare systems diagrams on paper to demonstrate their understandings of these interactions. Groups share their models with members of one other group and make modifications based on their discussions. Finally, students read text with scientific explanations and compare their explanations with the scientific explanations.

Sense making continues as teachers introduce students to the fieldwork that is central to this lesson. In our case, the school has a nearby, reestablished prairie. In fact, it abuts the school grounds and makes an ideal site for work because it provides the contrast of prairie and schoolyard. During this part of the lesson, we establish a belt transect[2] through the prairie and into the schoolyard. Students start writing in a field journal, beginning with general observations along the belt transect. We ask students to use some of what they learned in the population graphing activity and record what they see as potential links to their observations. These observations serve as an entry into the next learning target. We hold a general discussion about student observations, drawing connections to the previous activity and preparing to introduce the idea of biodiversity.

> *Note:* If you do not have a nearby ecosystem for study, you can conduct research in your schoolyard or in a nearby park, pond, or stream. Student observations and work in the schoolyard can be contrasted with more natural ecosystems, accessed via electronic resources and/or many networked ecological research projects. See the Recommended Resources on page 226, where you will find various web links and books to learn more about these procedures and those included in the rest of the lesson.

Students demonstrate understanding in a variety of ways during these activities. Their explanations and developed models themselves serve as demonstrations of understanding. Teacher questioning and student critiques act in the same way. Finally, the teacher can review field journals to analyze student thinking. If some students do not fully understand the concepts, we suggest that the teacher work with them in a small group on a group concept map of the key ideas. If Inspiration software is available, it could be used at this point. Those students who do show a deep understanding of the concepts can work on preparations for fieldwork and/or begin initial explorations about prairies.

Learning Target #2

Revisit Table 7.1 on page 220 and review Learning Target #2. To elicit student preconceptions, ask students to respond to some images. You can use images of your choice or those suggested by McCoy, McCoy, and Levey (2007) in the following activity. Display images of three different breeds of a similar species (e.g., dogs) that demonstrate genetic diversity, three different images of species from an ecosystem (we chose garter snake, goldfinch, and coyote) to demonstrate species diversity, and three habitats (e.g., prairie, deciduous forest, and desert) to illustrate ecosystem diversity. Ask students which set illustrates biodiversity. Since all three represent aspects of biodiversity, this should lead to a rich discussion. Students should be able to connect genetic diversity back to their understandings of natural selection. The focus of this lesson is on species diversity. The discussion should include students' ideas about why biodiversity—specifically species diversity and species richness—is important.

The activity we used to confront student preconceptions about biodiversity can be implemented at any school, even if under-resourced. Described by Richardson and Hari (2008), it studies the correlation between plants and arthropods and is easily conducted in urban settings. We briefly describe this activity here; but you can retrieve the full article for further detail.

For the activity, students place a brightly colored plastic bowl somewhere around the buildings where they live. Their bowl is filled with one cup of water, two teaspoons of salt, and a couple of drops of dish detergent. The bowls are left in place for 24 hours and will very likely collect various arthropods. (Students should be warned that they might not trap any arthropods; if that is the case, it is perfectly fine. Regardless, their results are part of the class data.)

At home, students place the collected samples into a jar and cover it with a lid. Students then use a one-meter-long piece of string with one end centered at the bowl. They work with a partner (e.g., parent or sibling) who holds the string over the center of the bowl, while they walk around the bowl at the length of the string, counting the number of plants and plants species within that circle. They record the data on a table provided to them. These data are naturally drawn from various habitats, since different students live in different areas and place their bowls in different settings. Students bring these data and samples to school and count and sort the samples. Each student's data are entered into a class spreadsheet and two graphs are generated: (1) arthropod richness versus plant richness and (2) arthropod abundance versus plant richness. These data are discussed by the class and connected to what students already know about biodiversity.

Next, we have students apply this understanding to the prairie through fieldwork and continuing to write in their field journals. They determine the index of biodiversity[3] for the prairie that adjoins the school, recording the species present between the two lines. Different groups are responsible for gathering data from portions of the belt transect and data are merged. This process acquaints students with the species present in the prairie and enhances their growing understanding of biodiversity.

When students have completed this work, they compile questions they have about the prairie area they studied. For instance, Does the makeup of the prairie change along the belt transect as the elevation changes (there is a slight slope)? The class discusses these questions, and each group identifies a question it would like to study.

Now, to make sure students incorporate these ideas into a broader under-standing about ecosystem stability and change, we have them carry out two sense-making activities.

1. Students conduct field research to find answers to their questions. They devel-op explanations and share them with the class. Then they use their results and those of the class to modify and extend their growing models of ecosystems.

2. Students conduct research, using text and online resources, to study prairies in our region historically and in the present. They note changes to the prairies over time and environmental factors that influenced those changes. They also consider changes to populations and communities. They then build this infor-mation into their growing models.

Students demonstrate understanding in a variety of ways during this portion of the lesson. Once again, they dialogue in small and large groups, and our probing ques-tions help them to develop their understandings. Their explanations and models help us to plan or possibly modify the lesson. Finally, we review their field journals and write descriptive comments and probing questions into the journals. If students require ad-ditional instruction, we identify the areas of their explanations and models that need clarification and design questions around those areas. We also identify sections of the text that are problematic and use reciprocal teaching to read and analyze the text. Then we meet in small groups for this additional instruction. Those students who demon-strate understanding can extend their learning by, for example, preparing and sending questions to scientists—both in the field and online—about their research. Newton's Ask a Scientist website (*www.newton.dep.anl.gov/aasquesv.htm*) is a good resource.

Learning Target #3

Learning Target #3 (Table 7.1) requires that we now consider natural disruptions to ecosystems and how these disruptions can impact ecosystems and the balance in them. We also look at the process that occurs when ecosystems recover.

We first elicit preconceptions, asking students to use their models to predict what would happen to a prairie ecosystem (perhaps ours) if impacted by a natural event. We provide individual students with one of two cases—either fire or extreme drought. They predict what they think will happen in the short and long term to the prairie and write a rationale for their predictions, based on their models.

We then confront student preconceptions. We place students in groups by case and ask them to share predictions with the group, to determine a group prediction, and to develop a group rationale. Students are thus required to hear alternative expla-nations, thereby confronting their own ideas and those of others.

Sense making (in particular, perceiving, interpreting, and organizing information) begins when we put students working on *different* cases into groups and ask them to share their predictions and rationales and to look for commonalities and differences. We then help students connect information by facilitating a brief class discussion of group ideas. This discussion is followed by an interactive lecture in which we use images of prairie succession, presentations, and whole-class discourse.

Sense making (in particular, retrieving, extending, and applying information) continues as students conduct a study using existent prairie research. We have other nearby prairies where ongoing research occurs but do not have the funding to allow multiple trips to the site. However, the SIMply Praire website contains rich data for student research. We chose to use selected data (*http://ed.fnal.gov/lasso/quadrats/study-searches.html*) and have students contrast selected prairies to our own in order to reinforce the concept of succession.[4] As students complete their research, we share findings via the website's online tools, update models, and develop a synthesized class model that summarizes understandings. [5]

Students demonstrate understanding in various ways that, as before, are embedded in the lesson. These include student predictions and written rationales (both individual and group), teacher questioning and probes during small- and large-group discussions, student online research sharing, and evolving models. The SIMply Prairie website provides resources we use if assessments show that some students need ongoing instruction. We also use guided questions to scaffold an inquiry for these students. In addition, we outline multiple extension activities for students are ready to continue learning.

Learning Target #4

Learning Target #4 is intended to get students started thinking about human impacts on an ecosystem (see Table 7.1). We elicit student understandings by returning to our belt transect. We ask individual students to make observations, compare the prairie transect portion to the schoolyard portion, and write an explanation for the differences between the two portions. They record observations and explanations in their field journals. They also add new questions that relate to these comparisons and explanations.

Students confront preconceptions during small-group discussions of observations and explanations. They identify a question for field research, make and implement a plan to gather data, and use the data to generate explanations.

Sense making occurs when students compare their findings to those of scientists (online and in text), generate a group report, and share the findings with the class via poster presentations. We facilitate a class discussion about the differences between the schoolyard and the prairie and ask students to describe what they think would be required to re-establish parts of the schoolyard as prairie. Students revisit the SIMply Prairie website, research information about re-established prairies, and devise a plan.

Finally, we ask students to apply this understanding to potential impacts of agriculture—specifically on biodiversity—in our state. They determine whether or not these impacts might be reversible or if the ecosystem might be irreversibly altered. They use online resources and questions posed to scientists to summarize their thinking. Finally, they revise their models to reflect any new understandings. These regional implications (as well as national and global environmental issues) are not the focus of this lesson, but this segment can lead to ongoing study of broader environmental issues.

Once again, embedded activities provide many types of evidence that demonstrate understanding. Field journals, models, and explanations continue to demonstrate students' degrees of understanding and to help us plan our instruction. Similarly, poster presentations and plans to re-establish prairie serve as formative assessments. Finally, questioning and probes during small- and large-group discussions continue to give us information about student understanding and the potential need for ongoing instruction. For students who need additional instruction, we use one-on-one and small-group work to analyze and modify their models. If additional supports are required, reading strategies using graphic organizers are employed as students are directed to specific text segments. Students ready to move on in their learning develop position papers on monoculture and its impact in our state.

Reflection and Application

We just completed the *responsive phase* for the last time. Let's consider the process we used and reflect on its application in your classroom. Review Table 7.1 before responding to the first question, and review Figure 7.7 before responding to the remaining questions.

1. How does the research review in Table 7.1 inform your instruction? What might you do differently in your current lesson on ecosystems, based on the research we summarized?
2. How well would the steps of the process in Figure 7.7 work for you? Would you need to modify them? If so, what might you do?
3. What about this iterative process makes sense to you? What works easily in your context?
4. What about this process challenges your instruction? What about the process makes it difficult and why?
5. If challenges exist, how would you overcome those challenges?

Closing

In Chapter 7, we modeled the entire Instructional Planning Framework, using "ecosystems and human impact" as the context. Earlier chapters showed how to implement different phases of the framework. Our intent in this book was to provide a framework and tools (Part I of the book), as well as a step-by-step orientation for using the framework and tools (Part II of the book). You might like to use Appendix A1 (pp. 244–245), which is a blank Teacher Work Template, and Appendix A2 (pp. 246–247), a list of the steps of the entire planning process.

We hope Chapter 7 clarified any of your remaining questions or concerns about the framework. Yes, you can use the Teacher Work Templates in each chapter to implement lessons and/or modify them for your own use, although our intent was not to develop ready-to-use lessons. Our ultimate hope is that you will make use of the framework and tools as you think through other hard-to-teach biology concepts.

Table 7.1

Teacher Work Template for "Interdependence—Environmental Systems and Human Impact"

Predictive Phase

		Lesson Topic—Interdependence: Environmental Systems and Human Impact	
Conceptual Target Development	National Standard(s) Addressed	*From 9–12 NSES:* • Organisms both cooperate and compete in ecosystems. The interrelationships and interdependencies of these organisms may generate ecosystems that are stable for hundreds or thousands of years. (p. 86) • Living organisms have the capacity to produce populations of infinite size, but environments and resources are finite. This fundamental tension has profound effects on the interactions between organisms. (p. 86) • Human beings live within the world's ecosystems. Increasingly, humans modify ecosystems as a result of population growth, technology, and consumption. Human destruction of habitats through direct harvesting, pollution, atmospheric changes, and other factors are threatening current global stability, and if not addressed, ecosystems will be irreversibly affected. (p. 86)	*From 9–12 Benchmarks:* • Ecosystems can be reasonably stable over hundreds or thousands of years. As any population of organisms grows, it is held in check by one or more environmental factors: depletion of food or nesting sites, increased loss to increased numbers of predators, or parasites. If a disaster such as flood or fire occurs, the damaged ecosystem is likely to recover in stages that eventually result in a system similar to the original one. (p. 117) • Like many complex systems, ecosystems tend to have cyclic fluctuations around a state of rough equilibrium. In the long run, however, ecosystems always change when climate changes or when one or more new species appear as a result of migration or local evolution. (p. 117) • Human beings are part of the earth's ecosystems. Human activities can, deliberately or inadvertently, alter the equilibrium in ecosystems. (p. 117)
	Previous Conceptual Learning	*From middle grade NSES:* • A population consists of all individuals of a species that occur together at a given place and time. All populations living together and the physical factors with which they interact compose an ecosystem. (p. 157) • The number of organisms an ecosystem can support depends on the resources available and abiotic factors, such as quantity of light and water, range of temperatures, and soil composition. Given adequate biotic and abiotic resources and no disease or predators, populations (including humans) increase at rapid rates. Lack of resources and other factors, such as predation and climate, limit the growth of populations in specific niches in the ecosystem. (p. 158) • When an area becomes overpopulated, the environment will become degraded due to the increased use of resources. (p. 168) • Causes of environmental degradation and resource depletion vary from region to region and from country to country. (p. 168)	*From middle grade Benchmarks:* • In all environments, organisms with similar needs may compete with one another for limited resources, including food, space, water, air, and shelter. (p. 117) • The world contains a wide diversity of physical conditions, which creates a wide variety of environments: freshwater, marine, forest, desert, grassland, mountain, and others. In any particular environment, the growth and survival of organisms depend on the physical conditions. (new set of Benchmarks[5D/M1b]) • Changes in environmental conditions can affect the survival of individual organisms and entire species. (p. 124) • Human activities, such as reducing the amount of forest cover, increasing the amount and variety of chemicals released into the atmosphere, and intensive farming, have changed the earth's lands, oceans, and atmosphere. Some of these changes have decreased the capacity of the environment to support some life forms. (p. 73)

Table 7.1 (continued)

	Knowledge and Skills	*From prior instruction in biology course:* Use of models in general and scientific models in particular, sources of variation (independent assortment, random fertilization, mutation), flow of energy and flow of matter in ecosystems, general understandings of population growth and intraspecific competition that are essential to natural selection
		Essential knowledge: See Learning Targets and unpack for embedded knowledge. **Subtopics that may be pruned**: climax community, "exponential growth curve," logistic growth curve, carrying capacity, density-dependent limiting and density-independent limiting **Essential vocabulary** (to apply and distinguish): *ecosystem, feedback* **Vocabulary that may be pruned**: See subtopics that may be pruned (listed above because some of these are both concepts and terms).
Essential Understandings		Ecosystems can remain relatively stable over long periods of time, fluctuating around a state of rough equilibrium. The roles and interactions of individual organisms and populations may change but ecosystems retain continuity. This can be disrupted by various natural factors or human interference. The ecosystem may gradually recover if the natural event is not too severe or the disruptive human influence is removed.
Criteria to Determine Understanding		• Accurately model the interactions in ecosystems that lead to a state of rough equilibrium. • Predict the impact of one ecosystem component on the interactions among organisms in the ecosystem. • Decide the long-term impact of a natural disruption on an ecosystem. • Propose a logical solution to a situation that results from human disruption in an ecosystem. • Justify the use of particular sources, data, and arguments as evidence for a claim. • Carefully plan and implement research, monitoring personal and group progress.

Responsive Phase

Identifying Student Preconceptions	Several good options include: • Have students individually construct circle maps, using "ecosystems" as the central term/concept. • Have students complete drawings in response to this prompt: "Make a drawing of an ecosystem that exists in our schoolyard and include annotations that describe your drawing." • Have each student complete a "Learning Goals Inventory" (Keeley 2008).

Table 7.1 (continued)

Learning Sequence Targets

Learning Target #1	Populations have the capacity to grow but are held in check by environmental factors/resources. This effects the interactions among organisms.

Research-Identified Misconceptions Addressed

- Some students think that populations exist in states of either constant growth or decline depending upon their position in a food chain (Munson 1991).
- Some students think that ecosystems are limitless resources, providing opportunities for limitless growth of a population (Munson 1991).
- Students may think that populations increase until limits are reached, then they crash and go extinct (McComas 2002).
- Some students think that all factors are limiting unless they are abundant, and that the least abundant factors are the most limiting (Eyster and Tashiro 1997).
- Some may think that density-dependent factors are biotic, and density-independent factors are abiotic (Lavoie 1997).
- Students may think that populations coexist in an ecological system because of their compatible needs and behaviors; they need to get along (Munson 1991).
- Some students of all ages think that populations of some organisms are numerous just so they are available to fulfill a food demand by another population (AAAS 1993).
- Students may think that the relative sizes of predator and prey populations have nothing to do with each other (Gallegos et al. 1994).
- They may also think that varying the population size of a species affects all other organisms to the same degree (Griffiths and Grant 1985).

Initial Instructional Plan

Eliciting Preconceptions: Teacher displays preinstructional graphic models and requires students to explain, in their science notebooks, the shapes of the curves (show both a logistic curve and a stabilized, oscillating curve resulting from intraspecific competition).

Confronting Preconceptions: Students share explanations, write group explanations, and share/critique explanations in a round-robin exercise. Write a class explanation. Student groups interpret and explain various graphs that show impact of different environment factors on population growth. Groups develop group explanations for the shape of their assigned graph.

Sense Making: Groups share and critique explanations. Teacher facilitates a class discussion to model how to synthesize ideas among graphs, using a think-aloud about two of the graphs. Groups use modeling software or systems diagrams on chart paper to create models that explain their synthesis of ideas. They then read selected text and compare their explanations to scientific explanations. Students establish a belt transect, crossing a prairie that abuts the school grounds and the schoolyard itself (*Note:* Any nearby selected ecosystem, including the schoolyard, can be used). They make observations and link observations to population graphing activity just completed.

Formative Assessment Plan (Demonstrating Understanding)

Teacher analyzes student explanations, models, and field journals. Teacher questioning and student critiques inform instruction. Student critiques serve as peer assessments

Table 7.1 (continued)

Learning Target #2	Ecosystems can be relatively stable over very long periods of time, even though the roles (e.g., competition and cooperation) and populations of organisms within the ecosystem can vary. Ecosystems fluctuate but in a cyclic way around a state of rough equilibrium.

Research-Identified Misconception Addressed

- Students may consider ecosystems, not as functioning whole, but as simply a collection of organisms (Brehm, Anderson, and DuBay 1986). They think in terms of separate components rather than the interconnected system.
- Students think predominately in a linear way rather than about cycles, interdependence, and systems (Driver et al. 1994).
- Students often think that communities change little over time (D'Avanzo 2003).
- Students may believe that organisms can change their structures to take advantage of a habitat or respond to changes in the environment by looking for a new environment (AAAS 1993).
- Some students think that varying the population size of a species may not affect an ecosystem, because some organisms are not important (Munson 1991).
- Some students think that population fluctuations in a river system community are due to seasonal changes, for example, phytoplankton dies off in winter. Some may also think there is a rapid increase in the number of top predators on a river system community as their food sources become depleted, and that this depletion contributes toward reestablishment of equilibrium (Webb and Boltt 1991).

Initial Instructional Plan

Eliciting Preconceptions: Students observe three sets of pictures that include three pictures each that demonstrate genetic diversity, species diversity, and ecosystem diversity and determine which (or all) illustrate biodiversity. Teacher facilitates class discussion that focuses on biodiversity, connecting to previous lessons on natural selection and stressing the importance of species diversity.

Confronting Preconceptions: Students collect arthropod samples outside their own home, as well as count numbers of plants and plant species surrounding the collection trap. Each student counts and sorts samples (at school). They share arthropod and plant count data as a class. Whole-class graphs of arthropod richness vs. plant richness and arthropod abundance vs. plant richness are developed and displayed. Data are discussed and the teacher facilitates the connections to previous understandings about biodiversity. Students determine the index of biodiversity for the prairie belt transect and become acquainted with the prairie species, recording observations and ideas in their field journal. Students generate questions they have about the prairie study area.

Sense Making: Students conduct field research to respond to a selected question, develop explanations, share explanations with the class, and use their own and class results to modify and/or extend their growing model. They then complete research (text and online) to study prairies of the region, historically and in the present. They consider changes through time and the factors that influence the changes. They use this information to further develop their model.

Formative Assessment Plan (Demonstrating Understanding)

Student small- and large-group dialogue and responses to the teacher's probing questions provide evidence of understanding and inform instruction. Student explanations, models, and field journals are analyzed to determine understanding and inform instruction

Table 7.1 (continued)

Learning Target #3	Various natural factors (including natural disasters, climate change, and the appearance of new species) can disrupt this equilibrium and the balance within the ecosystem can change. Depending on the severity of the disruption, the ecosystem can gradually recover to a system similar to the original system.

Research-Identified Misconceptions Addressed

- Many students fail to see the link between fluctuations in population size and related environmental issues (Munson 1991).
- Students may consider ecosystems, not a functioning whole, but as simply a collection of organisms (Brehm, Anderson, and DuBay 1986). They think in terms of separate components rather than the interconnected system.
- Students think predominately in a linear way rather than about cycles, interdependence, and systems (Driver et al. 1994).

Initial Instructional Plan

Eliciting Preconceptions: Students use their models to predict impact of a given natural event on a prairie ecosystem and provide a rationale for their prediction. Two different cases are used.

Confronting Preconceptions: Like-case groups share predictions, determine a group prediction, and develop a group rationale.

Sense Making: Different-case groups share predictions and rationales, comparing and contrasting their thinking. The teacher facilitates a class discussion of these ideas through an interactive lecture that introduces images of prairie succession. Students use online data and tools to conduct a virtual investigation, contrasting types of prairies and reinforcing the concept of succession. Students share findings via the online sharing tool. They update models and the class develops a synthesized model that summarizes understandings.

Formative Assessment Plan (Demonstrating Understanding)

Students demonstrate understanding in a variety of ways that includes their predictions and rationales (individual and group), teacher questioning and probes during small- and large-group discussions, student online research sharing, and evolving models. Each of these sources also serves to inform instruction.

Table 7.1 (continued)

Learning Target #4	Humans are part of the ecosystem, and our modifications to ecosystems can disrupt the established equilibrium. Ecosystems have the potential to recover from these disruptions, as they do when disrupted by natural factors. But sometimes the disruptive influences can overload the system's ability to maintain balance so ecosystems are irreversibly altered.

Research-Identified Misconceptions Addressed

- Many students fail to see the link between fluctuations in population size and related environmental issues (Munson 1991).
- It is a common misconception that humans are indestructible as a species (Brody 1994).
- Students may consider ecosystems, not a functioning whole, but as simply a collection of organisms (Brehm, Anderson, and DuBay 1986). They think in terms of separate components rather than the interconnected system.
- Students think predominately in a linear way rather than about cycles, interdependence, and systems (Driver et al. 1994).
- Learners have difficulty with comprehension of scale and geologic timeframes (Learmonth 2004, Mullis 2003), making more likely the perception that human impact is local and immediate.

Initial Instructional Plan

Eliciting Preconceptions: Students make observations, comparing the prairie and schoolyard components of the belt transect. They record observations, explanations, and questions in their field journal.

Confronting Preconceptions: Research groups discuss their various observations and explanations. They identify a group question, plan and implement research to gather and analyze data, and generate explanations for their findings.

Sense Making: Students compare their explanations to those of scientists, finalize their research reports, and share them via poster presentations. A whole-class discussion is used to summarize student findings and thinking about the differences between the prairie and schoolyard. Students develop a plan to re-establish prairie in some of the schoolyard. Finally, students extend and apply their thinking to a regional level by considering the impact of agriculture on the ecosystem. They research the degree of impact and determine what might be reversible or irreversible. They revise their models, one last time, based on these learning experiences.

Formative Assessment Plan (Demonstrating Understanding)

The various formative assessments available to demonstrate understanding and inform instruction include: field journals, models, explanations, poster presentations, plans to re-establish prairie, and questioning/probes during large- and small-group discussion.

Table 7.2

Potential Strategies to Identify Student Preconceptions

Potential Strategies	Summary of Research and Classroom Implications
Writing to Learn: Learning Logs	• They allow students to clarify ideas in and about science, related to conceptual, procedural and/or NOS understandings. • Learning logs can engage student thinking about a topic since they require students to focus on content in their writing, rather than on personal feelings.
Reading to Learn: Informational Text Strategies	Reading strategies that can be applied across disciplines include discussion strategies, active reading strategies, and organization strategies. Several of these strategies (including discussion webs, think-pair-share, anticipation guides, KWL, and concept diagrams) also help identify student preconceptions for teacher planning and elicit student preconceptions (allowing them to grapple with their own thinking).
Visual Tools: Brainstorming Webs	• These are generative and associative activities that help engage prior knowledge, skills, and understandings (Lipton and Wellman 1998). • Circle maps help students focus on and make connections between ideas. • Clustering allows students to explore and generate a network of initial ideas. • In mind mapping students represent relationships and conceptual knowledge, using both words and images. It can be used to determine prior knowledge as well as used during a lesson as students learn about the concepts.
Visual Tools: Task-Specific Organizers	• Some of these organizers are listed in "Informational Text Strategies" above. KWL's and anticipation guides fit this category and can be used to determine students' thinking prior to instruction. • Keeley (2008) outlines a FACT called "Learning Goals Inventory" that serves well to determine prior understandings since it asks students to inventory their ideas about a topic. The probing questions it includes deal with what students think they know about the topic; any familiar terminology, facts, concepts, or ideas about the topic; and any experiences they have had that helped them learn about the topic.
Drawing Out Thinking: Drawings and Annotated Drawings	• They may be best used when teaching nonobservable science concepts. • They are even more effective when coupled with verbal information (questioning/interviews). • Some students that might find it difficult to express themselves in words may be able to express themselves through drawing. • They provide information about specific misconceptions, helpful to both students and teachers. • They provide information to the teacher that helps determine what strategies best support student learning needs. • They are less biased than some strategies/assessments since students choose what they draw and draw from their own experiences. This also allows the teacher to respond to students' interests, background knowledge, and skills.

Table 7.3

Strategies to Elicit and Confront Preconceptions and for Sense Making and Demonstrating Understanding

Strategies	Summary of Research and Classroom Implications
Writing to Learn: Scientific Explanations	**Elicit and Confront:** Writing can be used to elicit preconceptions since it clarifies students' ideas and can be used to reflect on current understandings. **Sense Making:** In general, writing is a good strategy for sense making since it clarifies ideas and can be used to reflect on conceptual, procedural, and NOS understandings. Our focus on content, inquiry, and aspects of the NOS make writing appropriate for sense making in this lesson. In particular, constructing explanations results in improved understandings of inquiry and content. Since it is difficult to learn how to construct explanations, it helps to provide students a framework (e.g., claim, evidence, and reasoning that links claim to evidence). It also helps to generate criteria for explanations, make the framework explicit, model construction of explanations, and provide practice time to develop and critique explanations. **Demonstrating Understanding:** Student explanations themselves can be analyzed to determine level of understanding or misunderstanding. Peer critique of explanations based on pre-established criteria also serves as formative assessment.
Speaking to Learn: Large- and Small-Group Discourse	**Elicit and Confront:** Realistic and authentic problems (in our case, fieldwork and analysis of human impact on environment) provide focus for student discussion and can lead to productive follow-up activities. Accountable talk helps recognize and challenge misconceptions. **Sense Making:** Accountable talk deepens conversations and understanding of the topic studied. Accountable talk is promoted when students clarify, explain, justify proposals and challenges, demand evidence for claims, interpret each other's statements, etc. Discussion is enhanced with multiple viewpoints. Whole-class discussion works well in the context of an activity with shared experiences. Small-group discourse allows students to build on each other's ideas as they generate explanations. Use of both reflects the work of science and promotes development of shared understandings. Student-generated questions, open-ended questions, student choice of inquiry topics, and more time for student research and exploration encourage deeper discussion and investigation. All of this aligns with the lesson content, fieldwork, and our inquiry strategy. **Demonstrating Understanding:** Listening to small-group discourse and teacher questioning during small- and large-group discourse serves as formative assessment and informs instruction.

Table 7.3 (continued)

Strategies	Summary of Research and Classroom Implications
Models: Mental Models	***Elicit and Confront:*** Construction and critique of their own models promotes student conceptual development. Initial construction elicits/confronts preconceptions. Authentic inquiry engages students in construction, revision, and assessment of models. Peer discussion shows students alternative models, helpful in confronting preconceptions. ***Sense Making:*** Student conceptual development is promoted when they construct and critique their models. Construction elicits and confronts preconceptions. Authentic inquiry engages students in construction, revision, and assessment of their models. Pedagogies using various modes of modeling are most effective for content and NOS outcomes if students reflect on and discuss both their own models and those of scientists. Peer discussion provides students with alternative models and introduces criteria and evidence by which to distinguish among scientific models. A "think-aloud" approach shares the teacher's mental model with students, demonstrating how to think about a problem and plan an approach to solving it. ***Demonstrating Understanding:*** Listening and questioning during small-group discussion and one-on-one questioning probes students' thinking, determines level of understanding, and informs instruction.
Models: Visual Models	***Elicit and Confront:*** Graphic models elicit preconceptions when students are presented a graph, table or figure and asked to describe/interpret the image. Small-group interpretations surface alternate explanations and confront preconceptions. ***Sense Making:*** Developed models, when shared and critiqued, help students see connections among ideas, change as student learn more, and help teachers recognize what students know and don't know. ***Demonstrating Understanding:*** Listening and questioning during small-group discussion and one-on-one questioning, probes students' thinking, determines level of understanding, and informs instruction. The model itself and students' verbal critique of models demonstrate the level of student understanding.
Models: Dynamic Models	***Elicit and Confront:*** Dynamic models probe preconceptions and can be used individually or in small groups. Combining computer modeling with hands-on activities is effective. ***Sense Making:*** Modeling and visualization enable students to manipulate a variety of visual representations of abstract concepts and explore the concepts, bringing the study of science closer to the doing of science. They help instruction that involves concepts that are difficult to observe and simplify complex systems. They simulate the behavior of complex systems (like ecosystems) and improve problem-solving and process skills. Using simulations can promote misconceptions. It is important to facilitate students' analysis of the strengths and deficits of the model. STELLA and Model It are both software applications designed for systems modeling that allow students to develop their own models. Model It is designed to be accessible for precollege students. ***Demonstrating Understanding:*** Listening and questioning during small-group discussion and one-on-one questioning probes students' thinking, determines level of understanding, and informs instruction. Guiding questions during simulations allow for immediate modification of instruction. The model itself and students' verbal critique of models demonstrate the level of student understanding.

Table 7.3 (continued)

Strategies	Summary of Research and Classroom Implications
Nonlinguistic Representations: Concept Mapping	***Elicit and Confront Preconceptions:*** They help people differentiate misconceptions from accurate conceptions. Alternative explanations are shared when group mapping occurs, and this allows students to confront their own and others preconceptions. Or students can first build their own map (eliciting preconceptions) and then merge individual maps into a group map (confronting preconceptions). ***Sense Making:*** They establish meaningful patterns of learning and focus on the core concepts and concept relationships. They enhance metacognitive abilities and provide a reference for students to analyze their thinking, identify strengths and weaknesses, and set learning targets. They help elucidate the differences between alternative conceptions and the scientific conception, central to sense making. Merging individual maps into a group map promotes dialog and debate about alternative explanations, promoting sense making. Group construction allows students to confront peers' misunderstandings, leading to deeper understandings of their own. ***Demonstrating Understanding:*** Concept maps effectively identify student misconceptions and provide formative assessment data that inform instruction. They also allow students to correct each other's mistakes (peer assessment used formatively). Teacher questioning during map construction probes student thinking and guides instruction. The high levels of synthesis and evaluation required in map construction makes them powerful evaluation tools.
Nonlinguistic Representations: Systems Diagrams	***Elicit and Confront Preconceptions:*** When used for brainstorming, they elicit student preconceptions. ***Sense Making:*** Systems diagrams are essentially models. They represent complex situations more easily than text alone. They can be used to understand connectivity in a system, as well as diagnose, plan, implement, and communicate. Constructing diagrams in a group aids brainstorming, analysis, communication, and understanding. STELLA and Model It are dynamic systems diagramming software. But, without access to the software, systems diagrams serve the same purpose. ***Demonstrating Understanding:*** See concept maps.

Recommended Resources

Technology Applications and Websites

- A nice overview of the content in this chapter will be found in the Biology Mad website: *www.biologymad.com*. Select "A2 Biology" from the sidebar menu and then select "Ecosystems and Human Impact." This site provides general teacher information and graphs for use in Learning Target #1 in this chapter.

- Networked research projects available for student involvement include the following:

  - The Globe Program provides opportunities for several ongoing, authentic research projects (*www.globe.gov/r*).

- The U.S. Geological Survey offers the North American Amphibian Monitoring Program (NAAMP) at *www.pwrc.usgs.gov/naamp*, and the National Wildlife Federation hosts Frogwatch USA at *www.nwf.org/frogwatchusa*.

- BioQUEST offers opportunities to get involved in plant research efforts at the myPlantIT website (*www.myplantit.org*).

- The U.S. Forest Service I-Tree website (*www.itreetools.org*) incorporates two existing online monitoring programs—one to assess urban ecosystems and one to assess street tree populations. Both allow information about trees to be entered into a program that calculates the cost/benefit analysis of trees as they contribute to carbon sequestration, energy costs, and so forth.

- Pathfinder Science (*http://pathfinderscience.net/stream*) lets students share stream monitoring data. It uses different data sources: a visual survey, a chemical survey, biological monitoring, and volume/velocity of flow.

- The Cornell Lab of Ornithology offers Citizen Science with ongoing projects available for participation (*www.birds.cornell.edu*).

- The SIOExplorer Digital Library Project (*http://nsdl.sdsc.edu*) includes data, documents, and images from Scripps Institution of Oceanography expeditions.

- The Microbial Life project offers ideas and opportunities to integrate research and education (*http://serc.carleton.edu/microbelife/research_education/index.html*).

- There are great webcast surgeries, other health science resources, and examples of student research from the Cleveland Clinic at *www.clevelandclinic.org/civiceducation/realworld/real_world_connect.as*.

Build Your Library

NSTA Press has published several wonderful books that can serve as lesson resources. Among these are teacher and student editions of the Cornell Scientific Inquiry Series:

- *Assessing Toxic Risk* (Trautmann and the Environmental Inquiry Team 2001)

- *Decay and Renewal* (Trautmann and the Environmental Inquiry Team 2003)

- *Invasion Ecology* (Krasny and the Environmental Inquiry Team 2003)

- *Watershed Dynamics* (Carlsen, Trautman, and the Environmental Inquiry Team 2004)

In addition, *Resources for Environmental Literacy: Five Teaching Modules for Middle and High School Teachers* (ELC and NSTA 2007) offers many instructional ideas.

Another NSTA Press series worth your attention is the Global Environment Change series:

- *Global Environmental Change: Biodiversity* (NSTA and EPA 1997a)

- *Global Environmental Change: Carrying Capacity* (NSTA and EPA 1997b)

- *Global Environmental Change: Deforestation* (NSTA and EPA 1997c)
- *Global Environmental Change: Introduced Species* (NSTA and EPA 1998)

A classic resource for conducting schoolyard studies is *Biology Is Outdoors!* (Hancock 1991). This book directly or indirectly addresses each of these learning targets in this chapter.

Endnotes

1. We understand that you or your school district may not own the resources cited in this chapter. Selected maps from the *Atlas of Science Literacy* are available at the Project 2061 site, including the Interdependence of Life map on page 196, at *www. project2061.org/publications/atlas/sample/a2ch5.pdf.* The *Atlas of Science Literacy, Volume 1,* maps are at the National Science Digital Library website (*http://strandmaps.nsdl. org*). The *Pathways* books are available for purchase through the NSTA Science Store (*www.nsta.org/store*). Though the major work required for our planning process can be completed without them, they are great additions to any library and help clarify the National Science Education Standards.

2. Transects, in general, describe the distribution of species in a line across a habitat and are especially useful when there is a change in habitat. A belt transect records all species between two lines that run the length of the habitat.

3. The index of diversity considers the number of species present and the number of individuals for each species present. A good reference for the Simpson Diversity Index, which describes use of the formula and provides examples, is at the Offwell Woodland & Wildlife Trust website (*www.countrysideinfo.co.uk/simpsons.htm*).

4. This site also has an entire set of materials to help students implement a full investigation of their own. These resources and more (e.g., developed lessons, assessment tools) are at "Planning and Conducting Your Investigation" on the site (*http://ed.fnal. gov/ntep/f98/projects/fnal/student/invest.shtml*).

5. BLM has a CD ("Burning Issues") on the effects of fire on four ecosystems. It can be used as a replacement and/or additional activity for sense making. "Burning Issues" helps secondary students learn about the role of fire in ecosystems and the use of fire to manage natural areas. The program challenges users to learn about prescribed burns, wild-land fire suppression, the relationships between fire and invasive plant species, and building "firewise" homes. This CD contains four EcoTours of different biotic communities, an interactive field guide containing more than 300 slides and descriptions of organisms, four online activities, print materials for educators and students and much, much more. For further information go to *www.eea.freac.fsu.edu/bi.html.*

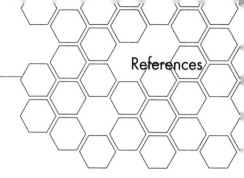

References

Ambron, J. 1987. Writing to improve learning in biology. *Journal of College Science Teaching* 16 (4): 263–266.

American Association for the Advancement of Science (AAAS). 1989. *Science for all Americans.* New York: Oxford University Press.

American Association for the Advancement of Science (AAAS). 1993. *Benchmarks for science literacy.* New York: Oxford University Press.

American Association for the Advancement of Science (AAAS). 2001a. *Atlas of science literacy.* Washington, DC: AAAS.

American Association for the Advancement of Science (AAAS). 2001b. *Designs for science literacy.* New York: Oxford University Press.

American Association for the Advancement of Science (AAAS). 2007a. Symposium: Learning progressions in environmental literacy. *2061 Connections* (July/August electronic newsletter). *www.project2061.org/publications/2061Connections/2007/2007-04a-resources.htm*

American Association for the Advancement of Science (AAAS). 2007b. *Atlas of science literacy.* Vol. 2. Washington, DC: AAAS.

Anderson, C. W. 2007. Environmental literacy learning progressions. Paper presented at the Knowledge Sharing Institute of the Center for Curriculum Studies in Science in Washington, D.C.

Anderson, D. L., K. M. Fisher, and G. J. Norman. 2002. Development and evaluation of the conceptual inventory of natural selection. *Journal of Research in Science Teaching* 39 (10): 952–978.

Anderson, R. D. 2007. Inquiry as an organizing theme for science curricula. In *Handbook of research on science education*, eds. S. K. Abell and N. G. Lederman, 807–830. Mahwah, NJ: Lawrence Erlbaum Associates.

Ardia, D. R. 2005. Natural selection and variation: A hands-on lesson using bird specimens. *The American Biology Teacher* 67 (8): 468–473.

Association for Supervision and Curriculum Development (ASCD). 2008. Analyzing classroom discourse to advance teaching and learning. *Education Update* 50 (2): 1, 3, and 7.

Atkinson, H., and S. Bannister. 1998. Concept maps and annotated drawings. *Primary Science Review* 51:3–5.

Bahar, M., A. H. Johnstone, and M. H. Hansell. 1999. Revisiting learning difficulties in biology. *Journal of Biological Education* 33 (2): 84–86.

Baird, J. R., and R. T. White. 1996. Metacognitive strategies in the classroom. In *Improving teaching and learning in science and mathematics*, eds. D. F. Treagust, R. Duit, and B. J. Fraser, 190–200. New York: Teachers College Press.

Baker, L. 2004. Reading comprehension and science inquiry: Metacognitive connections. In *Crossing borders in literacy and science instruction*, ed. E. W. Saul, 239–257. Newark, DE: International Reading Association and Arlington, VA: NSTA Press.

Banilower, E., K. Cohen, J. Pasley, and I. Weiss. 2008. *Effective science instruction: What does research tell us?* Portsmouth, NH: RMC Research Corporation, Center on Instruction.

Barker, M. 1985. *Where does wood come from? An introduction to photosynthesis for 3rd and 4th formers.* Hamilton, New Zealand: University of Waikato. Referenced in Wahanga Mahi Rangahau, *Curriculum, Learning and Effective Pedagogy: A Literature Review in Science Education* (Wellington, New Zealand: Ministry of Education).

Barker, M. 1986. The description and modification of children's ideas of plant nutrition. PhD diss., University of Waikato. Referenced in Wahanga Mahi Rangahau, *Curriculum, learning and effective pedagogy: A literature review in science education* (Wellington, New Zealand: Ministry of Education).

Barker, M. 1995. A plant is an animal standing on its head. *Journal of Biological Education* 29 (3): 203–208.

Barman, C. R., M. Stein, S. McNair, and N. S. Barman. 2006. Students' ideas about plants and plant growth. *The American Biology Teacher* 68 (2): 73–79.

Barton, M. L., and D. L. Jordan. 2001. *Teaching reading in science: A supplement to teaching reading in the content areas teacher's manual.* 2nd ed. Aurora, CO: McREL.

Berthelsen, B. 1999. Students' naive conceptions in life science. *MSTA Journal* 44 (1): 13–19.

Bishop, B., and C. Anderson. 1990. Student conceptions of natural selection and its role in evolution. *Journal of Research in Science Teaching* 27:415–427. Quoted in American Association for the Advancement of Science (AAAS), *Benchmarks for science literacy* (Washington, DC: National Academy Press, 1993), 343.

Blakey, E., and S. Spence. 1990. Developing megacognition. (ERIC Digest no. ED327218.) *www.ericdigests.org/pre-9218/developing.htm.*

Bransford, J., A. Brown, and R. R. Cocking. 1999. *How people learn: Brain, mind, experience, and school.* Washington, DC: National Academy Press.

Brehm, S., C. W. Anderson, and J. DuBay. 1986. *Ecology: A teaching module.* East Lansing, MI: Michigan State University–The Institute for Research on Teaching.

Brody, M. J. 1994. Student science knowledge related to the ecological crisis. *International Journal of Science Education* 21 (2): 16–26.

Brown, D. S. 2003. High school biology: A group approach to concept mapping. *The American Biology Teacher* 65 (3): 192–197.

Brumby, M. 1979. Problems in learning the concept of natural selection. *Journal of Biological Education* 13:119–122. Quoted in American Association for the Advancement of Science (AAAS), *Benchmarks for science literacy* (Washington, DC: National Academy Press, 1993), 343.

Bryson, B. 2003. *A short history of nearly everything.* New York: Broadway Books.

Bureau of Labor Statistics. 2000. Report on the youth labor force. U. S. Department of Labor. *www.bls.gov/opub/rylf/pdf/rylf2000.pdf*

Burke, K. A., T. J. Greenbowe, and B. M. Hand. 2005. Excerpts from the process of using inquiry and the science writing heuristic. Iowa State University. *http://avogadro.chem.iastate.edu/SWH/homepage.htm*

Burke, K. A., B. Hand, J. Poock, and T. Greenbowe. 2005. Using the science writing heuristic: Training chemistry teaching assistants. *Journal of College Science Teaching* 35 (1): 36–41.

NATIONAL SCIENCE TEACHERS ASSOCIATION

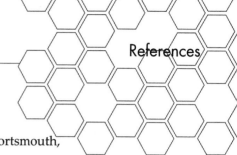

Bybee, R. W. 1997. *Achieving scientific literacy: From purposes to practices.* Portsmouth, NH: Heinemann.

Bybee, R. W. 2006. How inquiry can contribute to the prepared mind. *The American Biology Teacher* 68 (8): 454–457.

Cañas, A. J., and J. D. Novak. 2006. Re-examining the foundations for effective use of concept maps. Cmap Tools. *http://cmc.ihmc.us/cmc2006Papers/cmc2006-p247.pdf*

Carlsen, W. H. 2007. Language and science learning. In *Handbook of research on science education*, eds. S. K. Abell and N. G. Lederman, 57–74. Mahwah, NJ: Lawrence Erlbaum Associates.

Carlsen, W. S., N. M. Trautmann, and the Environmental Inquiry Team. 2004. *Watershed dynamics.* Student edition and teacher's guide. Arlington, VA: NSTA Press.

Carnegie Mellon University. 2003. Environmental literacy. Carnegie Mellon Environmental Decision Making, Science, and Technology. *http://telstar.ote.cmu.edu/environ/m1/s1/index.shtml*

Cartier, J. 2000. Research report: Using a modeling approach to explore scientific epistemology with high school biology student. Wisconsin Center for Education Research. *www.wcer.wisc.edu/NCISLA/publications/reports/ RR991.pdf*

Cawelti, G. C. 1999. *Handbook of research on improving student achievement.* 2nd ed. Arlington, VA: Educational Research Service.

Century, J. R., J. Flynn, D. S. Makang, M. Pasquale, K. M. Roblee, J. Winokur, and K. Worth. 2002. Supporting the science-literacy connection. In *Learning science and the science of learning,* ed. R. W. Bybee, 37–49. Arlington, VA: NSTA Press.

Chattopadhyay, A. 2005. Understanding of genetic information in higher secondary students in northeast India and the implications for genetics education. *Cell Biology Education* 4 (1): 97–104.

Chattopadhyay, A., and B. S. Mahajan. 2006. Student's understanding of DNA and DNA technologies after "fifty years of DNA double helix." Electronic proceedings of the International Conference to Review Research on Science, Technology, and Mathematics Education (epiSTEME1).

Chiappetta, E., and T. R. Koballa Jr. 2004. Quizzing students on the myths of science. *The Science Teacher* 71 (9): 58–61.

Chin, C., D. E. Brown, and C. B. Bertram. 2002. Student-generated questions: A meaningful aspect of learning in science. *International Journal of Science Education* 24 (5): 521–549.

Chinnici, J. P., S. Z. Neth, and L. R. Sherman. 2006. Using "chromosomal socks" to demonstrate ploidy in mitosis and meiosis. *The American Biology Teacher* 68 (2): 106–109.

Chinnici, J. P., J. W. Yes, and K. M. Torres. 2004. Students as "human chromosomes" in role-playing mitosis and meiosis. *The American Biology Teacher* 66 (1): 35–39.

Chubb, J. E., and T. Loveless. 2002. *Bridging the achievement gap.* Washington, DC: Brookings Institution Press.

Clough, E. E., and C. Wood-Robinson. 1985. Children's understanding of inheritance. *Journal of Biological Education* 19:304–310. Quoted in American Association for the Advancement of Science (AAAS), *Benchmarks for Science Literacy* (Washington, DC: National Academy Press, 1993), 343.

Clough, M. P., and J. K. Olson. 2004. The nature of science: Always part of the science story. *The Science Teacher* 71 (9): 28–31.

Coffey, J. E. 2006. Classroom assessment in the service of student learning. In *Teaching science in the 21st century,* eds. J. Rhoton and P. Shane, 39–51. Arlington, VA: NSTA Press.

Colbert, J. T., J. K. Olson, and M. P. Clough. 2007. Using the web to encourage student-generated questions in large-format introductory biology classes. *CBE Life Sciences Education* 6 (1): 42–48.

Colburn, A. 2004. Focusing labs on the nature of science: Laboratories can be structured to help students better understand the nature of science. *The Science Teacher* 71 (9): 32–35.

Committee on Undergraduate Science Education. 1997. Misconceptions as barriers to understanding science. *Science teaching reconsidered: A handbook.* Washington, DC: National Academy Press.

Cooper, R. A. 2004. How evolutionary biologists reconstruct history: Patterns and processes. *The American Biology Teacher* 66 (2): 101–108.

Costa, A. 2008. The thought-filled curriculum. *Educational Leadership* 65 (5): 20–24.

Cottrell, T. R. 2004. Capturing difficult botanical concepts with a net of previous knowledge. *The American Biology Teacher* 66 (6): 441–445.

D'Avanzo, C. 2003. Application of research on learning to college teaching: Ecological examples. *Bioscience* 53 (11): 1121–1128.

Davies, A. 2003. Learning through assessment: Assessment for learning in the science classroom. In *Everyday assessment in the science classroom,* eds. J. M. Atkin and J. E. Coffey, 13–25. Arlington, VA: NSTA Press.

DeFrono, R. D. 2006. Comprehension strategies and the scientist's notebook: Keys to assessing student understanding. In *Linking science and literacy in the K–8 classroom,* eds. R. Douglas, M. P. Klentschy, and K. Worth, with W. Binder, 127–147. Arlington, VA: NSTA Press.

Donovan, M. S., J. D. Bransford, and J. W. Pellegrino. 1999. *How people learn: Bridging research and practice.* Washington, DC: National Academy Press.

Driver, R. 1983. *The pupil as scientist?* Philadelphia, PA: Open University Press.

Driver, R., A. Squires, P. Rushworth, and V. Wood-Robinson. 1994. *Making sense of secondary science: Research into children's ideas.* London: Routledge.

Duit, R., and D. Treagust. 1998. Learning in science—from behaviourism towards social constructivism and beyond. In *International handbook of science education,* eds. K. Tobin, and B. Fraser, 3–25. Dordrecht, The Netherlands: Kluwer.

Duncan, R. G., and B. J. Reiser. 2003. Students' reasoning about phenomenon generated by complex systems: The case of molecular genetics. Paper presented at the annual international conference of the National Association for Research in Science Teaching in Philadelphia, PA.

Duncan, R. G., A. Rogat, and A. Yarden. 2007. Learning progression in genetics. Project 2061. *www.project2061.org/publications/2061Connections/2007/media/KSIdocs/golanduncan_ rogat_yarden_paper.pdf*

Duschl, R., H. Schweingruber, and A. Shouse. 2007. *Taking science to school: Learning and teaching science in grades K–8.* Washington, DC: National Academies Press.

Ebert-May, D. 2003. Radish problem. First II. *www.first2.org*

Ebert-May, D. 2006. Research on alternative conceptions in students: The carbon cycle. First II. *www.first2.org*

Ebert-May, D., K. Williams, and J. Batzli. 2002. Innovative teaching to achieve active learning in ecology. Presentation at the Ecological Society of America Workshop (08/02). First II. *www.first2.org*.

Edens, K. M., and E. F. Potter. 2003. Using descriptive drawings as a conceptual change strategy in elementary science. *School Science and Math Journal* 103 (3): 135–144.

Ekici, F., E. Ekici, and F. Aydin. 2007. Utility of concept cartoons in diagnosing and overcoming misconceptions related to photosynthesis. *International Journal of Environmental and Science Education* 2 (4): 111–124.

Eklund, J., A. Rogat, N. Alozie, and J. Krajcik. 2007. Promoting student scientific literacy of molecular genetics and genomics. Paper presented at the annual international conference of the National Association for Research in Science Teaching in New Orleans, LA.

Elrod, S. n.d. Genetics concepts inventory. Bioliteracy. *www.bioliteracy.net*

Environmental Literacy Council (ELC) and the National Science Teachers Association. 2007. *Resources for environmental literacy: Five teaching modules for middle and high school teachers.* Arlington, VA: NSTA Press.

Eyster, L. S., and J. S. Tashiro. 1997. Using manipulatives to teach quantitative concepts in ecology: A hands-on method for detecting and correcting misconceptions about limiting factors in eutrophication and vegetarianism. *The American Biology Teacher* 59 (6): 360–364.

Fink, P. A. 1990. An interactive, 3D model of protein synthesis. *The American Biology Teacher* 52 (5): 274–275.

Fisher, K. M. 1985. A misconception in biology: Amino acids and translation. *Journal of Research in Science Teaching* 22 (1): 53–62.

Fisher, K. M., J. H. Wandersee, and D. E. Moody. 2000. *Mapping biology knowledge.* Boston: Kluwer.

Fisher, K., and K. Williams. 2007. Inventorying conceptual understanding of basic biology ideas. Bioliteracy. *http://bioliteracy.net*

Flick, L. B. 1997. Understanding a generative learning model of instruction: A case study of elementary teacher planning. *Journal of Science Teacher Education* 7 (2): 95–122.

Freedman, R. L. H. 1994. *Open-ended questioning: A handbook for educators.* Menlo Park, CA: Addison-Wesley.

Friedrichsen, P. M., and B. Stone. 2004. Examining students' conceptions of molecular genetics in an introductory biology course for non-science majors: A self study. Paper presented at the annual international meeting of the National Association for Research in Science Teaching in Vancouver, WA.

Gallegos, L., M. E. Jerezano, and F. Flores. 1994. Preconceptions and relations used by children in the construction of food chains. *Journal of Research in Science Teaching* 31 (3): 259–272.

Gelbart, H., and A. Yarden. 2008. Learning genetics through a web-based research simulation in bioinformatics: How do students' approaches to learning influence their learning outcomes? Open University of Israel. *http://telem-pub.openu.ac.il/users/chais/2008/morning/4_3.pdf*

Gerking, J. 2004. Foreword to *Evolution in perspective: The science teacher's compendium*, ed. R.W. Bybee. Arlington, VA: NSTA Press.

Gilbert, S. W., and S. W. Ireton. 2003. *Understanding models in Earth and space science.* Arlington, VA: NSTA Press.

Gore, M. C. 2004. *Successful inclusion strategies for secondary and middle school teachers: Keys to help struggling learners access the curriculum.* Thousand Oaks, CA: Corwin Press.

Gregory, G. H., and E. Hammerman. 2008. *Differentiated instructional strategies for science, grades K–8.* Thousand Oaks, CA: Corwin Press.

Griffiths, A. K., and B. A. C. Grant. 1985. High school students' understanding of food webs: Identification of learning hierarchy and related misconceptions. *Journal of Research in Science Teaching* 22 (5): 421–436.

Groleau, R. 2001. How cells divide: Mitosis vs. meiosis. Videotape. Nova Online. *www.pbs.org/wgbh/nova/baby/divide.html*

Hale, M. S., and E. A. City. 2006. *The teacher's guide to leading student-centered discussions.* Thousand Oaks, CA: Corwin Press.

Hancock, J. M. 1991. *Biology is outdoors! A comprehensive resource for studying school environments.* Portland, ME: J. Weston Walch.

Hand, B. 2006. Using the science writing heuristic to promote understanding of science conceptual knowledge in middle school. In *Linking science and literacy in the K–8 classroom*, eds. R. Douglas, M. P. Klentschy, and K. Worth, with W. Binder, 117–125. Arlington, VA: NSTA Press.

Hargrove, T. Y., and C. Nesbit. 2003. *Science notebooks: Tools for increasing achievement across the curriculum.* Columbus, OH: ERIC Clearinghouse for Science, Mathematics and Environmental Education. ERIC Digest no. ED482720. *www.ericdigests.org/2004-4/notebooks.htm*

Harlen, W. 2001. *Primary science: Taking the plunge.* 2nd ed. Portsmouth, NH: Heinemann Educational Books.

Harrison, A. G., and R. K. Coll. 2008. *Using analogies in middle and secondary science classrooms: The FAR guide—An interesting way to teach with analogies.* Thousand Oaks, CA: Corwin Press.

Harrison, A. G., and D. F. Treagust. 2000. A typology of school science models. *International Journal of Science Education* 22 (9): 1011–1026.

Hartman, H. J., and N. A. Glasgow. 2002. *Tips for the science teacher: Research-based strategies to help students learn.* Thousand Oaks, CA: Corwin Press.

Harvard-Smithsonian Center for Astrophysics. 1995. *A Private Universe Project.* [Teacher workshop series.] Videotape. Burlington, VT: Annenberg/CPB Math and Science Collection.

Haury, D. L. 1996. *Teaching evolution in school science classes.* Columbus, OH: ERIC Clearinghouse for Science, Mathematics, and Environmental Education. ERIC Digest no. ED02148. *www.ericdigests.org/1998-1/evolution.htm*

Heritage, M. 2008. Learning progressions supporting instruction and formative assessment. Paper prepared for the Formative Assessment for Teachers and Students (FAST) Council of Chief State School Officers, Washington, DC.

Hershey, D. R. 2004. Avoid misconceptions when teaching about plants. ActionBioscience. org. *www.actionbioscience.org/education/hershey.html*

Hewson, P. W. 1992. Conceptual change in science teaching and teacher education. Paper presented at a meeting on "Research and Curriculum Development in Science Teaching," under the auspices of the National Center for Educational Research, Documentation, and Assessment at the Ministry for Education and Science, Madrid, Spain.

Hewson, P. W. 1996. Teaching for conceptual change. In *Improving teaching and learning in science and mathematics,* eds. D. F. Treagust, R. Duit, and B. J. Fraser, 131–140. New York: Teachers College Press.

Hilbish, T. J., and M. Goodwin. 1994. A simple demonstration of natural selection in the wild using the common dandelion. *The American Biology Teacher* 56 (5): 286–290.

Hipkins, R., R. Bolstad, R. Baker, A. Jones, M. Barker, B. Bell, R. Coll, B. Cooper, M. Forret, A. Harlow, I. Taylor, B. France, and M. Haigh. 2002. Curriculum, learning, and effective pedagogy: A literature review in science education. New Zealand Council for Educational Research. *www.nzcer.org.nz/default.php?products_id=559*

Holl, K., G. C. Daily, S. C. Daily, P. R. Ehrlich, and S. Bassin. 2002. Knowledge of and attitudes toward population growth and the environment: University students in Costa Rica and the United States. *Environmental Conservation* 26 (1): 66–74.

Horton, P., A. McConney, M. Gallo, A. Woods, G. Senn, and D. Hamelin. 1993. An investigation of the effectiveness of concept mapping as an instructional tool. *Science Education* 77 (1): 95–111.

Hyerle, D. 2000. *A field guide to using visual tools.* Alexandria, VA: Association for Supervision and Curriculum Development.

Ingram, M. 1993. *Bottle biology: An idea book for exploring the world through soda bottles and other recyclable materials.* Dubuque, IA: Kendall/Hunt.

International Centre for Development Oriented Research in Agriculture (ICRA). n.d. Systems diagrams: Guidelines. ICRA. *www.icra-edu.org/objects/anglolearn/Systems_Diagrams-Guidelines1.pdf*

Jensen, E. 1998. *Teaching with the brain in mind.* Alexandria, VA: Association for Curriculum and Supervision Development.

Jones, M. G., M. R. Falvo, A. R. Taylor, and B. P. Broadwell. 2007. *Nanoscale science: Activities for grades 6–12.* Arlington, VA: NSTA Press.

Keeley, P. 2005. *Science curriculum topic study: Bridging the gap between standards and practice.* Thousand Oaks, CA: Corwin Press.

Keeley, P. 2008. *Science formative assessment: 75 practical strategies for linking assessment, instruction, and learning.* Thousand Oaks, CA: Corwin Press.

Keeley, P., and F. Eberle. 2008. Using standards and cognitive research to inform the design and use of formative assessment probes. In *Assessing science learning,* eds. J. Coffey, R Douglas, and C. Stearns, 206–207. Arlington, VA: NSTA Press.

Keeley, P., F. Eberle, and C. Dorsey. 2008. *Uncovering student ideas in science. Vol. 3: Another 25 formative assessment probes.* Arlington, VA: NSTA Press.

Keeley, P., F. Eberle, and L. Farrin. 2005. *Uncovering student ideas in science. Vol. 1: 25 formative assessment probes.* Arlington, VA: NSTA Press.

Keeley, P., F. Eberle, and J. Tugel. 2007. *Uncovering student ideas in science. Vol. 2: 25 more formative assessment probes.* Arlington, VA: NSTA Press.

Keeley, P., and C. M. Rose. 2006. *Mathematics curriculum topic study: Bridging the gap between standards and practice.* Thousand Oaks, CA: Corwin Press.

Keogh, B., and S. Naylor. 1996. Teaching and learning in science: A new perspective. Paper presented at the annual conference for the British Education Research Association at the University of Lancaster, UK.

Keogh, B., and S. Naylor. 1999. Concept cartoons, teaching and learning in science: An evaluation. *International Journal of Science Education* 21 (4): 431–446.

Keogh, B., and S. Naylor. 2007. Talking and thinking in science. *School Science Review* 88 (324): 85–90.

Kindfield, A. C. H. 1994. Understanding a basic biological process: Expert and novice models of meiosis. *Science Education* 78 (3): 255–283.

Kirchhoff, A. 2008. Weaving in the story of science: Incorporating the nature of science into the classroom through stories about scientists, discoveries, and events. *The Science Teacher* 75 (3): 33–37.

Klentschy, M. P., and E. Moline-De la Torre. 2004. Students' science notebooks and the inquiry process. In *Crossing borders in literacy and science instruction,* ed. E.W. Saul, 340–354. Newark, DE: International Reading Association and Arlington, VA: NSTA Press.

Knippels, M. 2002. Coping with the abstract and complex nature of genetics in biology education: The yo-yo learning and teaching strategy. University of Utrecht. *www.library.uu.nl/digiarchief/dip/diss/2002-0930-094820/inhoud.htm*

Knippels, M., A. J. Waarlo, and K. Boersma. 2005. Design criteria for learning and teaching genetics. *Journal of Biological Education* 39 (3): 108–112.

Köse, S. 2008. Diagnosing student misconceptions: Using drawings as a research method. *World Applied Science Journal* 3 (2): 283–293.

Krajcik, J., P. C. Blumenfeld, R. W. Marx, K. M. Bass, and J. Fredricks. 1998. Inquiry in project-based science classrooms: Initial attempts by middle school students. *The Journal of the Learning Sciences* 7:313–350.

Krasny, M. E., and the Environmental Inquiry Team. 2003. *Invasion ecology.* Student edition and teacher's guide. Arlington, VA: NSTA Press.

Krueger, A., and J. Sutton. 2001. *EdThoughts: What we know about science teaching and learning.* Aurora, CO: McREL.

Lavoie, D. R. 1997. Using a modified concept mapping strategy to identify students' alternative scientific understandings of biology. Paper presented at the annual meeting of the National Association for Research in Science Teaching in Chicago, IL.

Layman, J., G. Ochoa, and H. Heikkinen. 1996. *Inquiry and learning: Realizing science standards in the classroom.* New York: National Center for Cross Disciplinary Teaching and Learning.

Lazear, D. 1991. *Seven ways of teaching: The artistry of teaching with multiple intelligences.* Palatine, IL: IRI/Skylight Publishing.

Learmonth, B. 2004. Using ecocentric literature in the middle school science class: Can we encourage eco-awareness without resorting to "The sky is falling"? University of New Mexico's Teacher Institute. *www.unm.edu/~abqteach/l&e/00-04-01.pdf*

Lederman, N. G. 2007. Nature of science: Past, present, and future. In *Handbook of research on science education,* eds. S. K. Abell and N. G. Lederman, 831–879. Mahwah, NJ: Lawrence Erlbaum Associates.

Lederman, N. G., and J. S. Lederman. 2004. Revising instruction to teach nature of science. *The Science Teacher* 71 (9): 36–39.

Lemke, J. L. 1990. *Talking science: Language, learning, and values.* Norwood, NJ: Ablex.

Lewis, J., and U. Kattmann. 2004. Traits, genes, particles, and information: Re-visiting students' understanding of genetics. *International Journal of Science Education* 26 (2): 195–206.

Lewis, J., J. Leach, and C. Wood-Robinson. 2000. Chromosomes: The missing link—people's understanding of mitosis, meiosis, and fertilization. *Journal of Biological Education* 34 (4): 189–199.

Lewis, J., and C. Wood-Robinson. 2000. Genes, chromosomes, cell division and inheritance—do students see any relationship? *International Journal of Science Education* 22 (2): 177–195.

Lipton, L., and B. Wellman. 2000. *Pathways to understanding: Patterns and practices in the learning-focused classroom.* 3rd ed. Sherman, CT: MiraVia.

Liu, X. 2006. Effects of combined hands-on laboratory and computer modeling on student learning of gas laws: A quasi-experimental study. *Journal of Science Education and Technology* 15 (1): 89–100.

Llewellyn, D. 2005. *Teaching high school science through inquiry: A case study approach.* Thousand Oaks, CA: Corwin Press.

Longden, B. 1982. Genetics—are there inherent learning difficulties? *Journal of Biological Education* 16 (2): 135–140.

Lowery, L. F. 1990. *The biological basis of thinking and learning.* Berkeley, CA: University of California Press.

Luft, J., R. L. Bell, and J. Gess-Newsome, eds. 2008. *Science as inquiry in the secondary setting.* Arlington, VA: NSTA Press.

Magnusson, S. J., and A. S. Palinscar. 2004. Learning from text designed to model scientific thinking in inquiry-based instruction. In *Crossing borders in literacy and science instruction,* ed. E.W. Saul, 316–339. Newark, DE: International Reading Association and Arlington, VA: NSTA Press.

Marzano, R. J. 1992. *A different kind of classroom: Teaching with dimensions of learning.* Alexandria, VA: Association for Supervision and Curriculum Development.

Marzano, R. J. 1997. *Dimensions of learning.* 2nd ed. Alexandria, VA: Association for Supervision and Curriculum Development.

Marzano, R. J., D. J. Pickering, and J. E. Pollock. 2001. *Classroom instruction that works: Research-based strategies for increasing student achievement.* Alexandria, VA: Association for Supervision and Curriculum Development.

Masilla, V. B., and H. Gardner. 2008. Disciplining the mind. *Educational Leadership* 65 (5): 14–19.

McComas, W. F. 2002. The ideal environmental science curriculum, 1. History, rationales, misconceptions and standards. *The American Biology Teacher* 64 (9): 665–672.

McComas, W. F. 2004. Keys to teaching the nature of science. *The Science Teacher* 71 (9): 24–27.

McConnell, S. 1993. Talking drawings: A strategy for assisting learners. *Journal of Reading* 36 (4): 260–269.

McCoy, M. W., K. A. McCoy, and D. J. Levey. 2007. Teaching biodiversity to students in inner city and under-resourced schools. *The American Biology Teacher* 69 (8): 473–476.

McKinney, D., and M. Michalovic. 2004. Teaching the stories of scientists and their discoveries. *The Science Teacher* 71 (9): 46–51.

McNair, S., and M. Stein. 2001. Drawing on their understanding: Using illustrations to invoke deeper thinking about plants. Pennsylvania State University. *http://edr1.educ. msu.edu/EnvironmentalLit/publicsite/html/paper.html.*

McNeill, K. L., and J. Krajcik. 2006. Supporting students' construction of scientific explanation through generic versus context-specific written scaffolds. Paper presented at the annual meeting of the American Educational Research Association in San Francisco, CA.

McNeill, K. L., and J. Krajcik. 2008. Inquiry and scientific explanations: Helping students use evidence and reasoning. In *Science as inquiry in the secondary setting,* eds. J. Luft, R.L. Bell, and J. Gess-Newsome, 121–133. Arlington, VA: NSTA Press.

McTighe, J., and G. Wiggins. 1999. *Understanding by design handbook.* Alexandria, VA: Association for Supervision and Curriculum Development..

McTighe, J., and G. Wiggins. 2004. *Understanding by design: Professional development workbook.* Alexandria, VA: Association for Supervision and Curriculum Development.

Mertens, T., and J. Walker. 1992. A paper-and-pencil strategy for teaching mitosis and meiosis, diagnosing learning problems and predicting examination performance. *The American Biology Teacher* 54 (8): 470–474.

Michaels, S., A. W. Shouse, and H. A. Schweingruber. 2007. *Ready, set science: Putting research to work in K–8 science classrooms.* Washington, DC: National Academies Press.

Milne, C. 2008. In praise of questions: Elevating the role of questions for inquiry in secondary school science. In *Science as inquiry in the secondary setting,* eds. J. Luft, R. L. Bell, and J. Gess-Newsome, 99–106. Arlington, VA: NSTA Press.

Mind Tools. n.d. Systems diagrams. Mind Tools. w*ww.mindtools.com/pages/article/ newTMC_04.htm*

Minstrell, J. 1989. Teaching science for understanding. In *Toward the thinking curriculum: Current cognitive research,* eds. L. B. Resnick and L. E. Klopfer, 129–149. Alexandria, VA: Association for Supervision and Curriculum Development.

Modell, H., J. Michael, and M. P. Wenderoth. 2005. Helping the learner to learn: The role of uncovering misconceptions. *The American Biology Teacher* 67 (1): 20–26.

Mohan, L., J. Chen, and C. W. Anderson. 2007. *Developing a K–12 learning progression for carbon cycling in socio-ecological systems.* Michigan State University, Environmental Literacy. *http://edr1.educ.msu.edu/EnvironmentalLit/index.htm*

Moore, J. 1993. *Science as a way of knowing: The foundations of modern biology.* Cambridge, MA: Harvard University Press.

Moreno, N. P., and B. Z. Tharp. 2006. How do students learn science? In *Teaching science in the 21st century,* eds. J. Rhoton and P. Shane, 291–305. Arlington, VA: NSTA Press.

Mortimer, E. F. 1995. Conceptual change or conceptual profile change? *Science and Education* 4 (3): 267–285.

Mortimer, E. F., and P. H. Scott. 2003. *Meaning making in secondary science classrooms.* London: Open University Press.

Mullis, K. 2003. *Dancing naked in the mind field.* New York: Random House.

Munson, B. H. 1991. Relationships between an individual's conceptual ecology and the individual's conceptions of ecology. PhD diss., University of Minnesota, Minneapolis.

National Academy of Sciences (NAS). 1998. *Teaching about evolution and the nature of science.* Washington, DC: National Academy Press.

National Academy of Sciences (NAS). 2007. *Rising above the gathering storm: Energizing and employing America for a brighter economic future.* Washington, DC: National Academies Press.

National Center for Mathematics and Science. 2002. Modeling for understanding in science education. *http://ncisla.wceruw.org/muse/models/index.html*

National Research Council (NRC). 1996. *National science education standards.* Washington, DC: National Academy Press.

National Research Council (NRC). 2000. *Inquiry and the National Science Education Standards.* Washington, DC: National Academy Press.

National Research Council (NRC). 2001a. *Classroom assessment and the National Science Education Standards.* Committee on Classroom Assessment and the National Science Education Standards. J. M. Atkin, P. Black, and J. Coffey, eds. Center for Education, Division of Behavioral and Social Sciences and Education. Washington, DC: National Academy Press.

National Research Council (NRC). 2001b. *Knowing what students know: The science and design of educational assessment.* Committee on the Foundations of Assessment, J. Pelligrino, N. Chudowsky, and R. Glaser, eds. Board on Testing and Assessment, Center for Education. Division of Behavioral and Social Sciences and Education. Washington, DC: National Academy Press.

National Research Council (NRC). 2005. *How students learn: Science in the classroom.* Committee on How People Learn, A Targeted Report for Teachers, M. S. Donovan and J. D. Bransford, eds. Division of Behavioral and Social Sciences and Education. Washington, DC: National Academies Press.

National Science Teachers Association (NSTA). 2003. NSTA position statement: The teaching of evolution. In *Evolution in Perspective: The Science Teacher's Compendium*, ed. R. W. Bybee, xix–xx. Arlington, VA: NSTA Press.

National Science Teachers Association (NSTA) and Environmental Protection Agency (EPA). 1997a. *Global environmental change: Biodiversity.* Arlington, VA: NSTA Press.

National Science Teachers Association (NSTA) and Environmental Protection Agency (EPA). 1997b. *Global environmental change: Carrying capacity.* Arlington, VA: NSTA Press.

National Science Teachers Association (NSTA) and Environmental Protection Agency (EPA). 1997c. *Global environmental change: Deforestation.* Arlington, VA: NSTA Press.

National Science Teachers Association (NSTA) and Environmental Protection Agency (EPA). 1998. *Global environmental change: Introduced species.* Arlington, VA: NSTA Press.

Nelson-Herber, J. 1986. Expanding and refining vocabulary in content areas. *Journal of Reading* 29 (7): 626–633.

Norris, S. P., L. M. Phillips, and J. F. Osborne. 2008. Scientific inquiry: The place of interpretation and argumentation. In *Science as inquiry in the secondary setting*, eds. J. Luft, R. L. Bell, and J. Gess-Newsome, 87–98. Arlington, VA: NSTA Press.

Novak, J. D. 1996. Concept mapping: A tool for improving science teaching and learning. In *Improving teaching and learning in science and mathematics,* eds. D. F. Treagust, R. Duit, and B. J. Fraser, 32–43. New York: Teachers College Press.

Novak, J. D. 1998. *Learning, creating, and using knowledge: Concept maps as facilitative tools in schools and corporations.* Mahwah, NJ: Lawrence Erlbaum.

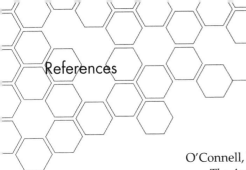

References

O'Connell, D. 2008. An inquiry-based approach to teaching photosynthesis and respiration. *The American Biology Teacher* 70 (6): 350–56.

O'Day, D. H. 2008. Using animation to teach biology: Past and future research on the attributes that underlie pedagogically sound animations. *The American Biology Teacher* 70 (5): 274–278.

Passmore, C., and J. Stewart. 2000. A course in evolutionary biology: Engaging students in the "practice" of evolution. *NCISLA Research Report No. 00-1.* National Center for Mathematics and Science. *http://ncisla.wceruw.org/publications/index.html*

Perkins, D. 2003. Making thinking visible. New Horizons for Learning. *www.newhorizons.org*

Posner, G., K. Strike, P. Hewson, and W. Gertzog. 1982. Accommodation of a scientific conception: Toward a theory of conceptual change. *Science Education* 66 (2): 211–27.

Rakow, S. J., ed. 2000. *NSTA pathways to the science standards.* Middle School Edition. 2nd ed. Arlington, VA: NSTA Press.

Rangahau, W. M. 2002. *Curriculum, learning and effective pedagogy: A literature review in science education.* Wellington, New Zealand: Ministry of Education.

Rhodes, D. 1995. Personal communication referenced in "Engaging students in conducting Socratic dialogues: Suggestions for science teachers." *Journal of Physics Teacher Education Online,* 4 (1), Autumn 2006. ISU Physics Teacher Education. *www.phy.ilstu.edu/pte*

Richardson, M. L., and J. Hari. 2008. Teaching students about biodiversity by studying the correlation between plants and arthropods. *The American Biology Teacher* 70 (4): 217–220.

Rico, G. 2000. *Writing the natural way.* New York: Putnam. Described in D. Hyerle, *A field guide to using visual tools.* Alexandria, VA: Association for Supervision and Curriculum Development, 2000, 44.

Ritchart, R., and D. Perkins. 2008. Making thinking visible. *Educational Leadership* 65 (5): 57–61.

Ritchart, R., and D. Perkins. n.d. Visible thinking: Engaged students, in-depth learning, better teaching. Council for Exceptional Children. *www.cec.sped.org/AM/Template.cfm?Section=Home*

Rolheiser, C., and J. A. Ross. n.d. Student self-evaluation: What research says and what practice shows. Center for Developmental Learning. *www.cdl.org/resource-library/articles/self_eval.php?type=subject&id=4*

Roseman, J. E., A. Caldwell, A. Gogos, and L. Kurth. 2006. Mapping a coherent learning progression for the molecular basis of heredity. Project 2061. *www.project2061.org/publications/articles/papers/narst2006.htm*

Ross, P. M., D. Tronson, and R. J. Ritchie. 2006. Modeling photosynthesis to increase conceptual understanding. *Journal of Biological Education* 40 (2): 84–88.

Rotbain, Y., G. Marbach-Ad, and R. Stavy. 2005. Understanding molecular genetics through a drawing-based activity. *Journal of Biological Education* 39 (4): 174–178.

Rowell, P. 1997. Learning in school science: The promises and practices of writing. *Studies in Science Education* 30:19–56.

Rudge, D. W., and E. M. Howe. 2004. Incorporating history into the science classroom. *The Science Teacher* 71 (9): 52–57.

Russell, A. W., G. M. A. Netherwood, and S. A. Robinson. 2004. Photosynthesis *In Silico.* Overcoming the challenges of photosynthesis education using a multimedia CD-ROM.

Bioscience Education eJournal 3 (30 April): Article 3–8. *www.bioscience.heacademy.ac.uk/journal/vol3/beej-3-8.aspx*

Schwendimann, B. A. 2008. Scaffolding interactive dynamic model to promote coherent connections in high school biology. Paper presented at the annual meeting of the American Educational Research Association in New York City.

Scotchmoor, J., and A. Janulaw. 2005. Understanding evolution. *The Science Teacher* 72 (9): 26–28.

Scott, P., H. Asoko, and R. Driver. 1992. Teaching for conceptual change: A review of strategies. In *Research in physics learning: Theoretical issues and empirical studies*, eds. R. Duit, F. Goldberg, and H. Niederer, 310–329. Kiel, Germany: IPN [Leibniz Institute for Science Education].

Scott, P., H. Asoko, and J. Leach. 2007. Student conceptions and conceptual learning in science. In *Handbook of research on science education*, eds. S. K. Abell and N. G. Lederman, 31–55. Mahwah, NJ: Lawrence Erlbaum Associates.

Scott, V. G., and M. K. Weishaar. 2008. Talking drawings as a university classroom assessment technique. *The Journal of Effective Teaching* 8 (1): 42–51. *www.uncwil.edu/cte/ET/articles/Vol8_1/Scott.htm*

Sinan, O., H. Aydin, and K. Gezer. 2007. Prospective science teachers' conceptual understanding about proteins and protein syntheis. *Journal of Applied Sciences* 7 (21): 3154–3166.

Singer, S., M. Hilton, and H. Schweingruber. 2007. *America's lab report: Investigations in high school science.* Washington, DC: National Academies Press.

Smith, M. U. 1991. Teaching cell division: Student difficulties and teaching recommendations. *Journal of College Science Teaching* 21 (1): 28–33.

Songer, N. B. 2007. Digital resources versus cognitive tools: A discussion of learning science with technology. In *Handbook of research on science education*, eds. S. K. Abell and N. G. Lederman, 471–491. Mahwah, NJ: Lawrence Erlbaum Associates.

Southwest Center for Education and the Natural Environment. 2004. *The inquiry process.* SCENE. *http://scene.asu.edu/habitat/inquiry.html*

Stein, M., and S. McNair. 2002. Science drawings as a tool for analyzing conceptual understanding. Paper presented at the annual meeting of the Association for the Education of Teachers of Science in Charlotte, NC.

Stow, W. 1997. Concept mapping as a tool for self-assessment? *Primary Science Review* 49:12–15.

Strike, K. A., and G. J. Posner. 1985. A conceptual change view of learning and understanding. In *Cognitive structure and conceptual change*, eds. L. West and R. Hamilton, 211–232. London: Academic Press.

Strike, K. A., and G. J. Posner. 1992. A revisionist theory of conceptual change. In *Philosophy of science, cognitive psychology and educational theory and practice*, eds. R. Duschl and R. Hamilton, 147–176. Albany, NY: State University of New York Press.

Sutherland, L. M., K. L. McNeill, and J. S. Krajcik. 2006. Supporting middle school students in developing scientific explanations. In *Linking science and literacy in the K–8 classroom*, eds. R. Douglas, M. P. Klentschy, and K. Worth, with W. Binder, 163–181. Arlington, VA: NSTA Press.

Swartz, R. J. 2008. Energizing learning. *Educational Leadership* 65 (5): 26–31.

Tanner, K., and D. Allen. 2005. Approaches to biology teaching and learning: Understanding the wrong answers—Teaching toward conceptual change. *Cell Biology Education* 4 (2): 112–117.

Texley, J., and A. Wild. 2004. *NSTA pathways to the science standards.* High School Edition. 2nd ed. Arlington, VA: NSTA Press.

Thier, M. 2002. *The new science literacy: Using language skills to help students learn science.* Portsmouth, NH: Heinemann.

Trautmann, N. M., and the Environmental Inquiry Team. 2001. *Assessing toxic risk.* Student edition and teacher's guide. Arlington, VA: NSTA Press.

Trautmann, N. M., and the Environmental Inquiry Team. 2003. *Decay and renewal.* Student edition and teacher's guide. Arlington, VA: NSTA Press.

Trunfio, P., B. Berenfeld, P. Kreikemeier, J. Moran, and S. Moodley. 2003. Molecular modeling and visualization tools in science education. Paper presented at the annual conference of the National Association for Research in Science Teaching in Philadelphia, PA.

University of California Berkeley. n.d. Misconceptions. *http://evolution.berkeley.edu/evosite/misconceps/index.shtml*

Visible Thinking. n.d. *www.pz.harvard.edu/vt/VisibleThinking_html_files/VisibleThinking1.html*

Vitale, M. R., and N. R. Romance. 2006. Research in science education: An interdisciplinary perspective. In *Teaching science in the 21st century,* eds. J. Rhoton and P. Shane, 329–351. Arlington, VA: NSTA Press.

Wallace, C. S., B. Hand, and E. Yang. 2004. The science writing heuristic: Using writing as a tool for learning in the laboratory. In *Crossing borders in literacy and science instruction,* ed. E. W. Saul, 355–367. Newark, DE: International Reading Association and Arlington, VA: NSTA Press.

Walsh, J. A., and B. D. Sattes. 2005. *Quality questioning: Research-based practice to engage every learner.* Thousand Oaks, CA: Corwin Press.

Wandersee, J. H., J. J. Mintzes, and J. D. Novak. 1994. Research on alternative conceptions in science. In *Handbook of research on science teaching and learning,* ed. D. L. Gabel, 177–210. New York: Simon and Schuster.

Wang, M. C., G. D. Haertel, and H. J. Walberg. 1993/1994. What helps students learn? *Educational Leadership* 51 (4) 74–79.

Webb, P., and G. Boltt. 1991. High school pupils' and first-year university students' responses to questions based on data analysis of an ecological case study. *Journal of Biological Education* 25 (2): 119–122.

Weiss, I. R., J. D. Pasley, P. S. Smith, E. R. Banilower, and D. J. Heck. 2003. Looking inside the classroom: A study of K–12 mathematics and science education in the United States. Horizon Research International, Inside the Classroom. *www.horizon-research.com/insidetheclassroom/reports/looking*

Wenning, C. J. 2005. *Whiteboarding and Socratic dialogues: Questions and answers.* ISU Physics Teacher Education Program. *www.phy.ilstu.edu/programs/ptefiles/publications/whiteboard_dialogues.pdf*

Wenning, C. J., T. W. Holbrook, and J. Stankevitz. 2006. Engaging students in conducting Socratic dialogues: Suggestions for science teachers. ISU Physics Teacher Education Program. *www.phy.ilstu.edu/pte/publications/engaging_students.pdf*

Westcott, D. J., and D. L. Cunningham. 2005. Recognizing student misconceptions about science and evolution. *Mountain Rise Electronic Journal* 2 (2) (Spring/Summer). *http://facctr.wcu.edu/mountainrise/archive/vol2no2/html/science_evolution.html*

WestEd and Council of Chief State School Officers. 2007. Science assessment and item specifications for the 2009 National Assessment of Educational Progress. Prepublication edition. National Assessment Governing Board contract #ED04CO0148.

Wiggins, G., and J. McTighe. 1998. *Understanding by design.* Alexandria, VA: Association for Supervision and Curriculum Development.

Williamson, B. n.d. The floating leaf disk assay for investigating photosynthesis. Exploring Life Community. *www.elbiology.com/labtools/Leafdisk.html*

Wilson, C. D., J. Zesaguli, and C. W. Anderson. 2006. The development of a K–12 learning progression for diversity in environmental systems. Michigan State University Environmental Literacy. *http://edr1.educ.msu.edu/EnvironmentalLit/publicsite/html/paperp2.html*

Windschitl, M. 2008. What is inquiry? A framework for thinking about authentic scientific practice in the classroom. In *Science as inquiry in the secondary setting,* eds. J. Luft, R.L. Bell, and J. Gess-Newsome, 1–20. Arlington, VA: NSTA Press.

Winokur, J., and K. Worth. 2006. Talk in the science classroom: Looking at what students and teachers need to know and be able to do. In *Linking science and literacy in the K–8 classroom,* eds. R. Douglas, M. P. Klentschy, and K. Worth, with W. Binder, 43–58. Arlington, VA: NSTA Press.

Wolfe, P. 2001. *Brain matters: Translating research into classroom practice.* Alexandria, VA: Association for Supervision and Curriculum Development.

Woodruff, E., and K. Meyer. 1997. Explanations from intra- and inter-group discourse: Students building knowledge in the science classroom. *Research in Science Education* 27 (1): 25–39.

Wright, A. W., and K. Bilica. 2007. Instructional tools to probe biology students' prior understanding. *The American Biology Teacher* 69 (1): 1–5.

Wuerth, M. 2004. Resources for teaching evolution. *The American Biology Teacher* 66 (2): 109–113.

Young, P. n.d. Visual thinking tools. San Diego State University's Encyclopedia of Educational Technology. *http://coe.sdsu.edu/eet/articles/VisThinkTools/start.htm*

Appendix A1

Teacher Work Template (Blank)

Lesson Topic—		
Predictive Phase		

Conceptual Target Development	National Standard(s) Addressed	*From 9–12 NSES:*	*From 9–12 Benchmarks:*
	Previous Conceptual Learning	*From middle grade NSES:*	*From middle grade Benchmarks:*
		From prior instruction in biology course:	
	Knowledge and Skills	*Essential knowledge:* See **Learning Targets** and unpack for embedded knowledge. *Subtopics that may be pruned:* *Essential vocabulary (to apply and distinguish):* *Vocabulary that may be pruned:*	
Essential Understandings			

Responsive Phase	
Identifying Student Preconceptions	

Learning Sequence Targets	
Learning Target #1	
Research-Identified Misconceptions Addressed	
Initial Instructional Plan	
Formative Assessment Plan *(Demonstrating Understanding)*	

Learning Target #2	
Research-Identified Misconceptions Addressed	
Initial Instructional Plan	
Formative Assessment Plan *(Demonstrating Understanding)*	

Learning Target #3	
Research-Identified Misconceptions Addressed	
Initial Instructional Plan	
Formative Assessment Plan *(Demonstrating Understanding)*	

Criteria to Determine Understanding	

Appendix A2

Steps of the Planning Process

1. Identify the essential understandings for the lesson (conceptual target).
   a. Begin with the descriptions of adult science literacy to determine an anchor goal.
   b. Consider the middle school and high school standards and benchmarks.
   c. Optional: Study existing research on learning progressions. A good resource is found in the 2061 Connections online newsletter (*www.project2061.org/publications/2061Connections/2007/2007-04a-resources.htm*) (AAAS 2007a).
   d. Dig a bit deeper and think about the concepts included in the standards.
   e. Decide what is essential and what can be pruned.

2. Develop a logical sequence of learning targets for the lesson.
   a. Consider first the middle school experiences that students *should* have had. (Your goal is to build on the understandings they have acquired, but of course you cannot assume that those understandings are in place.)
   b. Outline the key ideas embedded in the high school standards and benchmarks.
   c. Sequence the key ideas in a way to build student understanding.
   d. Consider connections from one lesson to the next.

3. Identify the criteria for demonstrating understanding. (*Note:* Steps b and c are completed later, after a review of research.)
   a. Identify one criterion for each Learning Target.
   b. Identify one criterion for your selected standards-based strategy (Inquiry, HOS, or NOS).
   c. Identify one criterion for your selected metacognitive strategy.

4. Determine the research-identified misconceptions.
   a. Review *Benchmarks for Science Literacy* (1993) for misconceptions discussed there. Chapter 15 of the book includes research findings organized by benchmark. You can read the book online at *www.project2061.org/publications/bsl/online/index.php?txtRef=&txtURlOld=%2Fpublications%2Fbsl%2Fonline%2Findex*.
   b. Complete a web search for misconceptions on the selected topic. Simply run a search for your topic and misconceptions (e.g., "photosynthesis + misconceptions"). If you run your search at Google Scholar (*http://scholar.google.com*), you will gain access to numerous resources. In some cases you will only access the abstract, but in others you will find the entire document. This process is more time-consuming than step #1 but yields additional resources.
   c. Obtain a copy of *Making Sense of Secondary Science: Research Into Children's Ideas* (Driver et al. 1994). This book is outlined by topic and provides a rich summary of research on children's ideas about these topics.

5. Select strategies to identify student preconceptions.
   a. Use the Instructional Strategy Sequencing Tool (p. 29) to identify possible strategies that work to identify student preconceptions.
   b. Find the strategies in the Sense-Making Strategy Tools (2.8–2.14, starting on p. 55).

   c. Carefully review the research and application recommendations for each of the identified strategies.

   d. Determine several strategies that fit well with the particular content you are teaching.

   e. Review the listed resources available to you to more fully understand the strategies and to determine what they might look like in application.

   f. Select one or two for use in your lesson.

6. Select remaining instructional strategies.

   a. Use the Instructional Strategy Sequencing Tool (p. 29) to identify possible strategies that work to *elicit and confront* student preconceptions, as well as strategies that work for *sense making* and *demonstrating understanding.* Finally, identify metacognitive and standards-based strategies to review.

   b. Find the strategies in the three Metacognitive Strategy Tools (2.2–2.4, starting on p. 33), the three Standards-Based Strategy Tools (2.5–2.7, starting on p. 43), and the seven Sense-Making Strategy Tools (2.8–2.14, starting on p. 55).

   c. Carefully review the research and application recommendations for each of the identified strategies.

   d. Determine several strategies that fit well with the particular content you are teaching.

   e. Review the listed resources available to you to more fully understand the strategies and to determine what they might look like in application.

   f. Select one metacognitive strategy, one standards-based strategy, and two or three sense-making strategies for use in your lesson (recall that these will be used to differentiate instruction and to provide further instruction if formative assessments indicate that students do not understand the learning targets).

   g. Determine one criterion to demonstrate understanding for each of your metacognitive and standards-based focuses. Add these to the existing criteria in the work template.

7. Implement the strategies

   a. Implement, for each learning target, the selected strategies to *elicit and confront preconceptions* and for *sense making* and *demonstrating understanding.* Gather data using the *formative assessment strategies* for a learning target.

   b. If formative assessments indicate that all students understand the concepts, move forward with the next learning target.

   c. If students do not understanding the ideas, then

- use a different strategy to provide additional learning experiences for the students or
- extend the learning for students who do demonstrate understanding and provide additional small-group and/or individualized instruction for those who still struggle to understand.

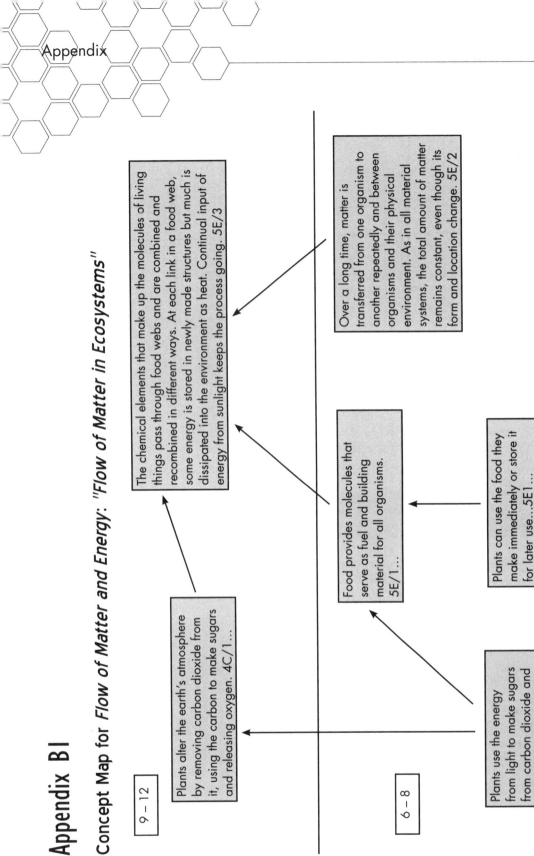

Appendix B1

Concept Map for *Flow of Matter and Energy: "Flow of Matter in Ecosystems"*

9 – 12

Plants alter the earth's atmosphere by removing carbon dioxide from it, using the carbon to make sugars and releasing oxygen. 4C/1.…

The chemical elements that make up the molecules of living things pass through food webs and are combined and recombined in different ways. At each link in a food web, some energy is stored in newly made structures but much is dissipated into the environment as heat. Continual input of energy from sunlight keeps the process going. 5E/3

Over a long time, matter is transferred from one organism to another repeatedly and between organisms and their physical environment. As in all material systems, the total amount of matter remains constant, even though its form and location change. 5E/2

Food provides molecules that serve as fuel and building material for all organisms. 5E/1.…

Plants can use the food they make immediately or store it for later use.…5E1.…

6 – 8

Plants use the energy from light to make sugars from carbon dioxide and water.…5E/1.…

plants making food   food web   matter cycle

Source: American Association for the Advancement of Science (AAAS). 2001. *Atlas of science literacy*. Washington, DC: AAAS, p. 77. Extract printed with permission.

Abbreviations: 4C/1, 5E/1, 5E/2, and 5E/3 refer to the chapter, section, and number of the corresponding goal statement in *Benchmarks for Science Literacy*. American Association for the Advancement of Science (AAAS). New York: Oxford University Press, 1993.

Appendix B2

Concept Map for *Evolution of Life: "Natural Selection"*

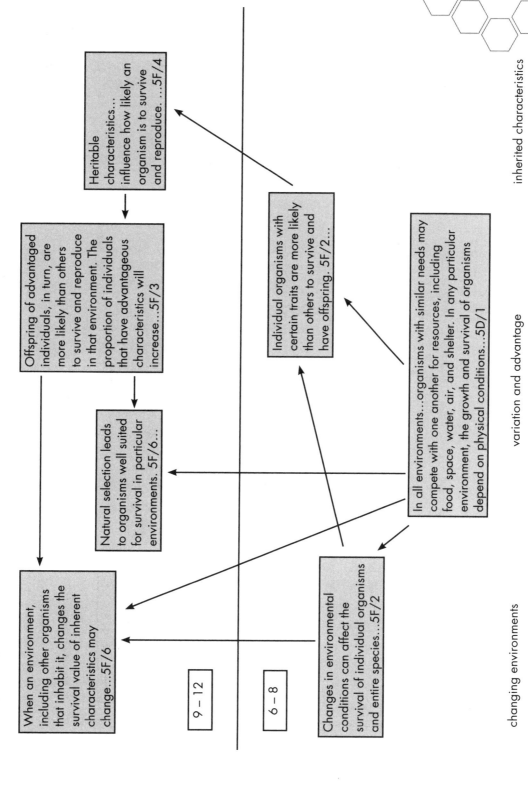

Heritable characteristics… influence how likely an organism is to survive and reproduce. …5F/4

Offspring of advantaged individuals, in turn, are more likely than others to survive and reproduce in that environment. The proportion of individuals that have advantageous characteristics will increase…5F/3

Individual organisms with certain traits are more likely than others to survive and have offspring. 5F/2…

Natural selection leads to organisms well suited for survival in particular environments. 5F/6…

When an environment, including other organisms that inhabit it, changes the survival value of inherent characteristics may change…5F/6

In all environments…organisms with similar needs may compete with one another for resources, including food, space, water, air, and shelter. In any particular environment, the growth and survival of organisms depend on physical conditions…5D/1

9 – 12

6 – 8

Changes in environmental conditions can affect the survival of individual organisms and entire species…5F/2

inherited characteristics

variation and advantage

changing environments

Source: American Association for the Advancement of Science (AAAS). 2001. *Atlas of science literacy*. Washington, DC: AAAS, p. 77. Extract printed with permission.

Abbreviations: 5D/1, 5F/2, 5F/3, 5F/4 and 5F/6 refer to the chapter, section, and number of the corresponding goal statement in *Benchmarks for Science Literacy*. American Association for the Advancement of Science (AAAS). New York: Oxford University Press, 1993.

Hard-to-Teach Biology Concepts

249

Appendix B3

Concept Map for *Cells:* *"Cell Functions"*

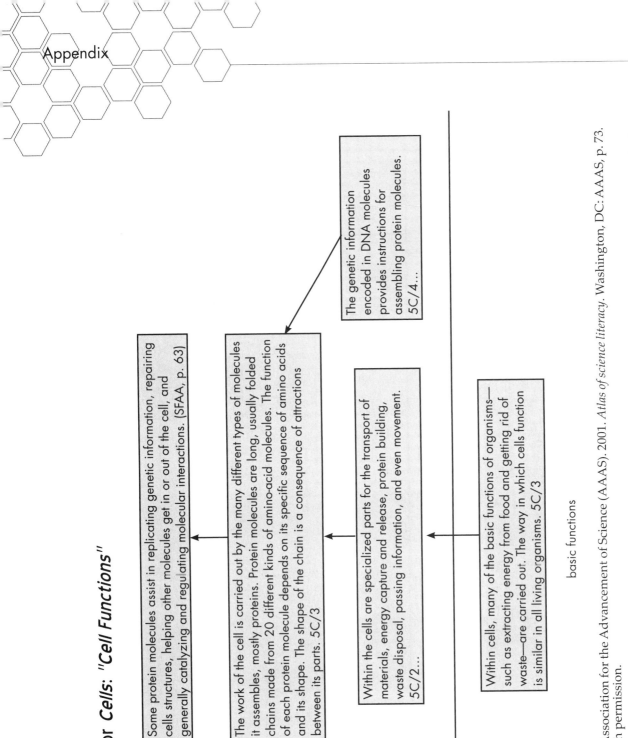

9 – 12

Some protein molecules assist in replicating genetic information, repairing cells structures, helping other molecules get in or out of the cell, and generally catalyzing and regulating molecular interactions. (SFAA, p. 63)

The work of the cell is carried out by the many different types of molecules it assembles, mostly proteins. Protein molecules are long, usually folded chains made from 20 different kinds of amino-acid molecules. The function of each protein molecule depends on its specific sequence of amino acids and its shape. The shape of the chain is a consequence of attractions between its parts. 5C/3

The genetic information encoded in DNA molecules provides instructions for assembling protein molecules. 5C/4...

Within the cells are specialized parts for the transport of materials, energy capture and release, protein building, waste disposal, passing information, and even movement. 5C/2...

Within cells, many of the basic functions of organisms—such as extracting energy from food and getting rid of waste—are carried out. The way in which cells function is similar in all living organisms. 5C/3

6 – 8

basic functions

Source: American Association for the Advancement of Science (AAAS). 2001. *Atlas of science literacy.* Washington, DC: AAAS, p. 73. Extract printed with permission.

Abbreviations: 5C/2, 5C/3, and 5C/4 refer to the chapter, section, and number of the corresponding goal statement in *Benchmarks for Science Literacy.* American Association for the Advancement of Science (AAAS). New York: Oxford University Press, 1993.

SFAA, p. 63, refers to the page on which the corresponding content in *Science for All Americans* will be found. American Association for the Advancement of Science (AAAS). New York: Oxford University Press, 1990.

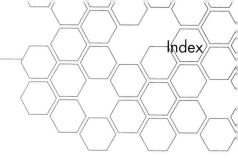

Index

Note: **Boldface** pages numbers indicate figures.

Analogies, 68–69
Annotated drawings, 83–84
Assessment, 27–28

Brainstorming webs, 25–26, 36, 72–74

Carbon cycling in environmental systems, **122**
Case studies, 95, **95**
Categorical organizers, 76–77
Cause-effect organizers, 76
Circle maps, 73–74
Classroom inquiry, essential features, 20
Clustering, 72
Comparison organizers, 77–78
Completing responsive phase, 132–140
Comprehension, 23–27, 31–33, 35, 86–87, 132–140, 209
    brainstorming webs, 25–26
    linguistic representations, 24
    nonlinguistic representations, 24–27
        drawing, 26
        kinesthetic activities, 26–27
        maps, 25–26
        models, 25
    task-specific organizers, 26
    thinking-process maps, 26
Concept cartoons, 85
Concept mapping, 79–80
Conceptual change, instructional planning framework, 3–14
    criteria demonstrating understanding, 6–7
    criteria for developing understanding, 7
    learning sequence, 6–7
    overview, 5–7

preconceptions
    comprehension strategies
        addressing, 7
        confronting, 7
        eliciting, 7
        identification of, 7
    research, 8–12
        predictive phase, 8–9
        responsive phase, 9–12
    target, 6–7
    understanding, criteria demonstrating, 6–7
Confronting preconceptions, 29–32, 128, 206–215, 224–226
Creative thinking, 18, 29, 36–37
    strategies supporting, 36–37
Creativity routines, 36
Critical thinking, 18, 29

Debriefing thinking process, 42
Demonstration experiments, 49
Description of assessment for preconceptions, 129–130
Descriptive organizers, 75
Diagrams, 70
Digging further into standards, 195–196
Drawing, 26, 83–84
Drawing out thinking, 83–85
Dynamic models, 25, 70–71

Ecosystems. *See* Socio-ecological systems
Eliciting preconceptions, 29–32, 128, 130–132, 206–215, 224–226
Energy, matter, flow of, 119–142
    carbon cycling in environmental systems, **122**

completing responsive phase, 132–140
comprehension, 132–140
confronting preconceptions, 128
description of assessment for
     preconceptions, 129–130
eliciting preconceptions, 128, 130–132
formative assessment plan, 136–139
identifying our students'
     preconceptions, 127–129
identifying preconceptions, 125, 128
initial instructional plan, 136–139
instructional planning framework,
     122–130
learning about research-identified
     misconceptions, 125–127
learning sequence targets, 134
library suggestions, 141
photosynthesis learning sequence, **124**
planning in predictive phase, **123**
preconceptions, 128
predictive phase, 122–124, 133–134
reflection, 124, 127, 130, 132
research-identified misconceptions,
     137–139
resources, 141
responsive phase, 125–130, 135–139
selection of topic, 120–121
steps for misconception literature
     review, **127**
strategies, 140
strategy selection, **128**
teacher work template, 133–139
technology applications, 141
websites, 141
Environmental systems, 191–228, **197**, 199,
201
     build on middle school experiences, 199
     comprehension strategies, 209
     conceptual targets, 194–198
     confronting preconceptions, 206–215,
          224–226
     criteria determining understanding, 200
     digging further into standards, 195–196
     ecosystems, 199–200
     eliciting preconceptions, 206–215,
          224–226

finalizing process to promote
     understanding, **207**
formative assessment plan, 219–222
high school standards, 194–195
     components of, 199–200
identifying preconceptions, **202,** 202–205
initial instructional plan, 219–222
instructional planning framework
     predictive phase, 193–201
     responsive phase, 201–215
learning sequence targets, 219
library suggestions, 227–228
logical learning sequence, 199–200
loop diagram, **197**
map for living environment, **196**
metacognitive approach strategies, 208
middle school standards, 194–195
planning in predictive phase, **193**
planning instruction for learning
     targets, 209
preconceptions, 206–215
     identifying, 223
predictive phase, 193–201, 217–218
pruning content, 198
reflection, 200–201, 205, 215
research-identified misconceptions,
     202–204, 219–222
research on learning progressions,
     197–198
resources, 226–228
responsive phase, 201–215, 218
selection of topic, 192
standards-based approach strategies,
     208–209
strategy selection, 206–208
teacher work predictive phase template,
     217–222
technology applications, 226–227
understanding, 224–226
websites, 226–227
Evidence, formulating explanations from,
     46–47
Evolution, 143–168
     comprehension, 156–158
     confronting preconceptions, 149, 151–158
     differential mortality, 154–156

eliciting preconceptions, 149, 151–158
formative assessment plan, 162–163
identifying preconceptions, 148–149
initial instructional plan, 161–163
instructional planning framework
    predictive phase, 146–148
    responsive phase, **145,** 148–166
learning sequence targets, 160–161
library suggestions, 167
natural selection learning sequence, **148**
planning in predictive phase, **147**
planning in responsive phase, **149**
population growth, 153
preconceptions, 149
reflection, 147–148, 150, 158–166
research-identified misconceptions, 149, 161–163
resources, 166–167
selection of topic, 144
teacher work template
    predictive phase, 159–160
    responsive phase, 161–163
teaching strategies, 164–166
technology applications, 166–167
websites, 166–167

Fairness routines, 34
Finalizing process to promote understanding, **207**
Focusing labs, 53–54
Formative assessment plan, 113–115, 136–139, 219–222

Genes, 169–190. *See also* Genetic variation
comprehension, strategies addressing preconceptions, 175–176
confronting preconceptions, 173–175
demonstrating understanding, 176–178
demonstrating understanding for learning targets, 178–180
eliciting preconceptions, 173–175
finalizing process to promote understanding, **180**
formative assessment plan, 186–188
identifying preconceptions, 173–175
initial instructional plan, 185–188

instructional planning framework
    predictive phase, 171–173
    responsive phase, 173–188
learning sequence, **173**
learning sequence targets, 185
learning targets, 178–182
library suggestions, 189
planned learning sequence, **177**
planning in predictive phase, **172**
planning in responsive phase, **174**
preconceptions, 173–175
    strategies addressing, 175–176
predictive phase, 171–173
protein synthesis instruction, case study, **171**
reflection, 173, 175, 180–188
research-identified misconceptions, 185–188
resources, 188–189
responsive phase, 173–188
selection of topic, 170
teacher work template, 183–188
technology applications, 188–189
websites, 188–189
Genetic variation, 93–118
adult science literacy, 96–97
case study, 95, **95**
conceptual target, 96–102
criteria, 104–107
    variation, 107
criteria for demonstrating understanding, **107**
expectations of adult science learning, **97**
experienced biology teacher with new assignment, **95**
formative assessment plan, 113–115
heredity map, **99**
high school science standards, 97–100
    components of, 103–104
initial instructional plan, 114–115
instructional planning framework
    predictive phase, **96,** 96–108
    responsive phase, 108–115, **109**
learning progressions research, 100–101
learning sequence, **104**
learning sequence targets, 111

library suggestions, 115–116
logical learning sequence, 102–104
map for heredity, **99**
middle school experiences, building on,
   103
middle school science standards,
   97–100
planning in predictive phase, **102, 107**
predictive phase, **96**
   planning, **102, 107**
reflection, 107–108
research-identified misconceptions,
   113–114
resources, 115–116
responsive phase, **109**
selection of topic, 94
teacher work template, 110–111
   responsive phase, 112–115
technology applications, 115
websites, 115
Graphs, 70
Group discussions, 62–64

Hands-on experiments, 86–87
Heredity map, **99**
High school standards, 97–100, 194–195
   components of, 103–104, 199–200
History of science, 21, 29, 49–50
History of science tools, 21–23
Human impact on environment, 191–228.
   See also Socio-ecological systems

Identification of knowledge bases, 38
Identifying preconceptions, 29–32, 125,
   127–129, **202,** 202–205
Informational text strategies, 59–60
Initial instructional plan, 114–115, 136–139,
   219–222
Inquiry, standards-based approaches,
   43–48
Inquiry tools, 19–21
Instructional approaches
   classroom inquiry, essential features of,
      20
   student understanding, 15–90
      assessment, 27–28

comprehension, 23–27
   brainstorming webs, 25–26
   linguistic representations, 24
   nonlinguistic representations, 24–27
      drawing, 26
      kinesthetic activities, 26–27
      maps, 25–26
      models, 25
   task-specific organizers, 26
   thinking-process maps, 26
instructional strategy sequencing,
   16–17
linguistic representational tools,
   23–27
   brainstorming webs, 25–26
   dynamic models, 25
   mental models, 25
   nonlinguistic representations,
      24–27
      drawing, 26
      graphic organizers, 25–26
      kinesthetic activities, 26–27
      mental models, 25
   physical models, 25
   task-specific organizers, 26
   thinking-process maps, 26
   verbal models, 25
   visual models, 25
metacognitive approach tools, 17–18
   creative thinking, 18
   critical thinking, 18
   self-regulated thinking, 18
nonlinguistic representational tools,
   23–27
resources, 87–88
   library suggestions, 88
   technology applications, 87
   websites, 87
standards-based approach tools,
   19–23
   history of science, 21–23
   inquiry tools, 19–21
   nature of science, 21–23
technology, 27
Instructional planning framework, **6,**
   122–130

conceptual change, 3–14
  criteria for developing
      understanding, 7
  instructional planning framework,
      overview, 5–7
  learning sequence, 6–7
  preconceptions
      comprehension strategies, 7
      confronting, 7
      eliciting, 7
      identification of, 7
  research, 8–12
      predictive phase, 8–9
      responsive phase, 9–12
  target, 6–7
  understanding, criteria
      demonstrating, 6–7
  predictive phase, **96,** 96–108, 193–201
  responsive phase, 108–115, **109,** 201–215
Instructional strategy sequencing, 16–17
Instructional strategy sequencing tool, 29–32
Interdependence of organisms, 191–228,
      197, 199, **201**
  build on middle school experiences, 199
  comprehension strategies, 209
  conceptual targets, 194–198
  confronting preconceptions, 206–215,
      224–226
  criteria determining understanding, 200
  digging further into standards, 195–196
  ecosystems, 199–200
  eliciting preconceptions, 206–215,
      224–226
  finalizing process to promote
      understanding, **207**
  formative assessment plan, 219–222
  high school standards, 194–195
      components of, 199–200
  identifying preconceptions, **202,** 202–205
  initial instructional plan, 219–222
  instructional planning framework
      predictive phase, 193–201
      responsive phase, 201–215
  learning sequence targets, 219
  library suggestions, 227–228
  logical learning sequence, 199–200

  loop diagram, **197**
  map for living environment, **196**
  metacognitive approach strategies, 208
  middle school standards, 194–195
  planning in predictive phase, **193**
  planning instruction for learning
      targets, 209
  preconceptions, 206–215
      identifying, 223
  predictive phase, 193–201, 217–218
  pruning content, 198
  reflection, 200–201, 205, 215
  research-identified misconceptions,
      202–204, 219–222
  research on learning progressions,
      197–198
  resources, 226–228
  responsive phase, 201–215, 218
  selection of topic, 192
  standards-based approach strategies,
      208–209
  strategy selection, 206–208
  teacher work predictive phase template,
      217–222
  technology applications, 226–227
  understanding, 224–226
  websites, 226–227

Journals, 39–40

Kinesthetics, 26–27, 32, 86–87
Knowledge bases, identification of, 38

Language, importance of, 52
Large-group discourse, 62–64
Learning about research-identified
      misconceptions, 125–127
Learning logs, 39–40, 55
Learning progressions research, 100–101
Learning sequence, 6–7, **104**
Learning sequence targets, 111, 134, 219
Library suggestions, 115–116, 141, 227–228
Linguistic representational tools, 23–27
  brainstorming webs, 25–26
  dynamic models, 25
  mental models, 25

nonlinguistic representations, 24–27
    drawing, 26
    graphic organizers, 25–26
    kinesthetic activities, 26–27
    mental models, 25
physical models, 25
task-specific organizers, 26
thinking-process maps, 26
verbal models, 25
visual models, 25
Linguistic representations, 24, 31, 55–65
Logical learning sequence, 102–104,
    199–200
Loop diagram, **197**

Map for cells, 250
Map for evolution of life, 249
Map for flow of matter, energy, 248
Map for living environment, **196**
Meiosis, 93–118
    adult science literacy, 96–97
    case study, 95, **95**
    conceptual target, 96–102
    criteria, 104–107
        variation, 107
    criteria for demonstrating
        understanding, **107**
    expectations of adult science learning, **97**
    experienced biology teacher with new
        assignment, **95**
    formative assessment plan, 113–115
    heredity map, **99**
    high school science standards, 97–100
        components of, 103–104
    initial instructional plan, 114–115
    instructional planning framework
        predictive phase, **96**, 96–108
        responsive phase, 108–115, **109**
    learning progressions research, 100–101
    learning sequence, **104**
    learning sequence targets, 111
    library suggestions, 115–116
    logical learning sequence, 102–104
    map for heredity, **99**
    middle school experiences, building on,
        103

middle school science standards,
    97–100
planning in predictive phase, **102, 107**
predictive phase, **96**
    planning, **102, 107**
reflection, 107–108
research-identified misconceptions,
    113–114
resources, 115–116
responsive phase, **109**
selection of topic, 94
teacher work template, 110–111
    responsive phase, 112–115
technology applications, 115
websites, 115
Mental models, 25, 66–67
Metacognitive approach tools, 17–18
    creative thinking, 18
    critical thinking, 18
    self-regulated thinking, 18
Metacognitive approaches, 29, 33–42, 208
Metaphors, 69
Middle school experiences, building on, 103
Middle school standards, 97–100, 194–195
Mind mapping, 72–73
Misconception literature review, **127**
Models, 25, 66–71
Molecular genetics, 169–190
    comprehension, strategies addressing
        preconceptions, 175–176
    confronting preconceptions, 173–175
    demonstrating understanding, 176–178
    demonstrating understanding for
        learning targets, 178–180
    eliciting preconceptions, 173–175
    finalizing process to promote
        understanding, **180**
    formative assessment plan, 186–188
    identifying preconceptions, 173–175
    initial instructional plan, 185–188
    instructional planning framework
        predictive phase, 171–173
        responsive phase, 173–188
    learning sequence, **173**
    learning sequence targets, 185
    learning targets, 178–182

---

library suggestions, 189
planned learning sequence, **177**
planning in predictive phase, **172**
planning in responsive phase, **174**
preconceptions, 173–175
  strategies addressing, 175–176
predictive phase, 171–173
protein synthesis instruction, case study, **171**
reflection, 173, 175, 180–188
research-identified misconceptions, 185–188
resources, 188–189
responsive phase, 173–188
selection of topic, 170
teacher work template, 183–188
technology applications, 188–189
websites, 188–189

Narratives, 49–50
Natural selection, 143–168
comprehension, 156–158
confronting preconceptions, 149, 151–158
differential mortality, 154–156
eliciting preconceptions, 149, 151–158
formative assessment plan, 162–163
identifying preconceptions, 148–149
initial instructional plan, 161–163
instructional planning framework
  predictive phase, 146–148
  responsive phase, **145,** 148–166
learning sequence targets, 160–161
library suggestions, 167
natural selection learning sequence, **148**
planning in predictive phase, **147**
planning in responsive phase, **149**
population growth, 153
preconceptions, 149
reflection, 147–148, 150, 158–166
research-identified misconceptions, 149, 161–163
resources, 166–167
selection of topic, 144
teacher work template
  predictive phase, 159–160
  responsive phase, 161–163

teaching strategies, 164–166
technology applications, 166–167
websites, 166–167
Nature of science, 22–23, 51–54
Nature of science tools, 21–23
Nonlinguistic representations, 23–27, 32, 66–85
drawing, 26
graphic organizers, 25–26
kinesthetic activities, 26–27
maps, 25–26
mental models, 25
models, 25

Photosynthesis, 119–142
carbon cycling in environmental systems, **122**
completing responsive phase, 132–140
comprehension, 132–140
confronting preconceptions, 128
description of assessment for preconceptions, 129–130
eliciting preconceptions, 128, 130–132
formative assessment plan, 136–139
identifying our students' preconceptions, 127–129
identifying preconceptions, 125, 128
initial instructional plan, 136–139
instructional planning framework, 122–130
learning about research-identified misconceptions, 125–127
learning sequence targets, 134
library suggestions, 141
photosynthesis learning sequence, **124**
planning in predictive phase, **123**
preconceptions, 128
predictive phase, 122–124, 133–134
reflection, 124, 127, 130, 132
research-identified misconceptions, 137–139
resources, 141
responsive phase, 125–130, 135–139
selection of topic, 120–121
steps for misconception literature review, **127**

strategies, 140
strategy selection, **128**
teacher work template, 133–139
technology applications, 141
websites, 141
Physical gestures, 86–87
Physical models, 25
Pictures, 70
Planning in predictive phase, **123, 193**
Planning instruction for learning targets, 209
Preconceptions, 29–32, 128, 206–215
    comprehension strategies, 7
    comprehension strategies addressing, 7
    confronting, 7
    eliciting, 7
    identification of, 7
    identifying, 223
Predictive phase, 122–124, 133–134, 193–201, 217–218
    planning, **102**
    planning in, **107**
Problem-solution organizers, 78
Proteins, 169–190
    comprehension, strategies addressing
        preconceptions, 175–176
    confronting preconceptions, 173–175
    demonstrating understanding, 176–178
    demonstrating understanding for
        learning targets, 178–180
    eliciting preconceptions, 173–175
    finalizing process to promote
        understanding, **180**
    formative assessment plan, 186–188
    identifying preconceptions, 173–175
    initial instructional plan, 185–188
    instructional planning framework
        predictive phase, 171–173
        responsive phase, 173–188
    learning sequence, **173**
    learning sequence targets, 185
    learning targets, 178–182
    library suggestions, 189
    planned learning sequence, **177**
    planning in predictive phase, **172**
    planning in responsive phase, **174**
    preconceptions, 173–175

        strategies addressing, 175–176
    predictive phase, 171–173
    protein synthesis instruction, case
        study, **171**
    reflection, 173, 175, 180–188
    research-identified misconceptions,
        185–188
    resources, 188–189
    responsive phase, 173–188
    selection of topic, 170
    teacher work template, 183–188
    technology applications, 188–189
    websites, 188–189
Pruning content, 198

Reading-to-learn tools, 31, 59–61
Reflection, 61, 107–108, 124, 127, 130, 132,
    200–201, 205, 215
Relational organizers, 77–78
Reproduction, 93–118
    adult science literacy, 96–97
    case studies, 95, **95**
    conceptual target, 96–102
    criteria, 104–107
        variation, 107
    criteria for demonstrating
        understanding, **107**
    expectations of adult science learning, **97**
    experienced biology teacher with new
        assignment, **95**
    formative assessment plan, 113–115
    heredity map, **99**
    high school science standards, 97–100
        components of, 103–104
    initial instructional plan, 114–115
    instructional planning framework
        predictive phase, **96,** 96–108
        responsive phase, 108–115, **109**
    learning progressions research, 100–101
    learning sequence, **104**
    learning sequence targets, 111
    library suggestions, 115–116
    logical learning sequence, 102–104
    map for heredity, **99**
    middle school experiences, building on,
        103

middle school science standards, 97–100
planning in predictive phase, **102, 107**
predictive phase, **96**
    planning, **102, 107**
reflection, 107–108
research-identified misconceptions,
    113–114
resources, 115–116
responsive phase, **109**
selection of topic, 94
teacher work template, 110–111
    responsive phase, 112–115
technology applications, 115
websites, 115
Research
    predictive phase, 8–9
    responsive phase, 9–12
Research-identified misconceptions, 113–
    114, 137–139, 202–204, 219–222
Research on learning progressions, 197–198
Resources, 87–88, 115–116, 141, 226–228
    library suggestions, 88
    technology applications, 87
    websites, 87
Responsive phase, 125–130, 135–139,
    201–215, 218

Science notebooks, 55–56
Science writing heuristic, 57
Scientific explanations, writing of, 56–57
Selection of topic, 94, 120–121, 192
Self-regulated thinking, 18, 29, 38–42
    strategies supporting, 38–42
Self-regulation, 41
Sense-making approaches. *See*
    Comprehension approaches
Sequential organizers, 75–76
Small-group discourse, 62–64
Socio-ecological systems, 191–228, **197,**
    199 **201**
    build on middle school experiences, 199
    comprehension strategies, 209
    conceptual targets, 194–198
    confronting preconceptions, 206–215,
        224–226
    criteria determining understanding, 200

digging further into standards, 195–196
ecosystems, 199–200
eliciting preconceptions, 206–215,
    224–226
finalizing process to promote
    understanding, **207**
formative assessment plan, 219–222
high school standards, 194–195
    components of, 199–200
identifying preconceptions, **202,** 202–205
initial instructional plan, 219–222
instructional planning framework
    predictive phase, 193–201
    responsive phase, 201–215
learning sequence targets, 219
library suggestions, 227–228
logical learning sequence, 199–200
loop diagram, **197**
map for living environment, **196**
metacognitive approach strategies, 208
middle school standards, 194–195
planning in predictive phase, **193**
planning instruction for learning
    targets, 209
preconceptions, 206–215
    identifying, 223
predictive phase, 193–201, 217–218
pruning content, 198
reflection, 200–201, 205, 215
research-identified misconceptions,
    202–204, 219–222
research on learning progressions,
    197–198
resources, 226–228
responsive phase, 201–215, 218
selection of topic, 192
standards-based approach strategies,
    208–209
strategy selection, 206–208
teacher work predictive phase template,
    217–222
technology applications, 226–227
understanding, 224–226
websites, 226–227
Socratic dialogue, 35, 37, 65
Speaking-to-learn tools, 31, 62–65

Standards-based approach strategies, 208–209
Standards-based approach tools, 19–23
  history of science, 21
  history of science tools, 21–23
  inquiry tools, 19–21
  nature of science, 22–23
  nature of science tools, 21–23
Steps of planning process, 246–247
Strategy selection, **128,** 206–208
Student questioning, 64–65
Student understanding, instructional approaches, 15–90
  assessment, 27–28
  comprehension, 23–27
    brainstorming webs, 25–26
    linguistic representations, 24
    nonlinguistic representations, 24–27
      drawing, 26
      kinesthetic activities, 26–27
      maps, 25–26
      models, 25
    task-specific organizers, 26
    thinking-process maps, 26
  features of classroom inquiry, 20
  instructional strategy sequencing, 16–17
  linguistic representational tools, 23–27
    brainstorming webs, 25–26
    dynamic models, 25
    mental models, 25
    nonlinguistic representations, 24–27
      drawing, 26
      graphic organizers, 25–26
      kinesthetic activities, 26–27
      mental models, 25
    physical models, 25
    task-specific organizers, 26
    thinking-process maps, 26
    verbal models, 25
    visual models, 25
  metacognitive approach tools, 17–18

    creative thinking, 18
    critical thinking, 18
    self-regulated thinking, 18
  nonlinguistic representational tools, 23–27
  resources, 87–88
    library suggestions, 88
    technology applications, 87
    websites, 87
  standards-based approach tools, 19–23
    history of science, 21
    history of science tools, 21–23
    inquiry tools, 19–21
    nature of science, 22–23
    nature of science tools, 21–23
  technology, 27
Systems diagrams, 80–81

Task-specific organizers, 26, 75–78
Teacher work template, 110–111, 133–139, 244–245
  responsive phase, 112–115
Teacher work predictive phase template, 217–222
Technology, 27, 115, 141, 226–227
Thinking maps, 26, 61, 79–82
Truth routines, 33

Understanding, 224–226
  criteria demonstrating, 6–7

Variation, genetic. *See* Genetic variation
Verbal models, 25, 68–69
Visible thinking, 33–34
Visual models, 25, 70
Vocabulary development, 58–59

Webs of brainstorming, 25–26
Websites, 115, 141, 226–227
Writing of scientific explanations, 56–57
Writing-to-learn tools, 31, 55–57